SH?#! Happens

TRAVELING WITH JOHN AND LESLIE

John Turzer

Table of Contents

Idaho, Oregon and Northern California Vacation
September 25th to October 6th 2016

ADDENDUM

Traveling from Henderson to Maui

FORWARD

When John and Leslie Turzer began their planned 39-day journey from Las Vegas to Europe and home again, it was in celebration of their 30th Wedding Anniversary. Frankly, I find it impossible to understand why they have waited so long. The Turzer's are *"equal opportunity fun people"* with a lust for life, liberty and the pursuit of happy endings. Their time spent on Maui is a tribute to their desire to expand the air beneath their wings; a way of sharing two lives and making them worthwhile and whole. They are simply good and enjoyable people who continue to live a remarkably pleasant marriage and life. Every day is a celebration; their Tour of Europe was just an extension of their sharing.

John is a devoted husband, father, grandfather, referee, umpire and sports nut! He also enjoys a reliable mid-handicap with his game of golf. Leslie is, as John is quick to admit, his Ace Wahine, the love of his life and the leader of the John Turzer Chowder and Marching Band!

I am delighted to have enjoyed reading these pages from their European experience. The antics of Leslie (the lady with the many pseudonyms based on the country in which they are visiting) are classic and, given that she had just begun to recover from hip surgery during their vacation, she pushed ahead to ensure they both enjoyed this special anniversary journey. What a trooper!

The Turzer's always enjoy themselves wherever they travel and they trust their adventures and experiences will be equally enjoyed when shared with friends and readers. Many of these friends have traveled the same routes and can easily recall the time they had and often compare these experiences with Leslie and John.

The transportation they take to meet the inner heart of Europe's most profound cities and even the lesser known stops along the way become the palette from which they can pain a unique mural seen through their eyes and captured in their words. The people whom they meet and discover to be either friends or acquaintances we all tend to have in common. Also we share the same foreign travel problems such as hotel accommodations, taxi's, buses, postage stamps and those who claim to be part of the postal service whose trust in your letters and post cards are often accompanied with a prayer or two. All together, we share the same thoughts, worries and laughter.

From London to Brussels, Germany, Prague, Vienna, Slovakia, Lake Como, Paris and home again, John and Leslie share every experience with their enjoyable and easy reading giving us a chance to help them celebrate more than a trip but rather a living and unique adventure. I am looking forward to their 35th Anniversary. If you can, John, please put the Far East on your travel agenda and, should you need either an interpreter, caddie or Gunga Din Baggage Carrier, I'm your guy! Lovely Leslie, *"keep beating that drum!"*

Aloha

Roman Divanti

INTRODUCTION

To celebrate our thirtieth wedding anniversary, Leslie and I decided to treat ourselves to a thirty-nine day adventure through eight European countries. The potential for great fun was unimaginable as was the probability of always slipping a bit *"off the rails"* and hoping no one would recognize us simply as *"those darn Americans"*.

To properly present the inspiration of this *book,* it is essential for the reader to understand that ours is an often coherent, detailed, and hopefully entertaining presentation of our excursions, a compilation of our many adventures ranging from, "what a great time we had" to "I can't believe *that* happened" situations and *"Sh?#! Happens"* situations encountered on our trip to Europe in 2013 and our Oregon and California coast trip in the Fall of 2016.

We visited so many wonderful cities and venues, shared so many experiences, met more people, ate more food, drank more adult beverages and yet somehow managed to take so many photos.

We sincerely hope you will enjoy *"our experiences"* as we relive the wonderful days and nights we spent in Europe and the Western United States. And now, onto Europe.

The Turzers

OUR EUROPEAN HOLIDAY
May — June 2013

Tuesday, May 14th -
A Long Day's Journey into Flight

Hello travel fans. Welcome to the start of our thirty-nine day adventure to Europe. A few years back, we enjoyed a *"sample"* of Europe as we cruised the Mediterranean for fourteen days. For this trip, we decided to do it **OUR** way, with no planned excursions. We will just use the European Rail System and a few rental cars to traverse London, Brussels, the German countryside, Prague, Vienna, Slovakia, Lake Como and Paris. So sit back, relax and enjoy our journey.

Keep in mind that country-hopping is not as simple as it may appear. There are many things one must do to prepare and carry out what will be, hopefully, a successful adventure. To accomplish this, you must have a worthwhile plan, and plenty of pizzazz. We have both—well, most of the time. Pizzazz, for sure.

Let's begin. We board the first segment of our journey in Las Vegas. Only 5,246 more miles to go. Flying first class on American Airlines through Dallas and then over the *"Pond"* onto The United Kingdom, we knew this was going to be a trip we'd remember for the rest of our lives. PLUS, we **LOVE** those Frequent Flyer Miles!

There is nothing like being spoiled in First Class: food, drinks, entertainment, and large seats that convert into beds! We eat everything that was put in front of us and sip various *"adult"* beverages. Tough choices ... read, sleep, watch a movie. Next stop London.

We are planning to visit a number of countries, each with their own culture, charm, food, sights and people. So, to *"fit right in"* and not be looked upon as American tourists on vacation (*"holiday"* in Canada and Europe), we decide to change our names to locally popular ones whenever we cross into a new country. With London our first stop, Leslie and John become Elizabeth, aka Betty and Paul.

This book is a detailed compilation of our adventures and our *"I cannot believe that happened situations"* that occurred on our trip to Europe in May and June 2013. The first three days nothing happened. But hold onto your hats, once the *"stuff"* starts happening, it does not let up. So, just enjoy the first three days of our trip and gear up for the excitement starting on day four.

***

Wednesday, May 15th -
Great Britain

HELLO, LONDON! After gathering our luggage, we then dash to the *"Tube"*, a quaint name for a series of eleven London Underground Metro Systems. From Heathrow Airport to our hotel check-in counter required twenty-three stops ... a one hour ride on the *"local"* subway. Sure wish we had gotten on an express train. Oh well, we finally reach our stop just two blocks from our hotel, The Mad Hatter.

Sleep deprivation has not yet kicked in. We caught a few winks lying down on the First Class seats that converted into individual beds. After settling in at the hotel, it's time to find the Hop-On-Hop-Off Bus to get an overview of London, a city of fourteen and a half million people covering 750 square miles! There is so much to see. We are in awe of everything, like kids in a candy store. Imagine that, from just one bus ride, we quickly understand why London is where the international community gathers. All that is required is time and money, and not necessarily in that order.

Betty and I plot some points of interest for tomorrow's first full day. I get the feeling we may do some heavy window shopping, reminding Betty how foolish an idea this is only because we can buy all the windows we need in Henderson at Home Depot. Plus, they will deliver. She simply wouldn't acknowledge my new-found

Churchillian sense of humour (don't be trivial, I did not misspell humor, after all, we are where the English language was created).

We find our way back to the hotel without getting lost. However, Betty's (remember the new name per country; there will be test at the end of the book so please **PAY ATTENTION** and if needed, take notes) new phrase, which will be repeated hundreds of times on this trip, is, *"ARE YOU SURE YOU KNOW WHERE WE ARE GOING?"* My standard reply is, *"YES, DEAR, TRUST ME."*

Our bodies and minds are wearing down as the eight-hour time difference kicks in. Betty is coming off a recent right hip replacement. We do not want to have her *"crash and burn"* on the first day. Rather than fight it, we grab a quick meal in the hotel's dining room and retire to our room. Sleep comes quickly as our heads hit the pillows.

***

Thursday, May 16th -
London

We awaken refreshed and ready to take on Her Majesty's vast capital city and are committed to a full day's surge of sightseeing adventures.

After breakfast, we head out to catch the Red Hop-On-Hop-Off Bus. Traffic in and about the city is brutal, virtually forcing many locals to ride their bikes to and from work, school or from point A to point B and home again. For those who do not own a bike, *"rent-a-bike"* racks are located throughout the city providing numerous locations for pickup and return. No money changes hands; the process is automated with prepaid key cards.

Bike riders are bundled from head to toe to keep warm during the early morning chill. Riders *"haul ass"* as they maneuver their way on the streets dodging busses and cars. Initially, we thought this was the Tour De England. Riding a bike in London is not for recreational bikers or even you, good buddy Steve Worthy.

We find our way to the Red Hop-On-Hop-Off Bus. The plan for today starts at Buckingham Palace to observe the daily parade leading to the *"Changing Of The Guard"* plus all that precedes it and follows. This is one of London's most popular attractions that epitomize the pomp and military ceremony for which Britain is famous. On our way to Buckingham Palace, we walk through a beautiful landscaped park filled with luscious flowers and tall, majestic trees. Swans enjoy the day by swimming gracefully on numerous lakes that dot the landscape. The scene is so surreal you feel like you are rubbing shoulders with the ghosts of the past. Upon leaving the park, we join the masses walking the parade route towards Buckingham Palace. Both sides of the half mile route are crowded with tourists of every age, culture, ethnicity and nationality.

We pause to watch the smartly synchronized marching band and soldier-mounted horses pass by. The guardsmen are dressed in uniforms pledging their historic symbols of generations in service. Some wear bearskin hats, scarlet tunics and boots. The scene is breathtaking. The horses are well-trained and clearly aware of their importance in this parade. The band plays inspirational *"fire up the crowd"* music. Their instruments are gleaming in the sunlight. Every soldier, every band member and every horse marches in unison. There is a sense of both entertainment and the rich delivery of an era that remains well beyond its calmed yet somehow euphoric and vast history. All of this ceremonial daily march is open to the public . . . unique and exquisite.

It doesn't take long before this brilliant procession of cavalry, foot-soldiers and the cadre of inspiring soldierly musicians to arrive at Buckingham Palace for the daily *"Changing Of The Guard"*. The crowd is twenty to thirty deep. The sun is out. We find an unobstructed view directly across the street, a spot that seems reserved just for us.

When the ceremony ends, the crowd disburses. We walk up and down the surrounding streets passing various government buildings. Everywhere we go, we hear numerous languages spoken. The world community is well represented in London.

Back on the Hop-On-Hop-Off Bus, we are anxious to visit our next stop, the remarkable Kensington Palace.

Betty almost learns the *"hard way"* to always carry change, as public toilets cost a few shillings. With Mother Nature calling, Betty finds herself ten shillings short of entering the relief station. Hmm ... ten shillings short sounds like a great idea for a Broadway show,

"Here I sit broken hearted, was ten shillings short and only" … nope, I don't need to share that vision with you. Sorry. Not to worry, Betty is resourceful. A lady sees her predicament and motions her over to literally *squeeze* in the turnstile with her. Both ladies start to giggle and then laugh out loud as they pass through the turnstile. I sure wish I had a video of that scene. Ha! It would go viral on YouTube in a heartbeat. By the way, Betty made a new friend.

Kensington Palace is a royal residence set in Kensington Gardens. It is the magnificent London home of the Duke and Duchess of Cambridge, William, Kate, their family and brother Prince Harry.

The State Rooms are open to the public. Our tour is led by a rather knowledgeable college educated guide who provides us all the *"scoop"* about the Royal Family. She is very familiar with the residence and history of the Palace and surrounding buildings.

Many of the rooms at Kensington Palace are filled with paintings and *objects d'art* belonging to the trust of the Royal Collection, including costumes and gowns worn in the 18th Century.

Our next destination is Stop Number Three which takes us to 87-135 Brompton Road, Knightsbridge, London SW1X 7XL, London, U.K., **HARRODS**, the famed department store that not only aims to please but is pleased to aim at your wallet and any other loose change you may happen to have. Harrods is one of the top department stores in the world and caters to the rich and famous. What pray tell, are we doing here decked out in our raincoats, jeans, baseball and sock hats, scarves and tennis shoes? The only thing absent from our modest attire was a neon sign signaling that we've just gotten off the boat, so to speak, and yes, we are rock-solid middle class American tourists clinging irrefutably to our American Express and other choices of plastic money. In total retrospect yet maintaining our dignity, I will admit that perhaps we are *"just a **LITTLE** bit"* out of place today. However, I prefer to believe they simply didn't recognize our wealth and fame. We do disguise it rather well if I say so myself.

It is fun to just look around and wonder, "Who buys this stuff at these outrageous prices?" Our one purchase, four gourmet chocolates, forced us to take out a second mortgage at the checkout register. So glad they have loan brokers on site ready to assist. The store occupies five acres and includes 330 departments including eat in and take away food establishments.

Betty is starting to fade. Her new hip is barking. We cut the stroll short after visiting seventy-five departments on the first floor. Gosh, there was only ... let me see, 330 minus 75 equals ... only 255 more to go! Let's get out of here.

Time to chill and let the hip calm down. Simultaneously, we both do a Dickie Vitale *"UT OH UT OH, give me a T.O. (time out) baby"* thing and take time for a biscuit and tea. For those who cannot relate to College Basketball Hall of Fame Coach, Dick Vitale, just ignore the comment and recognize his favorite studies in college did not include English or, for that matter, quite probably several other subjects unrelated to basketball.

Before heading back to the hotel, I convince Betty that we should set out for the Johnny Cupcakes shop for souvenirs requested by family members. We expertly navigate the Tube and alight at the right station. However, the shopping area that we are heading to is quite a distance away.

"Hi, Betty here. Along the way, Paul finds a William Hill Betting Shoppe. He descends the steps and enters the nondescript, i.e., tacky betting room. Most *"action"* taken here is on horse racing and soccer, which of course they curiously call football while resisting with vile determination even the use of the word *"soccer"*. Mind you, this is not a passing thing with Paul. He occasionally lays down a bet; however, he's never met a bet he didn't like. You can lay odds on that. Paul will now explain the procedures of legal wagering in the United Kingdom."

"Thank you, Betty." Where was I? Oh, yes.

To place a bet, the player must write his/her *"teams and odds"* on a preprinted slip of paper. This alone takes practice and talent. The bookmaker processes the bet and hands you back your betting slip. I made two bets, a three team MLB parley and a four teamer on the MLB and NBA Playoffs. Later that night, I learned that I *"hit"* the four teamer for eighty-three bucks!

Betty's hip finally gives out about two-thirds of the way to the quaint shopping area. The area is laid out like a small town with narrow streets. It is the home to many local merchants selling everything you can imagine and numerous *"locals"* bars and restaurants. My Lady Betty puts up her hands signaling for a *"T.O."* (Time Out. Remember Dickie Vitale?) and says, "See that restaurant bar? This is where I will be. Come back and pick me up." Low and behold, that's exactly what I did after buying overpriced Johnny Cupcakes shirts and hats for the Riverside crew back home. You see, I can follow instructions … not all the time and not always with a wholesome capacity to pay attention … but sometimes. **SLOWLY** making our way back to the Tube, we find a great restaurant filled with locals and enjoy another fabulous dinner. Fed and feeling bloated (i.e. ate too much but who is counting because … *"We Are On VACATION!"*), we head for the hotel to recharge our batteries and *"ice"* the barking hip. We have another well-planned day for tomorrow; however, for now it's time to sleep, per chance to dream.

***

Friday, May 17th -
London, On Our First Day Trip

Today we leave the city of London and visit the countryside, boarding an all-day bus trip to visit Stonehenge, Glastonbury Abbey and Village Avebury. Now, surely, everyone knows exactly where these places are located so I won't bother dragging all the details out just yet.

The English countryside is indeed beautiful. The landscape is dotted with rolling hills and fields highlighted with a variety of yellow flowers. Cattle and horses roam freely.

Time to get your maps out and follow us. Our first stop is Village Avebury, where I truly believe the words *"quaint"* and *"antiquity"* were coined. The Village is home to an authentic, charming sixteenth Century country manor estate complete with its own mini version of the famed Stonehenge. In a great sense, we were stepping into a time and witnessing how the English lived during those years when nothing we call *"modern"* existed. I can't imagine Betty doing the laundry in a barrel and hanging it on a clothes line to dry and then folding it while I was engrossed in some MLB, NBA or NFL OMG moment. Nor, I might add, can Betty.

Casually strolling the streets taking in the sights of Avebury, I spot a William Hill betting location. Not wanting to return to the London betting shoppe, I tried to cash my winning ticket. However, the staff did not know how to look up my winning ticket and pay me the eighty-three dollars. I was directed to return to the location where I placed my bet. Oh, I miss the sports books in Las Vegas.

Next stop Glastonbury Abbey. How Henry VIII could destroy this Abbey is beyond me. In its glory days, it must have been spellbinding. Just walking the grounds, we can appreciate all the imageries of the past, that same feeling I had in London while walking within the beautiful gardens and ponds sharing part of my day with ghosts of long ago.

New Age religion has moved into the town as crystal and witches signs lure you into the handful of handsome boutiques tempting you to browse and perhaps find something to take home as you leave. It's amazing how they knew we had credit cards.

On to Stonehenge. Wow! This is a mystical, pre-historic monument to who knows what. Archeologists have been studying this spot for hundreds of years, continuing to develop *theories* on what this reference to culture, society, spirituality and the human existence may be and still no one can say with any certainty what it specifically represents. No one knows who, how, why or to whom Stonehenge was built. However, present day Druids or Neo-Druidism followers consider this area as sacred and with parallel visceral beliefs.

Back on the bus and off to London savoring our day-long tour at Stonehenge. Within a few hours we would again be in London.

Navigating via the Tube, we exit at the right station and head by foot to the William Hill betting location where I placed my original (and winning) bet. On the bus ride back to London, I decide to handicap a few of today's games and plan to place a few more wagers, a single team bet and three, three-team MLB parleys. However, I arrived at 19:05, five minutes past closing time. *"What sports book closes at 19:00 (i.e. 7:00 PM in Las Vegas)?"* Naturally, and true to form, three of the four bets I planned to place **WON**! Would have been a nice payday.

Betty wants to return to the Lebanese restaurant where she had her *"time out"* yesterday. Her turn to pick where we eat. We head in that direction knowing full-well we must retrace our steps for the long walk back to the Tube.

The food is excellent. The staff is great. Each server is willing to converse with us without hesitation. This gives Betty the opportunity to ask approximately 10,000 (give or take a dozen or two) questions, which I must say, despite fear of minimizing whatever happiness I may be looking forward to in life. They dim the restaurant lights signifying they are closing and if they hadn't, believe me, we would still be sitting there. A good night's sleep awaits us at the Mad Hatter ... but first we must get there.

***

Saturday, May 18th -
Our Last Day in London

Today is our last full day in London. While Betty is getting ready for a full day of activities, I fall in love watching cricket.

Today's match is live from India. The Indian team is playing a team from Australia. Great pre-match show. I have no clue about the rules, how the game is played or how to keep score. Each team is supported by devoted, sometimes rabid fans, bands and cheerleaders. Cricket matches can last two to three days! Imagine the regimen and determination this requires. Watching these matches both inspires one's interests or demands a greater understanding of the word *"tolerance"*. Thus far, I am clinging to both interests of enthusiasm and tolerance.

The batter is using a three-pound bat! A typical major league baseball bat weighs a mere thirty-two to thirty-four ounces. A **BIG** dude from India scored 100 runs in the fewest pitches ever! His seventeen *"sixes"* was a first in cricket! This batter appeared to be the Barry Bonds of cricket . . . looked like he *"juiced"*. I still have no idea what he accomplished, but the avid cricket crowd did! After achieving this historic *"milestone"*, the color commentator spoke with the player about what had just occurred. And for spending time with the correspondent, the record setting batter was given a hat ... a fricking **HAT**. No gift certificate to a local eatery, no ten-minute romp through the local grocery store. No parade at Buckingham Palace. Nada, zero. Nothing! Just a simple *"on sale in the lobby"* fricking hat!

I watch the fans cheering and going nuts when certain things happen during the match. The broadcast team informs viewers that they can vote for *"new player of the year"* aka rookie of the year on Twitter and create a fantasy cricket team! I am *"hooked"* and want to join a cricket fantasy league . . . anyone else interested? Who among us knows how to keep score? This can be great fun. Oh, by the way, after it all took shape in front of my own unblinking eyes, I still haven't a clue what the big bloke accomplished, but somehow, I feel full of emotion and offer a *"way to go big fella"*.

A few more words on the subject and then we'll move on. You buying that?

Batters typically have huge, Popeye-like forearms, much like former Los Angeles Dodger, Steve Garvey. It looks like you score *"runs"* if you hit the ball over predetermined boundary lines. The pitcher (bowler) can really bring it. Fielders, who do not wear gloves, dive for the hard-as-a-rock cricket balls, get hurt, and then leave the game. If only I knew the rules maybe I could sign up to be a cricket referee. But for right now, I enjoy just being a new fan!

On this day, the pitcher was getting his *"ass"* kicked. The defense was so poor that the announcer said, "They are leaking runs." In time, this introduction to Cricket 101 shall pass as I learn both the rules and the local lingo.

During the match, the TV *"man on the field"* conducted live interviews with the coach from the cricket dugout or whatever they call it ... just like on the ESPN Sunday Night MLB game. There is no ESPN (baseball, NHL, NBA scores), just *"football"* aka don't call it soccer lest yee encounter the wrath of 60 million Brits.

Finally, Betty is ready to leave. Amen. We head out for our last day of adventure. But first, we head once more to the confines of our friendly William Hill betting location to cash in my winning ticket.

I had several *"cannot miss"* bets (locks) for today; however, since we are leaving in the morning for Brussels, time was more than important, it was essential. It would be impossible to collect my future winnings; therefore, betting today was not an option. Next time, I will get the William Hill London betting app for my IPhone5 and solve that problem.

We spend time at the Tower of London, pleased that an informative tour guide dressed in the official gear of yesteryear gives us a sense of the Tower's history. The complex, eleventh Century building was formerly the home of English Kings and Queens long before the current day Royals. Currently, the Tower houses the Crown Jewels (a definite *"whoa factor"*), the Royal Mint and Public Records. Some of the original homes within the walls are still used as full-time residence by the guards stationed there. Jolly-good duty, I am told.

After leaving the Tower of London, we walk across London Bridge, gaze back at Big Ben and head to the Tube to visit Westminster Abbey. The Abbey is only four subway stops away. Carefully, we descend three stories **DOWN** into the Tube to catch the subway. The train rolls into the heavily crowded station. The platform is jam-packed with locals and tourists. Inevitably. we find ourselves in our normally reserved location squarely in the back of the pack. As we approach the subway door, I *"feel"* someone push me on the lower left back to get on the train. I assumed it was Betty. Just as I enter the train and turn around, the subway door closes! **Low and behold, Betty is left standing on the platform.** Immediately I envision the French Connection scene with Gene Hackman pounding his fists on the subway as it pulls away with the French drug smuggler smiling and waving at him. The look on Betty's face was priceless with a mixed sense of fear and adventure and certainly curious asking, "What's next?" Thank goodness, I did not smile, wave good bye or take a picture.

This *"moment"* has now ushered in a new dilemma. I have the cell phone and money. Betty has her Tube ticket and hotel key. We did not create a plan should something like this happen. So, I have two choices: one, get off the subway at the next stop and go back to get her or two, go to our planned stop, get off and wait for her there. It is a *"Let's Make a Deal"* moment. Do I choose what's behind curtain number one or curtain number two? I choose curtain two. At the destination stop, four trains come and go; but, no Betty. I now surmise she is not coming to me. Hopefully, she is waiting for me four stops back at the original departure platform. I take the stairway over the tracks to the subway platform heading in the opposite direction. At least I didn't have to pay another fare. After getting on the next subway heading back to *"find her"*, my cell phone magically gets reception, who knows how. Well, Betty is very resourceful in a crisis. A text appears reading: *"Come get me. I am where you left me."* I ponder, but only briefly as the rationale of a borrowed phone enters my *"leaking"* brain reminding me that Betty is resourceful in many ways and always during a crisis. And to prove it, Betty took a moment to set her scene for me:

I scanned the crowd of people on the platform and noticed a mother and daughter decked out in Burberry clothes. I walked up to them and asked if they spoke English. "Sure do honey, we are from North Carolina!" I explained my dilemma and asked if they had a cell phone that was internationally activated as I needed to text my husband who got on the train without me. They were so nice. "Why, sure, sweetie, we understand a fellow American and damsel in distress."

Being deep in the Tube, there is no cell reception. So, the three of us ascended street side. Here I was able to text Paul.

Great poise and decision by Betty. We are united, none the worse for wear. **PLUS**, what a story. The whole incident took thirty minutes to reunite.

I was relieved to have Betty back and further relieved when she told me she had jokingly told them about a reward (which I equated with a ransom) reminding her that, *"It would have been money well spent."* Betty, employing the *"oh sure"* routine as expected, later admitted that she believed me. Oh, sure I thought.

Back to playing tourist. By the time we reach the Abbey, it is closed for the day. Bummer. Have to check it out on our next trip to London. We stroll the grounds and walk through the *"common area"* of an elite boy's boarding school.

Tomorrow we leave London for Brussels but not without considering that this day began rather early, was interrupted briefly and will continue with both major players walking into the early evening together. We find another great restaurant, fuel up and head back to the hotel to condense and pack up the numerous bags of *"just gotta have"* London souvenirs and belongings. Tomorrow, Brussels awaits us.

Before we close this chapter, let's look at what we learned of the people and other interesting observations during our four-day stay in London.

People in London speak the Queen's English. A most interesting statement that has managed to translate over a long period of time and help guide us through interesting periods of our own.

Examples:

Takeaway = Take out

Que up = Join the line

When Queing = Use both lanes (merging)

Give-way = Yield (while driving)

Bottled Water = Still or Sparkling?

Buggy = A carriage

Dual Carriage Way = Dual lanes of traffic in the same direction

Way Out Sign = Exit

Apartment for Let = Apartment for Rent

Sign on road: "Low Trees" Trimming not an option

Flyover = A road going over another road

People "flock" together = Not to be confused with "like sheep"

Real Estate Letting = Listing for Homes for Sale

Jumble Sale = Garage Sale

Every household pays 180 quid (pounds) yearly in support of the BBC Television.

Congestion Fee = A fee of about L7 per day to drive in London. Traffic has become more than an issue in London; it has become an annoyance and a controversy.

Many houses are located on leased land

Car Boot Sale = Selling objects out of the back on one's car much like a swap meet

Americans ask or say Help = Brit's say S.O.S.

Over-the-Brow of the Road = Over the top of the hill ahead

All public and private school children wear uniforms. There are confusing distinctions between public and private institutions and each are distinguished by public and/or private financial support.

Four years of college costs about L9,000. (Public)

The Tube subway announcement when approaching the next stop *"alight for"* and vs. *"the next stop is"*.

And, as almost a matter of comic relief but is part of the language: A woman's deodorant ad on a train may read: "My sweat terminates here two times when using Boots antiperspirant!" Way too much information for me.

A men's deodorant TV ad was even more descriptive: "Makes mens armpits multi-splendid!" It is a learning experience for certain! Until today I never knew my *"pits"* were multi-splendid.

Ya gotta love the Brit's. Their use of a faceted and distinguishing held-together language of dialogues, quips and other amazing use of words is remarkable simply because they surely understand it and couldn't care less if others don't and not the least surprised when others do. Confused thus far? Don't be, this is England, as it has been long before we arrived and shall remain long after we've gone.

***

Sunday, May 19th -
Heading for our next destination: Brussels, Belgium

Time to head to our next destination: Brussels. Once we cross the border into Belgium, we change our names to Derrick and Hettie. A quick two-hour train ride gets us to Brussels. European rail service is far superior to train service in the USA. Trains are clean, reliable, offer plenty of leg room and provide a very smooth ride. You can purchase reserved seats in advance.

Our hotel, the Exe Sabion, is located a few blocks from the train station. Rather than cab it, we hoof it. In addition to our luggage, we are carrying bags of London souvenirs. We are proud economy boosters, first timers who just cannot resist buying everyone *"something"* that they positively and absolutely do not need and likely will never use or display.

After checking in and dropping off our bags, we head up the street to an outdoor cafe. Smoking is very prevalent in Europe. Thus, no sooner do we sit down and get comfortable, two ladies take the table next to us and *"light-up"*. Just what the doctor ordered. Despite being exposed to the second-hand smoke, (as ex-smokers, we could get use to this and light up, **NOT**), we enjoy a satisfying lunch washed down by a few cold Leffe Belgium beers (my new favorite beer) and long forget about the gagging cigarette smoke.

Word to the wise. Gentlemen, should you decide to bring your wife to Brussels, be certain you visit on Sundays and Monday. Why you ask? Simple, **ALL** the stores are closed! You will *"miss-out"* on visiting numerous boutiques and contributing to the Brussels economy but consider the quality of life you will come to enjoy if only for a day or two! To be fair, I suppose this is applicable to a few husbands as well. I know we all like to shop, but I am not talking the sports stores or Target, I am talking Brussels.

We mosey around the city to gain our bearings. It is a brief but interesting … mosey. We enjoy a great dinner including Oysters-on-the-Half Shell, Lobster Bisque (*"to die for"*) and superbly grilled fish. Even though Hettie is on the DL (disabled list) and despite her recent hip replacement (mid-February), we walk the one-plus mile back to the hotel. She begins to fade, but I keep saying, "one more block," repeating this several times. Hettie is a *"Trooper"*. We barely make it. She decides a warm bath will aid her recovery. I live to obey her every wish. Really I do. Crazy I am not.

Let me tell you about Brussels *"bath tubs"*. They are long and deep and are complete with a three-meter diving board! As for the water pressure; oy vey, as my Yiddish speaking buddies Irv and Harvey in Vegas would say, and rightly so, "Oy vey" good grief. I thought the water would finally cover her aching body by morning.

Finally, out of her hot-to-ultimately lukewarm tub, Hettie is somewhat relieved but not fully. Her three month old hip is *"barking"*. She desperately needs an ice pack to help calm it down. So, I go on a mission to find ice cubes. Now catch this sports fans, the hotel staff has **NEVER** heard of ice cubes! Ice Cream but no ice cubes. Front desk personnel look at me as if I am speaking Chinese. Hotels, ICE? I guess we take certain things for granted in the USA, don't we?

The front desk *"employee of the month"* sends me on an *"adventure"* to a convenience store that allegedly remains open until 4:00. Well, to make a long story short, no such store exists. Feeling immense pressure to deliver *"in the clutch"* for my suffering Hettie, I see a Twenty-Star Hotel complete with people wearing upscale hotel uniforms and working arduously (unlike the front desk clerk at our hotel who sleeps in the back, and apparently often). What the heck. I have nothing to lose. So, I casually stroll into the lobby and ask the front desk person where I can buy ice cubes. He replies, "I can give you some for no cost!" My brain cells jump to attention. What a deal! **FREE ICE CUBES!** Mr. Front Desk Person sends a big, friendly chap to the kitchen. Within less than a minute, the *"Fetching Team Member"* returns with ice in one of the Twenty-Star Hotel's ice buckets. Clearly, they must think I am staying at their hotel. Ooops. Being quick on my feet and on occasion, possessing a sharp mind, I calmly ask for a plastic bag so I can ice my knee. A puzzled, confused look appears on the faces of the hotel staff. Their body language immediately tells me that there are **NO** plastic bags in this Twenty-Star Hotel. The front desk clerk then covers the bucket with one of their Twenty-Star Hotel cloth napkins and says, "Just leave it in the room." I thank him, adding, "That works for me." I pick up the napkin-covered Twenty-Star Hotel ice bucket and nonchalantly proceed to walk at something of a quicker pace past the front desk (opposite the room elevators) and toward the main entrance door leading to the sidewalk and street. In the background, I hear them saying, "Where is he going?" I escape, walk briskly, but not so quickly as to attract attention down the street and around the corner to our hotel, not knowing if they are hot on my heels or have called the cops. I just put my head down and go forward, choosing **NOT** to look back! I make it safely back to the room. Of course, I was privately promising to return the napkin and ice bucket first thing in the morning like a kid promising he'd be good from now on until Christmas. Like **NOT**. I make it safely back to the room. I am elated to know I wasn't pursued by anyone of consequence except for some guy in a long dark trench coat and hat. Derrick comes through in the clutch.

My return to the room is triumphant as I am welcomed as a hero. Hers. The ice is put to good use. A calm settles over the room. I am her hero despite my incessant looking through a corner of the closed curtains in anticipation that the hotel would soon be surrounded by cops and bell hops from the Twenty-Star Hotel up the street and around the corner. Their ice bucket became an important souvenir from our trip. We proudly display it in our Henderson living room.

P.S. You cannot make this stuff up!

***

Monday, May 20th -
Brussels

We awaken to a lazy, rainy day. I have no desire to attempt what is necessary, but it is time to do laundry and find a Post Office to mail all of our London souvenirs. Had we opted to use the hotel laundry service, it would have been cheaper to just throw away our clothes and buy new ones, an option I somehow would never ever consider.

We cab it to the local Laundromat. Hettie begins the laundry. I head out to grab coffee and something to munch on. Low and behold, I walk five blocks and do not pass or see a Starbucks, Dunkin' Donuts, 7-11, Wawa, Speedy Mart or any other convenience store. Not so much as a named brand gas station. Famished and craving caffeine, I find a bakery where I gain weight just eyeballing the case of *"fat free, sugar free (not!) more butter please cuz my cholesterol is way too low pastries"*. I have died and gone to Bakers Confectionary Heaven.

I grab some coffee and sweet rolls and race back to the Laundromat and my Hettie. Regrettably, along the way, I noticed that, in Brussels, it must not be a custom to carry a poop bag while walking pets. Thus, be aware and watch your step. You have been properly warned. Also, walking barefoot is not recommended.

Once the clothes are washed and dried, we head back to our hotel. Along we way, we ask numerous people including our *"Crackerjack"* hotel staff to direct us to the closest Brussels Post Office. My guess is that most people in Brussels **NEVER** go to the Post Office. A few people, including the hotel staff, direct us to the main train station, while others have no idea where one is located.

Following lunch, we try our luck at the Brussels subway and end up spending the afternoon at the European Union exhibit. Not being knowledgeable about European politics and governing, I learned how the EU works to help the twenty-seven member countries jointly work for the good of all member countries. The EU is, at this time, considering dropping Greece, Portugal and Spain for their nasty debt and huge entitlements, which they cannot sustain. Anyway, I am much smarter now, plus the education was fantastic and free!

We grab a Mercedes cab to take us back to the main train area for some window shopping. The very professional young driver of the cab is a well-dressed stud (per Hettie, and although I couldn't understand her rationale, I sat quietly feeling no obligation to correct her). The fellow was from Morocco. He owned the vehicle. This dude understood customer service. Plus, he charged €4 more than the regular yellow cab fare. His fee was not a factor. I was eager to pay. Don't you just love entrepreneurs?

Chocolate, chocolate everywhere. Some people have a drink and appetizer before dinner, but not us. To put it distinctly and without dodging any form of inquiry: We pig-out on Belgium Chocolate candy!

Time to contribute to the Belgium economy. Hettie decides to purchase (or, should I say, she selects and I pay) for a very nice necklace. Nothing that I would wear, mind you, but still quite nice.

While Hettie rests from a long day of walking and sightseeing, I head back to the marketplace and purchase a Euro scarf. I believe in the adage, *"When in Rome ... do as the Roman's do,"* so being in Europe I go *"Euro"* with my new, extra cool scarf. Not a terribly exciting tale, but one which I vividly recall. The scarf is, if nothing else, a conversation piece.

While heading back to the hotel, I ask numerous locals if they know where the local Post Office is located. Some have no clue, while others recommend the main train station around the corner. From our earlier inquiries, we know that there is no Post Office in the main train station. So far, the Post Office has not been found.

We enjoyed a great dinner at a local's bar. The meal included a bottle of wine, homemade lasagna, a healthy salad and of course, a Belgium waffle for dessert. This time, however, the waffle is served with ice cream **AND** extra whipped cream. It goes back to that *"when-in-Rome"* thing.

We meet a great bartender who is planning a fall trip to Las Vegas. Over the years, we have met many people who put stays in Vegas into their plans. Early tomorrow we are catching the train to Bruges. I hope Hettie wakes up in time.

Thought for the Day: Why do **ALL** European hotels put Americans farthest down the hall and not near emergency exits?

Final Thought for the Day: Try the Belgium waffles with the thick whipped cream and any flavored ice cream you choose. We live, so they say, only once, why not then enjoy a great and memorable dessert?

***

Tuesday, May 21st -
Brussels

Hettie slept in until 9:30 so we missed the 8:00 train to Bruges, the Venice of Belgium. Instead, we do the Hop-On-Hop-Off Bus, walk, shop and take in the sights. A lazy day, nothing planned, just mosey. I need a Coke Zero or a bottle of water. Anyone know where I can find the nearest 7-11? Please, don't say Queens, New York.

While out and about, we managed to spend two and a half Euro's for public potty use. How much did you spend today? Paying for public toilets ... what a pisser.

Hettie needs a *"T.O."* for R&R. I drop her off at the hotel and head out on a walking adventure. It's another cloudy, chilly day. On my self-guided walking tour, I can find either a rare structure or an optical illusion but a Post Office seems out of the equation. However, rather than dash back to the hotel and retrieve the souvenirs, for the next three hours I walk up and down the narrow streets, enjoy the architecture, public gathering squares, open air markets and the people and then make my way back to the hotel without getting lost. Being an Eagle Scout, I recall the best way not to get lost: drop breadcrumbs along the way so I could easily retrace my steps.

Tonight, we relax and enjoy in-room dining munching on cheese, crackers, fruit, and luncheon meat and wash it down with a bottle of vino. We are slaves to luxury.

***

Wednesday, May 22nd -
Brussels to Bruges

Today is our last day in Belgium and there *"ain't no stopping us now"*. We are off to Bruges. We arise, shower, dress warmly and hustle to the train station, arriving a few minutes early. Hettie heads to Starbucks while I scan my surroundings looking for the Post Office that hotel personnel and every man, woman and child on the streets of Brussels claims is located in the train station. Not finding it, I off-handedly ask someone at the ticket counter. Aha! Finally, an answer I can deal with and wouldn't you know it: The Post Office allegedly located in the train station **CLOSED** six months ago, and once again, no one, absolutely **NO ONE**, knows where the nearest Post Office can be found. Unbelievable!

Prior to catching up with Hettie, I decide to get some coffee, when suddenly, before my gaping eyes, something that never happens in the U.S.A. takes place. The train is apparently early, as in better than on time! As I rush down the steps carrying hot coffee and breakfast, I say to Hettie who is standing on the platform, "Oh, well, we just missed the train." "No, no we didn't," as she looks at the train pulling out of the station ... hang on tight, here comes the Leslie-ism, "Derrick," she says with her eyes fixed on the train schedule, "that was Train Car 2 and the information desk clerk said ours will be Train Car 4." The confusion begins as I remind her that, "No, no. Ours was Track 4, Car 2," watching the confusion on her face.

My double take was right out of a Jackie Gleason *"Honeymooners"* skit. I stopped just short of using the classic Ralph Kramden *"BANG ZOOM, You're Going to the Moon Alice, straight to the Moon!"* Hettie was **CLOSE**, but no cigar. Top five Leslie-ism. This one ranks right up there with the one from our trip to Yankee Stadium a few years back. During the seventh inning, she informs me, in no uncertain terms that the air temperature had dropped from ninety-four to eighty-one during the game. "Where do you see a thermometer?" I asked. "Right there on top of the scoreboard," she proudly points out. Hang on sports fans ... she was reading *"the speed of the pitch"* and not the temperature. I had to cover my face while muttering "Why me?"

We wait on the platform with coffee, breakfast and the knowledge that, should we leave this area, the next train scheduled for 8:21 will arrive early and thus leave us at the station once again.

Apparently, I look Euro, local, and above all, intellectual since people are asking **ME** which train to take to wherever they are going. Instantly, I become the translator of the departure schedules to those who speak German and French! Must be the Euro scarf and hat that I am wearing.

Something for the California Proposition people. As we enter the train station, *"Joe Porter"* is leaning on his wet mop proudly admiring his work. The stairs and floors are virtually glistening. Yes, the floor is wet and a tad slippery, but do we see any yellow "slippery floor/watch your step/caution tripod signs?" No. So, if you slip and fall here, they ask, "what, you stupid, you cannot see da floor is wet?" No lawyers, no big $$$ settlement, no disability, no setting yourself for life payments minus forty percent for the lawyers.

We board the train and soon arrive in Bruges, the capital city of West Flanders.

Bruges is indeed beautiful, with tons of history, a showplace everywhere you look and known as Venice of the North and much, much more. There are, at any given time, perhaps 118,000 residents in this colorful Western Netherland community. To call it a village may be appropriate, but truly it is a town and one to enjoy.

Great food, delicious chocolates (a prerequisite with us), and blocks and blocks of walking. After visiting a few museums and shops, we take a late afternoon canal boat cruise displaying the wonderful canal side of the village which includes the many homes, additional shops, restaurants and churches!

At the end of a great day, we board the train for our Brussels home. Then suddenly something magical happens. We take our seats and we meet Maggie, an eighty-seven-year old delight! A Belgian by birth, a free spirit by heart.

Let me tell you about Maggie. The moment we sit down, Maggie begins to converse with us through her limited English and hand signals, and from this comes the beginning of a wonderful forty-five-minute train ride and somewhat bi-lingual quest destined for life-long memories.

Maggie's English is good (far better than our French). She has been to the United States five times and has a remarkable memory, describing much of what she has experienced in her extraordinary life. She has a brother and family in the Philadelphia area and another brother and family settled in North Dakota; both moved to the United States following World War II. Go figure, Derrick's childhood turf was Philadelphia and Hettie was born in North Dakota. Was this just too coincidental, or what?

This sweet lady never married, and she never offered an explanation why, nor did we ask. She has cats waiting for her at home and this lovely lady loves tennis. She worked until age seventy-nine, managing a family shoe store she inherited from her parents who survived well enough in a town of approximately 4,000 good souls. Maggie lives in the house in which she was born and recalls vividly when, during WWII, the Germans invaded, taking possession of virtually everything. She can still remember that a German officer occupied a bedroom in their home and certainly, not by her family's choice. Imagine a young girl in such a circumstance and then to try to imagine it actually happened perhaps a million times during an era many of us cannot recall and never studied. Maggie's memories include her love for Americans because our army helped to liberate Belgium from its horrible invasion and dilemma.

This lovely lady is warm, friendly and apparently quite resilient. Believe me, it is easy to just sit and listen to her and never wish to interrupt a moment of her past. Her age somehow disappears as you speak with her. Her eyes are young yet had seen much. We can't help but notice how beautiful her skin is. She doesn't give you the impression of her advanced years; what is apparent is Maggie's heart and faith have persisted all her life. She asks us to write down where we live. When I scratch out Las Vegas, she tells us she and her brothers had been there. During their visit, they were horrified because one the brothers suddenly disappeared for no apparent reason. It wasn't until two in the morning that they found him at a blackjack table. Now, how could that ever happen in Las Vegas?

We hug and kiss goodbye at our train stop. Maggie reminds us how much she enjoyed the States and loved Americans. Without a doubt, we knew she could continue the conversation for another two hours. Hettie wants to put her in one of our suitcases and take her with us! The little lady is being picked up by yet another brother, a young brother who happened to be only eighty-five.

The last thing she tells us is, how after the war, many Belgium families took care of the graves of American soldiers. This coming Saturday is a Memorial Day for the soldiers of World War II. Maggie maintains a grave of one of the fallen heroes and stays in touch with his family, who reside in Pasadena, California. She is such a loving and gentle soul. We are more than pleased to meet and chat with her and remain delighted and honored.

Hettie and I enjoy our last dinner in Brussels at a quaint restaurant located in one of the many public squares I toured the day before. Today was a wonderful, memorable day. Tomorrow, we head to Würzburg to pick up a rental car for our driving trip through Germany. But first, we must figure out how to carry the ever-growing pile of *"stuff"* accumulated not only in London but in Brussels as well!

One Final Commentary/Diatribe/Dissertation About Our Brussels Hotel:

There were **NO** Ice Machines anywhere in the building and there was no free coffee in the lobby. Our room was also void of the familiar packets of coffee, creamers, sugar and anything resembling a coffee pot, cups, glasses or anything most people would consider taking with them as souvenirs.

We couldn't help but notice there exists a *"pulley system"* on the side of the hotel building operated by a dozen men raising five gallon buckets of water to the roof. It took a couple of days to figure it out. I thought they were a cleaning crew of some sort, but nothing could have been further from the truth.

Water pressure in this hotel is very low. Our room is one flight of steps up, commonly described as Floor One in Europe (vs. the second floor as we say in the USA). The water pressure is so low in the shower and bath that ... (just use your imagination and fill in the rest of the sentence). I can only imagine what the water pressure is like on the fourth floor.

The hotel staff were and remained clueless throughout our stay. It never occurred to them to locate the address of the closest Post Office. Unfortunately, as we learned the hard way, the staff had no idea that the Post Office allegedly located in the train station had been closed for the past six months! Moreover, UPS and FedEx were complete mysteries to these folks. None of the crackerjack staff had *"the smarts"* to open a phone directory, a cell phone or whatever they could use to locate such businesses.

Curiously, we came away from this entire experience almost pleased that the water and all the other little *"inconveniences"* occurred. Strange as it may seem, as we look back now, it is clear that we would have missed the comforts and thus missed the discomforts we should have anticipated from the beginning. Now, if any of this *"logic"* makes sense to you, please leave a message on my Facebook under "If something can go wrong, it will." The unambiguous promise of *"Murphy's Law"!*

***

Thursday, May 23rd -
Brussels to Würzburg

It's moving day once again. We are leaving Brussels for Würzburg, Germany to begin a three-day drive on the Romantic Highway through Germany, ending up in Munich.

Our cab driver managed to get us the station with time to spare. We hired two rather large dudes to assist in carrying our bags, luggage, and *"stuff"* (which we wanted to ship or mail) to the train. It was an inconvenience to be sure. Thank goodness that I had plenty of tip-money and the will to smile when thanking these *"haulers of heavy stuff"*. This was, however, another unexpected over budget travel cost.

We are heading to Germany with forty-plus pounds of souvenirs from London and Belgium, the infamous twenty-star hotel ice bucket, a beer mug, and other *"stuff"* purchased from whim and wit rather than common sense. Trust me when I say that I do not need to *"pump iron"* on this trip ... just do three sets of ten curls and bench press our luggage and the workout is a done deal.

With luggage and souvenirs in tow, we meander thru the train station to check the arrival/departure board. So, what do we find ... a message on the departure board showing our train number marked in **RED** . . . and a rather unnerving message: *"The train is now scheduled to leave from another station!"* Questions abound. Where is this *"other"* station? How do we get there? Why didn't we get a text or a call about the new location? Hello, Customer Service!

I find the train office and ask myself, "What exactly is going on? How do I get to speak to a human being?" There are so many people milling around and by this time I could only conclude that I needed a *"number"* to get service (as in waiting in a deli, bakery or at the dreaded DMV). Patience, I am told, is a virtue. I won't go there but for the moment I don't feel overwhelmed by that often-repeated prose.

After a brief delay, my number is called. I point to the departure board and ask, "On what track do we get the train to Germany?" Now, here it comes, and with all reasonable expectation: the customer service guy says, "I don't know anything about this," then proceeds to loudly call out to the other service agents, "Anyone know anything about the next train to Germany?" Great. Just great!

"Joe Boss Manager" comes out of his office and tells the agent what to do. We are instructed to go to Track 10, catch a local train and get off at the second stop. So off we go with the two porters hauling our *"stuff"*.

These are the moments specifically set into motion for people with hypertension, weak hearts, and patience and or the *"true grit"* of a couple looking for a challenge. None of these issues applied to us for the moment.

At times, it seems that, traveling with Hettie is like traveling with Lucy Ricardo. She asks, "Are you **SURE** you know where we are going?" Without taking a breath and exhaling, I thought of leaving her at the station. **"LUCIE, YES, I can read signs."** Success, we take the local train and arrive at the right station ... **HOWEVER** ... we cannot find our train number on the departure board, begging the question, where do we go from here? Another line, another customer service agent. **FINALLY**, we are pointed in the right direction.

Settling into our seats, we are greeted by Joe Conductor looking for our tickets. We show him, with modesty or hesitation, our Euro train passes and our First-Class seat upgrades. I would be presumptuous to ask or believe that all was in perfect order. It wasn't. The explanation being: "You were supposed to have the rail pass activated" (date stamp when *beginning* the trip, passport numbers, etc.).

Apparently, their interpretation of *"beginning the trip"* was *"prior to getting ON the train for the first segment of the trip"* and **NOT** when we boarded the train for the trip's first segment. So be it, we are bumbling American tourists and are unaware of this *"minor detail"*. Easy to fix right? Wrong travel fans, the conductor tells us that we must … gulp … **PAY FULL FARE!** "Now hold on, Mister Joe Conductor, this is just **NOT** gonna happen." It was smart that I didn't drop the "Don't you know who I am?" line on him. Why, here's why. He suddenly recognized me and apologized profusely, "Sorry Mr. Walter Mathieu. I did not recognize you at first. My apologies. Is there any chance that I may buy you a drink and serve you lunch?" The look in his eyes prevented me from introducing Hettie as my roomie Felix Unger aka Jack Lemmon.

When we purchased pre-assigned First-Class reserved seats, we expected coffee and something to eat at no charge. Wrong again, we have to pay for everything and have to tip the conductor/server.

After a few delays and moments of anxiety, we arrive in Frankfurt about **FIVE** minutes before our connection to Würzburg. Now catch this book-reading fans! We arrive on Track 18 seemingly trapped in the train car farthest from the main station corridor and we have to get to Track 9, the farthest track from where we are! The clock starts to *"tick, tick, tick"*. We are out of timeouts. We are weighed down trying to haul two bloated suitcases, a backpack and two stuffed carry-on bags. We cannot find a porter. The race is on to get to Track 9. The questions are, *"Will we make it and will Hettie's hip hold out?"*

Luckily, I am in great shape and am able to get us to the train with less than a minute to spare; however, we cannot find … you guessed it … our reserved seats! The conductor points us back to where we entered the train. We find two female squatters (literally) planted comfortably and I mean, like, spread out in our seats. While in most cases possession may be 9/10^{ths} of the law, not on my train, in my seats, on this day! Entering my mind were the words: "Ladies, may I have your attention please? Get the !*#&^ out of our seats!" Being the gentleman that I am, however, I simply inform them they were in our seats and usher them out ASAP. Our conductor suddenly becomes a team player, sees the situation and gives the ladies two options: jump from the moving train or be pushed out. They disappear briefly, leaving me to wonder which option they chose as they flew by the window. This incident was just another reminder that, *"When the going gets tough, the tough get going."*

Finally, we arrive in Würzburg and take a cab to our hotel, Novotel Würzburg. At the German border, we assumed new identities, Axel and Gertrude, aka Gertie. My next mission is obvious: find a German Post Office where we can send home what we most likely would throw away to begin with. It has become an obsession, the intense desire to find a Post Office, spend the money to ship the *"stuff"* back home and then get on with our lives! The front desk person informs me there is a Post Office nearby.

Success! There is a real German Post Office about a half mile down the street. Within thirty minutes, the *"stuff"* is packed and mailed.

We have dramatically lightened our load. It is time for dinner. As mentioned before, we are on a daily eating program that includes three solid meals, with, of course, dessert and a drink or three per day. We discover a quaint bistro near the hotel that serves what we consider gourmet pizza and daily specials. The walls are covered with old American movie star pictures. Three *"locals"* sit at the next table. We engage in friendly conversation with Annette. Joining her is her dog, her husband who, by now is two-sheets to the wind, and another male friend who crossed that border sometime earlier. The bar allows dogs and provides a large dish of water. Annette, it turns out, is an English teacher at the local high school. She is easy and fun to talk with ... like we were friends for ages. She tells us that most high school students graduate. Education is very important. Her students would love to visit America. Annette and her husband have a cat and the one dog. They live on the fourth floor of a no-elevator building. She says the obvious, "It keeps me in shape." Not to my surprise, we learn that most Germans speak English and have no problem conversing with tourists from the west. Needless to say, we enjoy a pleasant evening with the locals.

Gertie and I take a slow sojourn to our hotel for a jacuzzi soak and, finally, bed. Tomorrow we pick up our rental car and drive the Romantic Highway ... lots of castles and colorful landscape. "Guten nacht." P.S. The Post Office and local bistro did not take credit cards. Bring some cash with you. Gertie should be finished washing dishes and loading the mail trucks by morning. I will be sure to pick her up on our way out of town.

***

Friday, May 24th -
Würzburg and Driving Through the German Countryside

We awaken to the sounds of church bells and a vision of something we have not seen in a while: the sun.

The hotel has English speaking TV from the UK, but my favorite is Sponge Bob Square Pants in German. I cannot believe I have not seen Sports Center since May 13th. Can someone text me a Chris Berman, *"Back, back, back, back ... GONE!"* audio? That would be much appreciated.

Also, there is no sports talk radio in Germany ... "Hi, this is Axel in Würzburg. First-time caller, long-time listener. Love your show. Let's breakdown today's IPL (India Professional League) cricket match between the India Warriors and the West Aussie Kangaroos."

Another New Experience: Driving in Germany

Gertie and I pick up our travel accommodations for the next three days, a VW automatic station wagon with built-in GPS. Off we go down the Autobahn towards Rotenberg, an ancient walled city and super tourist trap where we most likely (like 99.9%) will contribute heavily to the local economy.

Again, not without incident . . . not five minutes into our journey, a minor issue becomes a serious dilemma. The car's cigarette lighter doesn't work, making it impossible to charge our IPhone5 or iPad. This *"could"* be a problem later in the day.

Along the way, we stop at a local coffee shop (not Starbucks, Dunkin' Donuts, etc.). Great sweet rolls (we are sugar and carb loading for lots of walking later). The little town also provides clean and **FREE** potty service.

Leaving town, I head down a one-way street the wrong direction (what did you expect?), then incur the wrath of a local truck driver. "You stupid Americano, you are driving ze vrong vay!" I shrug my shoulders in an informal manner of apology, but much to my chagrin, shoulder shrugging must have a completely different meaning in Germany, witness to his universal *"bird"* response. For the life of me, I will forever wonder how he deduced we were Americans. Was it something I was wearing? Was my music on and playing too loud?

Oh well, I guess we didn't make new friends. Meanwhile, we are back on the Romantic Highway looking for castles and enjoying the positively gorgeous and lush countryside. Can't wait for lunch. The thought of devouring one of those large German soft pretzels while absorbing the flavors of sauerkraut and sausages then downing all with a cold one or two absorbs me!

A short time later, we arrive in Rotenberg, a charming twelfth century walled city with cobblestone roads. The old streets are *"just great"* for Gertie's new hip. I don't mind carrying her *"piggy back"* style. Many tourists must think we are a local attraction of some unknown origin and they take photos and video of this unusual sight as we schlep across the old village city. I will check later and see if we've gone viral on YouTube.

Suddenly and without warning, the breakfast coffee kicks in. I desperately **NEED** a potty. I ask a shopkeeper to direct me to the nearest public toilet. What's new, for the fifty-fourth time so far in

Europe, I get bad directions. I think Europeans like to screw with us. So, I cannot locate the potty. Things are getting tense. Alas, a road construction site with a porta potty. I ask Hans the foreman (only guy not leaning on a shovel, leaving me to believe he is the boss) for permission to use their porta potty. He gives me the right shoulder shrug coupled with a double bob of his head directed at the potty indicating *"Cool, ok, have at it, be my guest."* Unbeknownst to Hans, I would have paid big € to use it. His loss, my gain.

Back to the walled city where we listen to birds singing in German. We met the local cats, spend some Euros on souvenirs and indulge in a super bratwurst with sauerkraut sandwich topped with spicy mustard. Dessert is a large German soft pretzel with extra salt. Heartburn is just around the corner. Anyone have Rolaids?

We stroll to the outskirts of the city and meet a charming couple from London. They are in their seventies and are on *"Holiday"* that includes … get this … camping (roughing it, or *"camping"* for Gertie is a room at the Holiday Inn). We take pictures for each other and listen to stories. I particularly love the WWII stories from those who lived it. It is a not just a snapshot or picture in time, it is touching the reality that it existed. The husband tells of how he would ask American soldiers as they passed by or huddled in the small towns, "Got some gum, chum?" He is quick to tell us that he hadn't a hint at first of what he was talking about but soon caught on. His brother was apparently familiar with these few words and put him up to it. Once again, we learn how the Europeans love Americans for saving their continent from Hitler.

We bid adieu to this friendly town of Rotenberg and head back to the Romantic Highway. It isn't long before we come upon a small town. We find the local Best Buy type store and buy a new cigarette lighter phone charger for the car. Of course, it does not solve our problem. And should you be wondering, "No, I wasn't the least bit surprised. *"Murphy's Law"* gets us again. After all, nothing seems to go right for us."

We return to the store. The manager provides super service, attempting to lend a hand to make this gadget work. No luck. I received a refund minus a fifty percent restocking and packaging fee. What can I say?

Back on the road, out of the middle of nowhere, we find a VW dealer! Now, we're talking! I go into a super clean and well-decorated car dealership and explain my dilemma to a friendly receptionist. She says, "Please wait in the lounge," then brings me coffee in a real mug with napkin and saucer! Gertie sees the treatment I am getting and wants her free cup of coffee too. In less than five-minutes Hans, a mechanic, greets us and asks how he can assist us. He is well-dressed, absent of grease on his hands, pants, shirt or shoes. He seems a nice enough fellow. I am certain he had the solution to our *"electrical"* problem. I explain the problem with the cigarette lighter, suggesting there may be a bad fuse or the rental car company somehow disabled it so no one smokes in their car. He changes the fuse for the ridiculously low price .63 Euros. Yes. Point .63 Euros! Yes, it turned out to be a blown fuse. Again, I was right.

We are back in business, charging the phone and iPad. The countryside is punctuated with rolling hills, farms, trees and the occasional farmer Johan driving his tractor down the two-lane country road! We drive by numerous large solar farms, a view of the future. The dark green hillsides are visible through a light mist and are covered with a light dusting of snow. As we continue south, we see the snow-covered Alps in the distance. How majestic they look.

It is approaching time for dinner; however, there is a castle in the distance. Of course, we decide to check it out. Driving down a two-lane, no shoulder country road, we round a bend and are greeted by hundreds of sheep being shepherded by a real sheep herder wearing the appropriate garb (double breasted tan trench coat, raised collar and belted at the waist), Sheppard's hat and a curved staff in hand. He is assisted by two large sheep-herding dogs. We are forced to stop. The herder taps his stick on the ground. The sheep *"bitch and moan"* a bit but move to the side of the road while the dogs direct the stragglers. It is an amusing moment and not one we often (like **NEVER**) see at home.

Success. The castle is, in reality, a restaurant. The free parking lot is a long walk from the entrance. So, being the concerned husband that I am, I drop Fraulein Gertie off near the door and then park the car. Please note, there is no Valet Parking, another potential part-time business opportunity.

A wedding reception is in full swing in one of the castle's private dining areas. I formulate a plan so we can crash the reception and perhaps secure free food and drink. We nonchalantly enter the room, greet the groom Stephan and his lovely bride Hannah.

My hand fully, extended, I warmly greet the groom and introduce myself. "Vei Gates, I am Axel Lieberschlichler, your second cousin twice removed from your father's side with my wife Fraulein Gertie. We have come all the way from Bratislava, Slovakia (a real town for you doubters) to be at your wedding. Congrats, vie gates und guten abend."

Unfortunately, Stephan doesn't buy the story. I tend to believe it was either because we are not exactly dressed for the occasion, my German is lousy or the fact that his real second cousin twice removed from his father's side is standing next to us. So, rather than take up more of their valuable time, I explain that I am simply joking, "We wanted to wish you both every happiness. Guten abend." We bolted for the door before the **BIG** dude can roll up his sleeves to usher us out!

After escaping with our lives intact, we discover the main restaurant. Gertie and I enjoy a lovely dinner with *"to die for"* homemade mushroom soup (cholesterol count went up big time but well worth it; *"Bless me father for I have sinned and will probably do it again"*), pork tenderloins, fish and lots of potatoes. I guess that is how the Germans fill themselves up. I could become a double-wide on this diet.

Back on the road and heading south, we are in search of accommodations for the evening. I discover another great business opportunity: signs one-half kilometer before highway exit ramps indicating hotels, gas, food, etc.

We play the *"get-off-and-on"* highway exit game while looking for a motel/hotel. Most the neighborhoods remind me of '40s World War II movie scenes. Sleeping in the car is becoming an option, a long-shot option, but one nonetheless.

Travel distance today: 275 kilometers. We are close to giving up the hotel search but just then, out of nowhere, we see a large, well-lit sign, *"Holiday Inn Express"*. We are saved! We immediately envision a real bed, real pillows, super shower with great water pressure and soft fluffy towels. The dream comes true! We are in Holiday Inn Express Heaven. We just may decide to commute from here for the rest of the trip.

***

Saturday, May 25th -
Romantic Highway
Through Germany

We awake after a good night's sleep. While dressing, I watch BBC World News to catch on what's happening around the globe. I am getting way too interested in international news stories, international business opportunities and global and foreign stock markets. I may take a course or two in these subjects when we get home. As a reporter said after discussing the Polish Stock Market, "Enough of the stats, let's get on with the story."

As at all Holiday Inn Express hotels, breakfast is **FREE**. It's just like traveling in the USA. The breakfast buffet includes a variety of lunch meats and cheese, breads, pastries, delicious soft pretzels, yogurts and grains.

The coffee machine offers a variety of options. Unfortunately, there are three tour buses filled with traveling students staying at the hotel, thus the buffet line snakes out the door and around the block. I choose to wait. It is cold outside and I did not bring my jacket and *"bitchin"* Euro scarf and hat.

Internet service is slow. Tough to log onto. I asked the young lady at the front desk about this. She points to the crowd and states the obvious, "lots of people logged on." I guess they need more Campbell soup cans tied together and more hamsters spinning the wheels to improve bandwidth and productivity. Another business opportunity, roadside sign maker by day, computer Internet provider geek at night. All I need are the soup cans and the hamsters.

Now, catch this: The bar in the lobby is open 24/7. Did I really leave Las Vegas or am I dreaming? The bar is hosted by the check-in employee. She also multi-tasks in the morning by clearing breakfast dishes from the lobby area, and now, she is mopping the floor. Can anyone imagine the boss having employees' multi-task at home? "Yo, not my job, dude, get off my ass or I will call the shop steward. Now, back off, Charlie!" Try that in Germany and you may never be heard from or seen again!

We say goodbye to the Holiday Inn Express and head south towards Rusden. It is *"Visit Friendly Castles Day."* There is no holding us back.

Along the way, we just *"have to"* stop for a Coke, the ever-present, ever-enjoyable soft pretzel, and while we are at it, a sponge cake rolled with strawberry cream, very light and low calorie *"in my dreams"*. At least we shared.

It is near noon when Gertie and I arrive at Ludwig's castle *"some-where"* in Bavaria. We cram into a bus taking us and about eighty other tourists to the top of the hill where the castle is located. We both now know how the tomatoes feel when crammed into a tiny tin can. Our driver, Dale Jr. (NASCAR), is driving up a steep one-lane curved road at 200 km/per hour. We arrive unscathed at what we believe is the top. **NOT**. We must hoof it straight up the final half mile. Gertie's hip is barking so loud, people wonder if she has a dog in her bag. Our pace slows as we fall back just a bit. I am so proud how well Gertie handled this part of the trek. She is a real *"gamer"*.

At the top of the hill, we walk onto a suspension bridge hanging over a huge gorge that drops miles to a river filled with rapids. What a view! Castles and the Alps. Two for the price of one! We are not certain of the weight capacity of the suspension bridge; however, it is no secret that a few of the floor boards are loose, causing us to look at each other and say, "Enough, not for us, we're out of here."

The Ludwig Castle tour wait is two and one half hours. We learn that on our next trip, it is highly advisable (required) to buy tickets in advance rather than just show up unannounced. Waiting two and one half hours for the tour is not an option. So, we head down the steep, winding hill via horse drawn carriage and get off at the ticket office.

Discovering we can reserve tickets for a Sunday morning tour, we take a *thumbs vote* and unanimously agree to *"book it Dano"*.

King Ludwig's summer castle, which was remodeled in the 1860's, has tour openings within the hour. We decide, *"what the heck, let's do it"*. We purchase the tickets and wait for the short time to pass.

To get to this castle, we take the only mode of transportation available (other than walking), a two horse-drawn carriage. On the way, Phillip, one of the two horses, lifts his tail, relieves himself and leaves a fragrance which lingers, thankfully, for only a brief period. Next time, we sit in the back of the coach. The horses are working very hard to get us up the tree-lined steep hill. Other tourists chose option two, accepting the challenge of hoofing it up the hill. The view is incredible. It doesn't get much *bitte!*

We learn that it took laborers fifteen years to rebuild this twelfth century *"summer home"*. The forty-five minute castle tour is truly fantastic. A big shout out to our friend, Culleen, for recommending the Romantic Highway drive and castle visits.

Six o'clock, it's time to find a place to stay. We head to town and locate a great Bavarian-style hotel complete with a large bedroom, internet in the common TV room, and to seal the deal, a washer and dryer (our clothes are ready to walk to the Czech Republic, just ask anyone who is within ten feet or so of us).

The waitresses wear Bavarian style dresses. Dinner is excellent and includes a salad bar, liver patty soup, pork schnitzel fried potatoes, cold brews and superb sauerkraut. Gertie had a *"perfect"* steak and

French onion soup. *"Yum City"* from the moment we sat down to imbibe. After a long day of castle chasing, it's good to relax and enjoy a wonderful meal, especially with my dear Gertie.

Laundry time. The washer and dryer are located in the basement in the employees' locker room. The operating instructions are in German. After unsuccessfully attempting various options to start the machine, we track down the front desk person to give us a crash course in how to operate the machine. While waiting for the washer to complete its cycle, I engage Gertie in a spirited game of table tennis.

Tonight is the United European Football Association aka soccer Champions League Final from Wembley Stadium in London. For the first time ever, this is an all-German final: Dortmund vs. Munich. Fans staying at the hotel anxiously await the start of the game that will begin in about twenty minutes. The Germans are rabid fans for their teams! Being an *"athletic supporter"*, I will be *"glued-to-the-tube"* as will ninety percent of Germany!

***

Sunday, May 26th -
Romantic Highway to Munich

Gertie and I are super impressed with our hotel room and are not being redundant in our many praises.

The Bavarian flavored, well-appointed extra-large room has a knotted pine tongue and grooved wooden ceiling, hardwood floors, a double shower, and to top it off, a free breakfast buffet! Can I love a place more? I wish we could take this with us!

We planned to rise at 7:00 and tour Ludwig's Castle; however, my little *Liebling schnitzel* dumpling Fraulein Gertie is kaput from climbing up the steep hills yesterday. So, like General Douglas MacArthur once said, "Ludwig, we shall return, but not just now, some day for sure."

Our preference this morning is the breakfast buffet. We have a reserved table. Cool! Scanning the fare, our choices include dry cereals, various rolls and breads, pastries, soft boiled brown eggs, fresh cut fruit, juices, soft (you guessed it) pretzels, yogurt, cheeses, European luncheon meats and something that I have no idea what to call it and thus elected not to try it.

We find ourselves more than nourished and stuffed. What else is new, after all as Gertie frequently (like at every meal) says, *"We Are On Vacation"*. Yes, and I am turning into a doublewide (mobile home talk for the uninformed). Without much ado, we check out and pack up the car for our drive to Munich.

Heading out, we notice we are running low on Euros (about €10 between us) and like all of Greece, we search for a bank willing to provide us with the necessary cash to carry on. We are stock piling our € coins for public potties in lieu of pulling off the road and watering the trees. No problem, we stop at a local bank ATM Machine but ... our Wells Fargo ATM and MasterCard credit cards are both rejected. No problem, small town, Sunday, whatever, we will try again when we get to Munich. Think about it for a moment. Small German town, credit and ATM cards rejected, you try to remain cool but somehow deep down inside you *"feel"* something is not right . . . just can't put my finger on it ... but ... this **COULD** turn out to be a long and rather challenging day.

The drive to Munich takes us through the magnificent German landscape, an impossible view to describe or even find proper superlatives for without expanding the bounds of hyperbole. Interpretation for most readers: this place is great. Period. But, nevertheless, I will give it my best shot.

Right now, we want you to sit back and relax while you visualize this: You are driving down a narrow, windy two-lane road through the German countryside, which is graced by snow covered Alps on one side and rolling farmland dotted with a few homes and barns on the other while listening to the latest James Bond theme song, *"Skyfall"*. Now take the next step as a participant in a multiple-choice reader participation scene: (option 1) you are either being chased by the bad guys who are spraying your bullet-proof car with rapid machine gun fire or (option 2) you are being chased by the *Politzia* (cops) with their Euro blasting Politzia siren on ... you know, the *"uga-uga-uga"* your hear in all the foreign movie chase scenes. It does not get much better than this!

We keep seeing signs for Ashfardt. We learn that Ashfardt is not a city in German or an ass fart. It simply means *"Exit"*.

Arriving in Munich, we are greeted with the applause of rain. What else is new? Seems like the rain clouds know exactly where we are all the time. I missed the turn off for our exit; however, the Fraulein GPS lady re-routed us to our abode for the night, The Kings Hotel. Could not get there without her. The hotel is right around the corner from the train station where we depart from in the morning and one block from where we return the rental car, but first, we need to fill the tank.

The GPS Lady routes us to a local Shell station where (best you tighten up your seat belt), we experience the most impossible and implausible concept ... customers **PUMP GAS FIRST** and then they pay! A throw-back to a time in America when such traits were common and they even washed your damn windows and checked your tires and oil! I asked the attendant, "What if I pump the gas and take off without paying?" She looked at me as though I was crazy. "No one does that," she replied. What a novel idea, the trust-worthy concept. "Cash or credit?", she asked. Done deal.

A few final remembrances from the Romantic Highway drive from
Würzburg to Munich

Germans are serious about recycling. When you purchase a bottle of Coke, for example, they charge $.14 cents per bottle recycling fee. When you return the bottle, the refund is given back to the purchaser or bearer of the bottle. And I thought $.05 per can or bottle was steep in Maui! Wow.

I really enjoy CNN Worldwide News. I admit I am ignorant on international events and politics; however, I have learned a great deal in just a few weeks by tuning into the CNN news network plus reading two weekly newspapers. There really is a *"Big World"* out there.

Throughout our journey, I have learned about economic prob-lems, human rights issues, religious intolerance, infrastructures needing to be upgraded, etc . From now on, I will stay more abreast of what is happening throughout the globe.

We return the rental car and check into The Kings Hotel. Across the street is Munich's finest Gentlemen's Club offering the best *"table dances"* in Munich. But it is Sunday and the establishment is closed. Here's the upshot, and really, fasten your *"diversity"* seat belt; right next door to the Gentlemen's Club is a Arab Social Club. Go figure how they found a way to *"co-exist"*.

Gertie and I walk over to check out the train station where we catch the bus on Monday for Prague (the bus for some unknown reason, is about two hours faster than the train. Must be a **REAL** *"local train"* I guess).

Like most European cities, the train station is often a central part of the community, very large and typically offers many contemporary takeaway food and beverage options including Starbucks and Burger King. This breaks our streak of four days, ten hours and thirty-two seconds without seeing a Starbucks. But who's counting?

Being a tad low on funds, we locate the ATM machines and after numerous attempts, you guessed it, our Wells Fargo cards are again rejected. What's Wells Fargo's problem? I *"collect call"* Wells Fargo customer service demanding an answer. Agent #1 has no clue what to do (holiday weekend help on the international desk), so I ask to talk to someone more knowledgeable. Person #2 does some checking and tells us the ATM cards in our possession have not been *"activated"*. She proceeds to sprinkle her magic fingers on the keyboard and *"activates them"*. Great, we are now back in the Euro game. My blood pressure returns to normal and my heart rate to sixty-five beats per minute.

Not so fast. Not being a particularly trusting soul, I ask her to remain on the line while I try to use the cards to get some cash. Alas, the cards still do not work. She continues to research the problem. After a few minutes, she informs us the cards we have will not work because they have **EXPIRED**. Immediately if not sooner, the blood pressure soars to unknown heights and my heart now beats at 130 beats per minute. Air is being sucked out of my lungs.

"Hold on Missy, our Wells Fargo branch manager specifically told us to use these **NEW CARDS** which were allegedly activated on May 10th for our Europe trip. The cards are supposed to be good for forty-five days and are linked to a specific savings account. For security reasons, the branch manager told us to use these cards. Our names are not printed on the cards and should they be stolen or lost, no problem. Additionally, we provided the branch manager our European country itinerary that Wells Fargo required to trace card usage. We were additionally told to leave our *"normal"* Wells Fargo ATM cards in our Nevada safe deposit box for additional security. Lady, I am down to 1 Euro. Get me a Supervisor ASAP!" I move up the chain of command, talk to a new agent, same story. The third agent tells me to call the same number collect on Monday from 8:00 to 19:00 West Coast time and ask for the ATM Emergency department. I really want you to participate in this dilemma. That's right ... it gets worse!

Monday is the Memorial Day Holiday. Banks in the USA are closed. It looks as though we have a major job to do when we get to Prague tomorrow. **NOT**. Before hanging up, I ask the agent to email my branch manager and ask that HE email ME. The agent asks, "Why?" My reply was simple and straight forward: "I need to let him know he *"screwed up"* **ROYALLY** and needs to overnight us new ATM cards that will work, plus, if this collect call uses up my cell minutes (forty-five and counting), Wells Fargo will reimburse me the excess on my ATT cell phone bill!" Could I have been any more specific? Were there any vagaries in my reply? After today, I have come to believe that customer service, especially on a holiday weekend, is a euphemism for *"call us back later"*.

Since we have been *"shut out"* by Wells Fargo, we attempt to get cash by using our MasterCard. I specifically set-up this option as a back-up in case the ATM cards did not work ... a brilliant idea given to Gertie by a world traveling friend. As you by now have guessed, the MasterCard would **NOT** give us a cash advance. So, I collect call

MasterCard to report that our credit card cash advance option is not working. Low and behold, the customer service agent informs me that our card has been *"flagged"* for *"fraud warning"* because the cash advance was requested in Europe. "But I alerted MasterCard fraud department we were traveling through Europe on certain dates and cities," I bellowed in frustration. I could feel the veins in my neck expanding, my heart racing and my patience, which has never been real high, at an all-time low. "Never mind, just get the fraud freeze off." The agent confirms she has removed the freeze; however, the doubting soul deep within me says "**WAIT**, hang on while I try the card." Well, it doesn't take a rocket scientist to figure out the Card would **NOT** dispense a cash advance. Upon further research, the agent advises me that even though she removed the Fraud Alert, the transaction was rejected because, "You tried more than four times in one day to get cash!" Now strap on your seat belt and make it tight, "You have to wait twenty-four hours until 15:30 Europe time on Monday to use the card! There is **NOTHING** I can do about this." Gasp, gag and a few other unacceptable expletives rush through my mind. Why is all of this happening to us today?

There are times in our lives when defeat may be nothing more than a bitter pill. It is a game, a sporting event whereby customers and ATM service reps compete for either the final word or participate in/or add to the agony of Americans tourist suffering wildly far from home.

These one-sided competitors often show no remorse and take no stock in what they can possibly do to the heart and soul of travelers who must find refuge and travel blindly into the night. That's my story and I deny anyone to claim that I am wrong (or kind of wrong).

At this juncture, the familiar *"rock and a hard place"*, we now have an executive decision to make and it surrounds itself with *"freeing up the potty fund"*. In the scheme of things, we have two options: 1. picking through trash cans in search of two empty containers and cardboard that will allow us to set up two USA beggar's shops in the train station, or 2. simply take up pick-pocketing.

Consider this, the train station is packed with Germans returning from wherever they traveled including London where, the night before, they watched Munich defeat Dortmund 2-1 thus winning United European Football Association aka soccer Champions League Final from Wembley Stadium. The win came in the waning moments with a goal in the eighty-ninth and final minute of the game. Remember their game is called football, not soccer. Calling football soccer in Europe could get you strung up on a lamp post.

After five seconds of careful deliberation, we choose option 1 and set up shop in the train station offering hugs, knuckle fist bumps, handshakes and high and low fives. Singing and dancing with Americans is where I draw the line. The humiliation factor begins to set in. Imagine your soul mate walking about clamoring, "Touch an American for two Euros." It's pathetic but it worked. I refuse to believe she was as good as she claimed she could be.

Gertie sets up shop on the opposite side of the station for maximum exposure. We hope to raise fifty Euros before dinner. She looks great, a babushka lay over her brown hair, a pathetic look of poverty and starvation rampant across her now sad looking face.

GREAT NEWS sports fans, Gertie returned to our room after *"working"* the train crowd effectively panhandling ninety-five Euros. She beat her quota by nearly double, and by God, I couldn't have been more proud of her!

With cash in hand, it is time for a drink or three and dinner. While I nursed a German Pilsner, Gertie celebrates her over the top panhandling day by polishing off three quarters of a bottle of red wine. Hard day at the train station but it was worth it. But wait. It's Sunday. The hotel restaurant only serves a limited menu. No problem though, we can charge it to the room. Saved again.

During our meal, we are *"entertained"* by two elderly men sitting on the sidewalk next to our window table. Both are uninvited, are *"drunk as skunks"* and are leaning on each other and crying.

After dinner, we take a stroll. I can't recall if it was of our conversation, the beer or just plain stupidity but, we stopped at the local *Politzia* station and asked if they could turn on the siren for fifteen to twenty seconds to allow me to record it for a movie (a very, very low budget effort).

The desk sergeant said I would first have to commit a crime. While the *Politzia* would be chasing me, I could use the iPhone5 to record the siren. Respectfully, I declined their scenario but ... there is always the adventurous and *"will try anything once"* Gertie. I will run it by her. Who knows, we may get the recording before we leave for Prague at 13:00 tomorrow. I really wanted a recording of the blaring *"uga-uga-uga"* siren.

Back in our room, we labor to figure out the Euro Krieg single cup coffee pot. So far, we have not followed the directions even though they are in English. We put water in the wrong slot. I am a klutz when it comes to anything this *"high-tech"*. I just hope we can get out of town quickly and disappear before they assess the damage and charge us 300 Euros for the coffee pot that is now kaput. Guten Abend und Auf Wiedersehen ... Good Night and Good Bye.

A last-minute share ... I heard this quotation on CNN and liked it: "Do what comes naturally to never limit yourself." I hope my grandchildren read this and remember it.

Finally, another Euro business opportunity: there was a two plus hour wait for Ludwig's castle tour tickets. Become an entrepreneur ticket scalper. "Tickets. Who needs tickets? Get your tickets here. Who has extra tickets?"

***

Monday, May 27th -
Munich to Prague

We are finally on our way to the Czech Republic, formerly Czechoslovakia, and a country with a long and very storied history. Prague is one of the larger cities in Europe, complete with castles, country homes, farms, great food, a whole different language and, as we will soon find out, their own currency!

We settle in our reserved seats for the four-hour bus trip. Our Greyhound style bus provides a smooth, comfortable ride. We locate an electrical outlet near the window seat and charge the IPhone5 and iPad. We are still in Germany. I am still looking over my shoulder visa vi the coffee maker fiasco at the hotel. Gertie needs something to drink. She places a water bottle on top of the postcard-size, flimsy tray table. A quick right-hand sends the bottled water overboard against the window and down the wall to, of all things, the electric outlet. Without warning, the lights inside the bus begin to flicker. The passengers are concerned and clearly nervous as most look around wondering if we are being *"high-jacked"*. From the front, back and center of the bus, three undercover Bus Marshals, with guns drawn, jump up, then closely assess the situation. Both of us quite naturally assume the same role as the other passengers and look completely innocent of any possible involvement.

Ever see a Glock aimed at your general direction? Don't think about it. Realizing what occurred, I leap to my feet and almost trip over my words, pleading with my hands up claiming: "Nothing is kaput … just a Gertie-ism surfacing in an unlikely place."

The Head Bus Marshal Dude (i.e., the largest) orders us to sit down and demands we show him our passports. I hate to use the word, but given its universal meaning and the circumstance, we felt like the Gestapo chose to appear and raise its ugly head. Marshal Two, is the techie guy in this threesome. He pulls out a 1990 Apple computer, shoots an antenna out the window and enters our info. In a few minutes (seems like hours, as . . . they have not put away their Glocks) later, Marshal Two gives a *"thumbs up"* to the head dude. I hope and pray this means we are ok, i.e., do not stop the bus and take them away. Further, since they holster their weapons, I trust this *"situation"* is over. Normal breathing returns. The bus driver cranks up the bus. We are on our way once more and our passports returned. The drastic horror of the moment came full-circle and a sense of normalcy and recognizable breathing and heart beat returns. But, there is always a ***"BUT"***, we are officially *"ordered"* **NOT** to move and breathe every third breath. "We will be watching you," was etched on the Marshal's faces. I could only imagine they sensed a reasonable look of fear in our eyes. We know how to follow directions, so we did not fail to do as told.

Without a doubt, somewhere, the Secret Politzia have made a note about this incident in a black book now earmarked for future reference. With our luck, they also forwarded our information to the EU main security headquarters so that all member countries can monitor our whereabouts. Oh well, nothing we can do about it now. The Czech border is close. Soon it will be time to leave German soil and start a new beginning.

We cross over the border from Germany into the Czech Republic and notice there is not a great difference in landscape and countryside. The only distinction being we are no longer under the suspicion of the Bus Marshals or the German Secret Politzia.

For security and another reasons, we cannot reveal that we joined the CIA yesterday to increase our cash flow. Upon entering the Czech Republic, we decide it is best we change our identity . . . we are now Petra and Stefen. We decide to save Katarina and Wolfgang for our stay in Austria.

We disembark the bus at the 1930s Prague main train station. So, this is what the world looked like way back then. We have entered the time zone of a black and white 1930's European spy movie. Curious how one's mind races to an era when there existed no peace accords in this region of the world. The fear runs rampant when given a chance to do so.

It is rush hour in Prague. You would think there would be a long line of taxi cabs waiting if not for the madding crowd, at least for us.

The only cab available is, you guessed it, a *"gypsy cab"*, unlicensed and ready to *"take us for a ride"* (aka long hauling in Las Vegas). Petra steps up her game and comes to the rescue as she negotiates the fare down from €20 to €15 for what turns out to be a €6 fare. The absence of a meter makes this type of short-term high jacking possible. More often than not, it seems like everything happens to us . . . from a near terrorist attack on the bus to a gypsy cab driver creating his own form of terrorism on tourists. My kind of movie. I am, however, reminded of the old *"beater cabs"* we used while in Fiji, but that's another story for another day.

We arrive at The Friday Hotel, our home for the next four nights. The hotel is located adjacent to a walking path shopping area. I quickly learned to speak great Czech as I read the signs lining the walkway:

McDonald's Adidas, Prada, Subway. Casino with Texas Hold 'em at 7:00 pm. What a country!

We check (no pun intended) into our hotel and ascend three stories in an elevator built a **LONG** time ago. There is barely enough room for the both us of and our suitcases. We squeeze in ... people's body shapes back in the 1930's were much smaller than today's larger, physically fit frames. We walk down the hallway to our room passing marble statues of a large tiger cat and giraffe. Slightly outdated but what the heck, they tried to decorate ... and the statues matched the dated wallpaper. Enough ... let's just hope the key to the room works. Surprise, it opens the door on the first try! We can unpack for the first time in three nights. Our room overlooks the shopping area. I can easily take notes on places to go and things to see. Up the street we see open fire food carts selling hot dogs, kielbasa, old Prague ham, deserts, beer and more. Cart food is good, in my opinion. Petra overrules my dining decision and opts for an ornate restaurant attached to the concert hall just three blocks down the walkway. Great choice. Oh, how I wanted to try the Old Prague ham. We will be here for four days so I make it a priority to try this Czech delicacy.

After dinner, I drop Petra back at the hotel. My next job is, you guessed it, search, for what else, an ice machine so Petra can ice-down her replaced hip and her barking like mad knees.

So, off I go on my *"find some ice"* journey. Just like our Brussels hotel, this hotel does not have an ice machine. A few blocks away, I find ice at a local liqueur store; however, it is not for sale. I use pantomime to negotiate two small bags for two Euros. We strike a deal. Ah, the underground cash economy is a worldwide symbol of entrepreneurship. On the way back to the room, ice in hand, I stop at a cart vendor selling super *"to die for"* fruit crepes. How I love super, *"ready to eat"* yummies. Also, I pick up a bottle of chilled Champagne from the front desk. Back to the room, there is an extra-large bath tub with a built-in jacuzzi. I will leave the rest to your imagination. Or perhaps not.

The Champagne and crepes were excellent, and sharing them with my Petra made me feel like James Bond. The only thing missing were the martini glasses and the non-filter cigarettes.

Dale, my friend, Prague needs you. Czech craftsmanship leaves much to be desired. There is a handyman job just waiting here for you. Trust me, you can close your One Day Shade operation and set up shop here. You'd become a **BIG-TIME** Czech entrepreneur in the underground *"cash only"* economy. There is plenty of work, starting with the hotel rooms.

***

Tuesday, May 28th -
Prague

Today is our first full day in the capital city of the Czech Republic. I have become something of a note taker, especially during the day, assuring it will not be easy for us to get lost. Getting confused or lost, wondering where I am, who I am, and what's the time now in Henderson or Maui, everything suddenly becomes relevant and infinitely important.

After showering and dressing, Petra and I head to the dining room. Our room stay includes a free breakfast buffet . . . many tasty things to choose from. As usual, we try two of everything. **FREE** or **INCLUDED IN THE ROOM PRICE** is an excellent price on any menu.

It is sunny in Prague today. No need to go with the *"Euro Look"* forcing me to leave my bitchin scarf and hat in the hotel. Today is short-sleeve weather. At last, I get to wear something different since leaving Las Vegas on May 14th. I went full bore American today: Adidas, Reebok and UNLV hat. No point in not showing off we are full-blooded Americana tourists!

Meanwhile, Wells Fargo has not resolved the problem with our debit cards. I spoke with a banker in our Henderson branch. My concern with re-activating the ATM cards in our possession is clearly a priority. He completely understood the situation and assured me that the problem would be resolved. His other claim, which continues to ring in my head was: "I'll get back to you today." Common sense told me not to hold my breath but hope for the best.

Time to catch the Hop-On-Hop-Off Bus to give us a lay of the land and main sights in Prague. There is so much to see. We know the city will be there waiting for us and has been for I don't know how many centuries.

We begin with a twenty-minute *"show and tell walk"* from the Old Town Square, a version of St. Mark's Square in Venice, complete with many cafe style restaurants, souvenir shops, toss in a few, as in three, churches and hustling tourist companies offering a variety of tours.

What is abundantly clear, the Prague tourist area per square foot, or whatever unit of measure they use, has more entrepreneurs and souvenir shops each selling the same tee shirts, bags, cups and iconic junk that can be seen in New York City or San Francisco! In just fifteen short minute's reconnaissance, I am pleased to report that Prague has successfully discovered capitalism. It is *"alive and well"* after years of communist rule.

Known for its Old Town Square, *"The City of One Hundred Spires"* is a feast for the eyes. There is a 15th century clock that offers something of a show every hour of the day, assuring it to be a tourist attraction. Altogether, Prague is absolutely a good part of our European itinerary.

The walking tour leads us to the bus and during the sixty minute ride, we see the main *"tourist traps"*, which is a misnomer simply because many of the tourists wish to find themselves strolling and window shopping, church hunting and generally enjoy the show. They are not trapped; they are willing participants in the game.

We head back to the Old Town Square for lunch and yet another tour, this one designated as our *"Afternoon Tour"*. Petra and I enjoy two warm *"hunks or chunks"* of Old Prague Ham and rye bread washed down with a cold brew. The juicy, Old Prague Ham is cooked on a wood fire stove. It's amazing how this ancient process preserves numerous flavors and juices. Delicious.

Our after lunch stroll/tour is a walking journey through the historical Jewish quarter area. Eight hundred years of history that truly speaks volumes about not only a people but of a nation and history steeped in important values and challenges. Time was not always kind to the people or the structures, yet the people survive and most of the buildings remain. Place your hand on almost any given wall and you've touched the work of a carpenter or a mason many centuries old.

Our tour guide is a young, well-educated Albanian lady working on her Ph.D. Her exemplary discussion and tour was instrumental in educating us. It is sad to say the Jewish people endured so much oppression and suffering. We are learning so much on this tour.

Next, since this is the warmest day of our trip, we take a relaxing Vltava riverboat cruise. The sun is beaming brightly. The coats, scarves, sock hats and gloves are off. It doesn't get much better!

In our very early days, we no-doubt rushed everywhere. It didn't matter if it was someplace important or not, we just had no time to waste getting *"there"*. However, today in Prague (and a few other delightful places), we put all the glitz and promises aside, look deeply into ourselves and then casually we stroll.

Heading back to the Old Town Square, we stopped at the Post Office to mail those all-important postcards and headed for a light dinner before going to a Mozart and Strauss concert with a touch of ballet and opera. We were seriously thinking of following the old adage, when in Prague, do as the local Czech's do . . . eat a favorite Czech delicacy such as pig's knee and kraut with dumplings or boiled or grilled pig's knuckles. However, common sense took hold. We opted for fish.

Earlier in the day, we purchased concert tickets for the evening performance. The super high tech reservation system consisted of a crumpled letter-size piece of paper showing the rows, sections and seat numbers. Naturally, we selected two prime, on the aisle reserved seats. Using his trusty black ball point pen, Klaus, the Ticketmaster person *"X'd"* off our seats declaring for one and all to know *"These seats are taken!"* and manually wrote out our tickets. Ah, the good old days of personal seat-selection and no seven and a half dollar per person Ticketmaster charge.

It was a great show, certainly well worth the price and the upgrade in our sophistication as musical enthusiasts. We were hoping to get back stage and meet the composers, Mozart and Strauss, but I was told they left early. Pity. Regardless, Stefan pulled a Petra and left the camera in the room. Next time we'll get selfies of us and those composers.

Long before the curtain falls, we are ready for what else, dessert and coffee (what the hell is up with these tiny cups and zero refills?).

Catch this. The dessert cart dude, let's call him Josef, is an independent contractor working from his manually driven (i.e. push it youselfa) two-story refrigerated dessert cart. We pay him for the three-day old dried out cheesecake and realize it is all show business (explaining the lack of frills and tiny cups) while writing it off as merely a bad experience. The real waiter brings warm apple strudel and ice cream. Hallelujah! Much better choice and thus the end of day one in Prague.

P.S. The Citibank MasterCard cash advance works! Who cares about the usury mob oriented fees and interest charges? Later I may have to reconsider this issue but for now . . . we are back in the cash game.

First day Observations of Prague

We found a **FREE** clean potty and marked the location on our map. This was a key move for us.

Alley streets look nasty at night. We met someone who was robbed in such a place late last night. Guess where we will not go.

We left our red, morning stretching cord on the bed. We found a note from the maid, "How do you use and where do I get one? Can I trade you for something? How about ice cubes?"

Banks close Noon til' 13:00 for lunch.

The Czech Republic is number one in per capita beer consumption (160 liters per person) and the number one smoking country in the world. Smoking is allowed in restaurants. We are reformed smokers but still enjoy breathing in second hand smoke.

Eighty percent of the population are atheists. Hence there is little use for the collection plates in their underused churches.

Many early and mid-twentieth century buildings throughout the city are drab Communist architecture sharply contrasting with the historical architecture and newer modern buildings.

No new structures can be built without approval from UNESCO, the United Nations Educational, Scientific and Cultural Organization, a specialized agency of the U.N. based in Paris.

In 1989, Czechoslovakia renounced communism and became a democracy. In 1993, Slovakia became a separate country, leaving a bordered space now known as the Czech Republic.

The Czech Republic has its own currency, choosing not to adopt the Euro. This becomes a problem. I spent a fortune in money-changing fees as I converted U.S. Dollars into Euros and then converted my Euros into Czech Crown *Koruna,* abbreviated Kc. When the process of converting begins so, too, does the complexity of currency exchange. The back and forth will cost a bundle and I can't help but feel I am being ripped off. It cost, for example, a whopping two and a half Euros for a sixteen ounce bottle of water! This is about four American dollars … kind of like being a captive tourist in a Las Vegas Strip Casino at home.

Prague's main train station looks like something out of the 1930's-40's. It was like looking at a black and white movie with all its charm and dank appearance. I can visualize the security guards in their uniforms. Each looks official with their swag. The Secret *Politzia* in tan trench coats, tucked over-the-eye dark grey Fedora hats with a two inch black band, mustaches, smoking non-filtered cigarettes and holding a folded newspaper under their left arm. The others (extras in movie lingo) are most certainly out of central casting. If you close your eyes, you can *"feel it"*.

We observed a large transmission tower built for Communist Free Radio, an oxymoron if you consider the source of the transmissions. Free? Communist? The broadcasting was nothing more than Communist propaganda spread throughout the land. It seems Communist and Free Radio just don't jibe, thus the oxymoron(s).

Many people use public transportation. Trolley cars are packed with riders going to and from work, shopping trips or visiting friends.

Folks in these parts eat tons of breads, rolls and pastries. Lunch meats and cheeses are always on the breakfast buffets.

No one rides a bike in Prague. Why, many crazy drivers create traffic mayhem. I got a sneaky suspicion that Prague car drivers accumulate points for hitting all foreign tourists. Higher points are awarded when running into slow-footed Americans ... easy targets and often in abundance.

***

Wednesday, May 29th -
Prague

We begin our day with stretching and CNN Worldwide TV News which differs *"just slightly"* from what we see and hear in America (much more independent reporting . . . just gives you the facts versus the liberal slanted Clinton News Network (CNN) at home). We also get NHL and NBA playoff highlights but NO MLB. Still, this is better than nothing. I do love the news here. I am learning so much about the world in which we live.

Our breakfast buffet hostess is tall, has great posture, strong calves, and shoulders back and walks self-assured with a purpose and a pleasant smile. I ask our waitress if she is an athlete. She says she was a former ballet dancer. She is a multi-tasking breakfast hostess seating people (you must be *"on the list"* and of course, we are) clearing dishes, bringing out clean plates, silverware and setting tables. It's all quite efficient. And yes, Petra is giving me *"that look"* which clearly indicates, *"Just eat your breakfast so we can go"*.

We head back to the square to pick up the Hop-On-Hop-Off Bus to begin our castle and monastery tours. But first, we watch a dancing troupe of young men and women perform, something we don't often see in Henderson. Very well done, amazingly athletic and energetic.

Today's tour guide gives us a brief history of a 600-year old astronomical clock atop a church in the square. Visualize the many clocks, churches, synagogues and other charms of the Old World and it becomes clear that this *"one of a kind"* dial is very much a part of a time we can scarcely imagine but can well appreciate.

The Hop-On-Hop-Off Bus is a great deal for tourists. Two days of bus service plus four walking tours and a boat ride. Of course, the rain has returned; but, it is not cold or windy, making it *"tolerable"*.

During our castle tour, we meet four Malaysian ladies who become my new best friends ... it must be the Euro hat, scarf and appreciably notable walking stick. This is yet another great tour led by a university educated Czech gentleman named Adam who made certain, I am happy to say, that we visited a large cathedral that remains active today while the others apparently exist to just collect dust. In a land where atheism is king, the church remains a place of solace and comfort for those whose beliefs may be just a tad deeper and certainly more *"inwardly profound"* than expressed openly. Just saying.

A note about Czech wages. It is obvious that people work hard in the services sector and tourism but, frankly they don't make a great deal of money. Here are the stats provided by our college educated guide who happens to work about six-hours each day, five-days a week.

Tours start at 10:00 and usually end by 16:00 or 17:00. Should no tour be scheduled or organized, the guides go home. The stats in U.S. dollars are:

$1,300 - $1,400 monthly in wages. Thirty percent to Uncle Czech, which covers medical insurance, schooling and other government provided services. I have yet to see a firehouse but am told by our guide they do exist. $300 - $400 rent for small accommodations out of the city. No need to own a car. Public transportation, including busses, trolley cars, subways and rail service provide excellent means to move about the area. After discussing these numbers, it appears there is not much money left over for food, entertainment and utilities. Home ownership is not a priority. "Why do I need to own? I can rise every morning and move about and go anywhere easily." His live-in girlfriend chips in to help pay the bills. It is, in the final analysis, an interesting life-style philosophy worth considering. I am confident there aren't a lot of bankruptcies or repossessions here. It seems to me a *"no-stress life"* much like Maui but without golf courses, beaches and the ocean.

Next stop, St. Norbert's monastery for a quick look around and then lunch. The monastic members of Norbert's have their own brewery to help finance maintenance of the building and the grounds. We were fortunate enough to enjoy a meal of wild fowl sausage, onion soup and bread and, of course, their home-made beers, which include year-round and seasonal brews. Why not, we sampled numerous beers. The castle, the monks, the beer and the food ... Ah, God does move in wonderful, albeit strange ways. If I could, I would contribute to this beer brewing religious sanctuary and take a *"charitable contribution tax deduction"* on my Form 1040.

Back on the Hop-On-Hop-Off Bus. Prague has the world's largest outdoor stadium with 240,000 seats. The Great Strahov Stadium, erected in 1926, however, is in very poor condition and needs repair as evidenced by crumbling concrete steps making it unsafe to hold events but rather stand only as *"what could have and should have been"*.

I learned that the Czech government plans to renovate the Stadium and add shops and restaurants in an effort towards creating a gathering place primarily for tourists and perhaps at some date in the future, sporting events.

The Stadium renovation plans include a massive HD TV screen running the length of its interior held up by giant sky-hooks, much like Jerry Jones's Cowboy Stadium in Dallas. I cannot wait to see the finished results. Nor, I believe, can all of Prague!

We decide to get off the bus and stroll, picking up fruit, meat, cheese, wine and crackers for an in-room relaxing evening picnic. Need to recharge batteries. Great idea, Petra.

Back at the Prague *"ranch"*, we have yet to hear from our otherwise reliable Wells Fargo bankers in Henderson. I ask our house sitter and cat enabler, Diane, to stop by the bank and ask the manager to advise us on how to activate our de-activated ATM cards. The manager and I email back and forth. I call to tell him the story of our Munich experience on Sunday and all the crazy. fruitless phone calls between us and Wells Fargo *"customer service"*. After checking out our situation, he tells us he **CANNOT** (like NO, NADA, NOT, NFW) activate the de-activated cards since **new cards were mailed to us**!

Great! We are in Prague; our regular ATM cards are in the safe deposit box in Henderson and we have **NO** clue where the new cards may happen to be. Is there **NO** justice in this world?

Now catch this (better yet fasten your seatbelt), the Branch Manager's solution to this mess, "Can you contact friends or relatives to wire you money?" His *"solution"* sets me over the boiling point ... I remind him we did exactly what we were told by Wells personnel! I asked him to create new ATM cards and overnight to us. I would give permission to two bank employees who I know to enter the password for the new cards. He runs my solution up the corporate flag pole and says, "No can do, against bank policy." Every human being has a boiling point. Some may take seconds, others moments and while others months. Guess which group I can be found in? So here's where I go next. Let me get this straight, I remind him that there are over three hundred million people in the USA and for some strange corporate policy reason, he cannot get **ONE** to enter a password for us? His reply was faintly apologetic, "Sorry policy is policy." And if my last name was Wells or Fargo ... same reply, "Sorry policy is policy." What I found most curious is that there is no telephone listing for Wells Fargo Corporate Headquarters in San Francisco. I can fully understand why. That damn phone would be ringing off the hook 24/7.

"Frustrated" is too soft a word for what is transpiring; however, it is the best I can come up with now. I call our cat enabler and house sitter, Diane. She checks the mail and finds the new cards. There is a God. She takes them to the bank and in no uncertain terms, has the bank send the correct bank cards to us via FedEx on their Euro (nickel). With tracking number in hand, I alert the hotel staff in Vienna to be certain they are on the lookout for our package. It should arrive in two days, the same day we are schedule to arrive in Austria. Quadruple shout out to Diane. Thanks. You're a lifesaver even if you are spoiling our already spoiled cat, Tee.

With the ATM card situation handled, it was time for dinner . . . a relaxing, private evening in our room having a picnic.

Questions of the day: Will the bank cards be waiting for us in Austria? Will they work? Is there a God? Will we be back in the cash game? Let's see if FedEx can find us in Vienna on Friday. Film at 23:00.

Closing this chapter of our adventure, we wish to share a few meaningless bits of information about Prague:

Construction of the main church in the Old Square began in 1365. It took 158 years, so they say, to complete. Union job, I guess. The right side of the tower is bigger, called Adam and left side of the tower is Eve. There is a biblical message in there somewhere. Size matters?

A double Petra/Stefan: riding on the Hop-On-Hop-Off Bus wondering why we cannot hear the guide talking ... ten minutes later we realize that we should have put on our earphones ... ten minutes earlier. The tour is offered in nine languages. I looked for Japanese but realized I was out of my element.

The Intercontinental Hotel in Prague was built under the Communist Regime. Drab architecture. Another reason for disliking Communists.

Anyone going to Home Depot today? Our hotel needs two-dozen light bulbs. Many are out in the dining room making us wonder if it could be a deliberate attempt at something we just don't wish to think about. Or, is it simply a Prague conservation measure: fewer light bulbs, lower monthly cost. Whatever, works for me.

I visited a high-end indoor shopping mall. I love these emerging capitalists . . . it did not take them long to *"get it"* and relieve me of a few Czech Crown *Koruna*.

Yesterday in the market square, I see primary school kids on a field trip. I wave and give them a thumbs up, the international *"what's up"* sign. I get one response, the fickle finger of fate, from the tallest kid with the bad haircut who also happens to look like the class bully. As he passes, he taps another boy's shoulder and says in Czech, "I just give Americano the Czech bird! That was cool ... made my day." I hope the little snot head gets an F on his field trip report.

We decide to walk down two flights of steps to the lobby area in lieu of taking the undersized elevator. While the steps from floor 2 to floor 1 were **VERY** steep, it gave credence to the thought that the person who designed the steps to the ground floor, known as floor 0 in Europe, must have had a few too many that day. The stairway layout was almost a 150-degree angle with a sharp curve at the end plus the handrail was not anchored to the floor. I trust this had to have been a remnant from the old Communist regime, perhaps an indoor skiing training course for both downhill and giant slalom.

***

Thursday, May 30th -
Prague

Temperature dropping today by ten degrees. I decide to go *"FULL"* Euro and wear my new hat and scarf to match my dark grey Adidas pullover shirt and black designer waterproof jacket and walking stick. I am learning that a walking stick is … wait for it … my new Shtick … adding class and variety to my demeanor. The lower portion of my emblazed attire includes, Reebok navy sweats and their high-end athletic walking shoes. Yes, homey, I am **VERY** label conscience.

Today, our last full day in Prague turns into a lazy walking around kind of day . . . nothing spectacular. So rather than bore you with meaningless tidbits of nothing, let's move on to some other *"Prague observations"*.

The unsecured wireless Internet service in our room is putting it mildly, **SLOW** and often has a mind to just disconnect for no apparent reason. Their *"wireless system"* seems to be a cross between two Campbell soup cans tied together and an old AOL dial-up network. Patience is the operative word, learning that once you send an email, you can look out the window and see the text float by on some kind of electronic magic carpet. This, my friends, is Czech Republic progress.

I believe only two rooms can be logged onto the Internet at one time (four story hotel). Should two devices in the same room try to log on, the system shuts down and the Secret Politzia show up unannounced. Luckily, we *"just missed them"*. Exiting our room, we passed them in the hall. However, since I was dressed in my Euro gear, additionally carrying my ski-type walking poles, they just nodded, allowing us to squeeze by them in the two-foot-wide hallway. It was refreshing to learn that even the Secret Politzia can demonstrate manners. One even tipped his hat to Petra. It was a moving moment. Almost literally!

I learned today that my stunning Euro attire has placed me as a finalist for the Spring 2013 Mr. Euro Tourist Contest in the sixty to sixty-four age group. Please vote for me on the Internet: www. mreurotouristspring2013.cz.

Petra is concerned people can peek into our room. "Dumpling, we are on the second floor" (really on the third floor due to the unusual fact that in Europe the ground floor is 0). Little did she know that after she fell asleep last night, a large crowd gathered below our window chanting and clapping **MORE, MORE** in various languages. Why, who knows. I suspect they may have heard the roar of intermittent snoring. I guess Petra was right, people can see in. And, upon further investigation, I discovered a hidden camera put there by the Secret Politzia broadcasting live from our room onto a fifty-square meter HD quality screen in the shopping plaza. Check YouTube for a copy. I just know that the video has gone viral. Our fifteen minutes of fame may be desired by many but cherished by few.

I think I just figured out the Secret Politzia guys, you know, the characters in tan trench costs with the collar pulled up, grey/black Fedora top hat tucked over their brow slightly to the right, mustached, and smoking an unfiltered cigarette with a rolled-up newspaper under their right arm, not their left arm. Left arm paper holder guys are Eastern European left over Secret Politzia . . . that's how you tell the difference. Most are in their early fifties . . . leftovers from the Communist reign. They probably don't even know that the commies have left and moved back to Russia . . . some people just have a hard time with change. From now on, we either ignore them or give them a wave and go about our merry way.

The Prague sports store refund policy: I needed to return a knee wrap that I purchased the previous day. Petra did not care for the style or look. Whatever. Well, when an American tourist buys something and wants to return it, the store clerk says, "We no givea da money back even if you have your receipt and bought item twelve hours ago . . . that's the way it works here . . . go find an *"I Love Prague"* tee shirt for about 199 Czech Crown *Koruna,* about ten dollars." I should have just cut my losses; but Petra goes wild and buys a two-year supply of socks in multiple styles and colors. We go all the way to Prague to buy socks! She won't buy the *"I love Prague"* tee shirt . . . . just socks! I wind up spending another 1,500 Czech Crown *Koruna* for freaking socks. Although I cannot ask the Guinness people, I am confident Petra sets a personal record for the longest time ever in a sporting goods store in of all places ... Prague! Next time, we are **NOT** going to try on each pair to see how they look and feel . . . they are just socks, dumpling Fräulein, just socks! We take in all the sights, more than dabble in the finest cuisine, endure a major ATM fiasco and we conclude our stay in Prague where she buys **SOCKS**!

If they consolidated the money in most European countries to Euros, they need to seriously consider consolidating the languages. Just when I was really getting great in Germany with my Danka (thanks), Guten (good) and Guten Abends (Goodnight) etc., (three years high school German), I run into another consonant ridden language ... Czech. Also, the Czechs did not adopt the Euro as their national currency. So every time we buy something, I use my IPhone5 Euro/Czech Crown *Koruna* conversion app to see how much I am getting ripped off.

Potty time . . . we find one; however, all users must pay upon exit. The price is negotiable with this restroom monitor lady. I reach into my pocket for some change fearing bodily harm if I *"pee and dash"*, knowing I was being watched by someone somewhere, somehow. I give her a combo of Euros and Czech Crown *Koruna*. Well, I guess I overdid it. She jumps up, hugs me tightly, kisses both cheeks, gathers her things and heads for the door only to turn once again to thank me in a mysterious but well-placed language. For the rest of the day the potty, due to my generosity and her giddy response, is free to everyone. Danka Herr Stefen.

Petra decides to *"chill"* back at the room. I, however, continue to explore the area. On my travels, I managed to discover a Dick's type sporting goods store. **NO** golf stuff, one small shelf of baseball gear, but lots of tennis, darts, exercise equipment, bikes, skateboards, roller blades, soccer (i.e. football) goodies and virtually every color and style of athletic shoes. Nike, Adidas, Quicksilver and Roxy have the lion's share of the apparel shelves. Euro sizes are far different than the U.S.A. Unfortunately, I found out I do not have a *"stud Euro body"*, so the hiking pants that stop just below the knee return to the rack. I guess I will stick with the relaxed fitting sweat pants (elastic waist and draw string) versus the *"Joe Euro"* appearance of studly masculinity.

Has anyone seen the Prague glasses cleaning lady? This is a clever scam that reaches just beyond the unbelievable. There is a gal in Prague who, given the opening, will present you with a product that, when sprayed on your glasses is guaranteed to **FOREVER** prevent fogging, scratches and smudges from ever ruining your glasses and interrupting your day. For the mere amount of 125 Czech Crown *Koruna,* this miracle can happen for you. And, as a bonus, you will receive a second bottle free! The key word which superimposed my original thought of, if you have one that will do the job, why does one need another? But that's simply a logical question best left in the past. **FREE** was the optimum word. Plus, after the demonstration, it is a *"hafta have item"*, so you guessed it, I buy. Well, guess what folks, my glasses keep fogging up. They have become scratched like my cat Tee had a field day on them and the finger prints and smudges are now a permanent part of the lenses and will **NOT** come out no matter how much solution I spritz on them and no matter hard I try to rub them out! It just gets worse. I have to buy a white cane and hire the services of a Czech Sheppard to lead me around the city. My seeing eye dog is on order . . . there is a huge backup thanks to this gypsy lady, who, by the way, could tell me my fortune and get it right. I need to get her photo to the Secret Politzia but I cannot **SEE** my pictures! The Politzia are aware of her activities but they can't seem to sort her out from the madding crowd of native hucksters. There is a sucker born every day. Today just happened to be my day. 125 Czech Crown *Koruna* wasted, gone.

Time for our last dinner in Prague. It is a cold, rainy night. Many restaurants are crowded and each with long waiting lists. I try my favorite line, "What, you don't know who I AM?" on five hostesses to no avail. I guess they just didn't recognize talent when they see it. Finally, we come upon an old barrel shaped restaurant, *"buy"* the sales pitch from the outside host and enter the cave-like structure. Surprise, the dining room is comfortable. Carefully studying the menu, I decide to do the *"Czech"* thing. My meal consists of Czech style goulash, pork liver pate on fresh rye bread and a fresh chilled salad, while Petra goes *"Midwest USA"* with fresh trout (minus its head) and chicken noodle soup. The meal is great, the ambiance *"different"*. We head back into the dreary, cold, windy night and without any further stops, get to the hotel and retire for the night.

***

Friday, May 31st -
Prague to Vienna

We rise, stretch, bathe, dress, pack up and enjoy a hasty but enjoyable, free buffet breakfast. Today, we travel to Vienna and rather than deal with the gypsy cab drivers (a more colorful way of saying illegal cab owners), the hotel front desk gets us a limo to the train station. Well, our limo driver pulls a Petra: an unexpected but assured action that somehow comes out of nowhere and simply performs its often comical, sometimes annoying act.

The driver picks us up early; his anxiety to have us move along quickly is annoying as he insists, "Let's go, we go, now!" At breakneck speed, we are ushered into the car. He completes loading the trunk, moves quickly behind the wheel, and asks, "Airport?" The air stood still as I could feel an urge to strangle come upon me. "No. Not the airport. The train station," I reply. There is a blank stare and a voiceless response as he realizes we are not the passengers he was scheduled to pick up. The look of panic fills his eyes while he somehow nonchalantly calls his dispatcher and receives, what we determine is a well-deserved reaming in his native language. The driver, like a good soldier, *"takes the bullet"*, assuring us there is no problem and drives us directly to the train station. Somewhere in the back of our minds, we think briefly of the poor people waiting at the hotel for a limo to the airport who, more than likely, will miss their flight to Transylvania and get stuck in Prague until next week when the next plane goes there! This, my friends, is the effect we have when people encounter Petra and Stefan. It isn't a curse, it is more a pebble in your shoe just when you don't need nor want it. We just cannot get out of Prague without a few more Petra's. Indulge me as I attempt to explain.

Secret Politzia walk around the train station not with pistols and heavily shaded glasses, but rather with stubby automatic rifles slung over their shoulders. I ask three questions, nothing provocative, but rather mundane, every day questions: The cops make notes in a secret black book, inspect our passports, and strip search me in public. No one in the train station reacts. I am not certain how to take this. Should I be insulted or is this just so common an incident that it leaves no room for surprise or draws any attention?

Stefan needs twenty Czech Crown *Koruna* for potty. I perform my duty, take ten steps and Mother Nature calls again. I plead with the attendant to no avail. "No re-entry without pay." I have no leverage ("You pay again or leave") so again I sort out the change in my pocket, fidgeting for another twenty Czech Crown *Koruna*. Clearly, they have you by *"the potty needs"* and come hell or high water, they win.

On a lighter note and from out-of-nowhere, Dumpling Petra decides to chime in about something only she could have noted: "Six months ago, you couldn't get Stefan (aka John) to try Facebook. This morning at breakfast, he mistyped his password and in a near panic said, "Oh, my God. I can't get into Facebook!!" I started laughing so hard I nearly drew the attention of the entire dining room and staff. Mr. Euro has become addicted! This has little bearing on much but nonetheless it is, in its way, a footnote in our lives and I thought it fair enough to include for now."

Entering Austria, we have an odd sense of entering an entirely different nation; the view and the scenery seems different, refreshing in a way that we know we will be comforted by the people and the sights. Vienna is a name that has its own charm. We are anxious to see it all.

We made it alive and well to Vienna without much ado on our five-hour train ride. Euro train service is so great and easy to use. Lovely views along the way, small farms, lakes, small boats, animals and locals. I love the open space.

Stefan and Petra, as has happened in every other stop along the way, change their names and become Wolfgang and Katarina. We depart the train, gather our luggage and take a Mercedes cab to Hotel' Palais Strudlhop, our home away from home for the next four nights.

A mere ten-minutes in Vienna, Katarina pulls her first Leslie-ism. She has a need to ask the cab driver a question. After all, she has a **VERY** inquisitive mind. His reply was not meant to be curt but to the point: "Only speak Dutch" (while living and driving tourists in Austria?). So, what does Katarina do? You guessed it. Yes, you guessed right sports fans, she asks him another long, compound question slightly shorter than the Gettysburg Address in **ENGLISH**! To which I react, "Katarina, didn't you hear him, he speaks only Dutch! Are your ears clogged? Were you not paying attention?" The look on her face was not one of surprise but one of complete surprise as she assessed the moment and then agreed, sitting back to enjoy the rest of the brief ride. Under her breath, I was certain I heard, "Dutch my backside … he understood me." Perhaps she was right.

We arrive at our destination, Hotel' Palais Strudlhop where great news awaits. The bank cards are waiting for us! We can quit our day jobs at last. Panhandling can be a chore, especially if you work the wrong neighborhoods.

Laundry day and it's my turn. Question to myself: What is it with Europeans and their inability to give accurate directions; how do I get from here to there and back again, for example.

The professional front desk young lady provides me with some *"lefts and rights"* on the location of the local Laundromat. With a suitcase of dirty laundry in hand, I head toward the main drag in our part of town. At the traffic light, I see a bank and guess what, the bank cards **WORK**!

I leave the bank and instead of following my *"gut"* and turn right at the light, I ask a local couple where the local Laundromat is located. Understand that I am hauling about dirty laundry, more than enough change and I am in the middle of Vienna talking to people in a foreign language (in actuality, two, mine and theirs). Taking their advice I am either nearing the Hungarian border or I am going around in circles. Their fifteen minute wild goose chase turns out to be the **OPPOSITE DIRECTION** from where I wish to be. In my zest for a rational answer I quite naturally assume this must be *"Screw with American Tourists Day"*, which is typically any day ending in the letter *"y"*.

I finally realize that once more, I have been duped. So, I seek out someone who speaks English. This turns out to be a chore in itself. The newly acquired directions head me **BACK** toward the bank, another fifteen minute trek. Finally, however, I am heading in the right direction and positively giddy that Katarina decided to stay at the hotel and ice her barking hip. Yes, **FINALLY** a Euro hotel with **ICE** from the bar. If she had made this ill-fated walk with me, there is **NO** doubt that I would have had to sign over the Maui condo to her.

I am closing in on the Laundromat. Along the way, I see a convenience store. Being a smart shopper, I load up on laundry detergent and that all important, yes you must use per Katarina, fabric softener. I reconfirm the directions; however, concerned the street I am told to turn on is **NOT** the street where the Laundromat should be. I have now invested a good forty-five minutes in this journey to the unknown so I do the next logical thing and ask yet another stranger. At this point, what the hell do I have to lose? She points at the same street noting the street name **CHANGES** in the middle of the fricking block! How did I **NOT** know that? Isn't that a normal occurrence in every city . . . street names changing in the middle of the block? Shame on me for **NOT** knowing that. At last, before my very eyes, there is the Laundromat waiting just for me.

Now begins the battle of the washers. I have three choices, small machines, large machines and a combo washer/dryer. Being a well-trained house husband who handles this chore at home, I go with the small machine for the whites and the large for the dark clothes. I add the soap without a measuring cup (a special talent of mine), a few handfuls that should be enough and perhaps yet another half handful more just in case. I do, however, carefully measure a full capful of softener. That was simple enough. Now, all I must do now is navigate the high-tech panel that controls the operation of twenty-four washers and dryers! After a few kicks, the machines comply. The money I save on doing our laundry can easily go toward another foreign adventure. Back in 1988 while visiting New Zealand, I was shocked to see the outrageous charge incurred for in-hotel laundry service. Trust me, without a doubt, we could have each purchased a completely new wardrobe for the price we paid to launder undergarments, socks, jeans and a few shirts. Ace Leslie still laughs her ass off when recalling that moment.

After today's management of machines, coins, detergent and softener and after being duped into taking the long, wrong way to the Laundromat, I have a well-earned advanced degree in *"Laundromat Machines In Vienna"*.

While sitting idly by on an ancient, olive green plastic chair, waiting for the washers to do their thing, I befriend a recent college graduate from Wisconsin traveling through Europe with friends. She drew the *"short straw"* thus, it was her turn to do laundry. We strike up a conversation. Clearly, she understood two significant characteristics uniquely mine: (1) I am an experienced U.S. tourist, and (2) I am a certified Austrian Laundromat Expert.

I offer to share my detergent and softener, considering it a simple and harmless gesture. She looks at me with wide eyes and a wry smile, her eyes widened and in disbelief as though to ask, "What's up, old man?" and then points to the sign on the wall stating, *"Laundry detergent and softener automatically ADDED during the wash cycle."* Okay, my excuse had to be that my German may not be *"up to speed"* but my embarrassment for both my lack of knowledge and the money wasted in a nearby store made me look like a foreigner, which, of course, I am.

To top it off, I break out in a cold sweat when my imagination takes over. I can *"see"* the combination of my detergent and theirs, my softener and theirs combined in several machines. The potential for a nightmare of bubbles in a mad escape from the machines filling the room was terrifying. The mess would be horrendous, the potential damage to the equipment and flooring huge. How could I escape with our laundry without be caught? Clearly, the Secret Politzia would NOT like this. Fortunately, as the sayings goes, *"It all comes out in the wash."* No bubbles, no flood, no need for Noah's ark and no soapy buildup on the garments. Relief, time to breath normally again. After a short time, the clothes are dried. My chores for the day are done. Each article of clothing is as soft as a new baby's butt.

Now catch this. Remember the forty-five plus minute walk from the hotel to wherever and then back on the right track to the Laundromat? Well, sports fans, my walk back to the hotel took a total of nine minutes thirty-two seconds, as in just over nine fricking minutes! Laundry in tow, my life is once again intact. The laundry room incident, in my mind, just like they say in Vegas, *"never happened"* and I wasn't going to share my *"dumb ass"* story with anyone.

While returning to the hotel, I pass by a Russian restaurant that looks terrific. I make an executive decision . . . this is where we will eat tonight. A five minute stroll gets us there. Everything on the menu looks great. The ambiance couldn't have been better. Katarina chimes in with her assessment of the fare. Her proclamation is apparently unanimous throughout the restaurant: "This food is to die for!" We engage in lively conversation with the owner and learn about the history of the restaurant starting in the 1930's and through the World War II years. The staff royally spoils us. The owner has the staff bring their sampler appetizer tray which includes caviar to our table. Second course, a freshly made salad. For the main course, he highly recommends the fresh salmon with wild mushroom sauce. We both choose the recommended dish. Needless to say, it is excellent. Following the main course, a dessert sampler plate arrives tableside. All of the mini-choices are to die for. Last but not least, the waiter brings out complimentary shots of Russian vodka to top off the meal and the evening!

Katarina and Stefan very much enjoy the Russian music played during dinner. We convince the waiter, for a small fee, to download what was being played onto a CD.

A long day traveling from Prague; however, another great day as we expand our world here in Vienna. Sleepy time.

***

Saturday, June 1st -
Vienna

Today is our first full day in Vienna. Did I fail to mention that our hotel room is as large as our Maui condo? Nearly all the comforts of home minus Kapalua and Wailea, the beach and golf courses.

The brochure reads: *"breakfast included"*. Need I say more? Katarina tries to lower my expectations, "Don't be disappointed but it sounds more like breakfast rolls and coffee." Accepting her assessment while anticipating this reality, we head for the breakfast room with limited expectations.

When we arrive, we find a dining room comparable to the Waldorf-Astoria main dining room! The Buffet is fit for a King (me) and a Queen (Katarina). Everything is elegant.

The coffee maker machine has many buttons offering numerous choices; you can even fly to the moon if you can read German! I offer my "Guten Morgens" to anyone within earshot along with my normal modest flair, receiving a few *"good mornings"* in return. Admittedly, I begin a running conversation with a lovely young Fräulein about the speed of the coffee machine and its choices.

As our conversation progresses (beyond my established five words of German), I sense trouble ahead. Not to worry, I am both resourceful and quick on my feet. I reply with a "U-betcha," accompanied with a north and south head nod followed by a well-pronounced

"Yah". By golly, it works! My German is great and improving by the minute.

There is so much to see in Vienna. This is not simply a grand European city, it can easily be called an iconic European capital for several reasons.

Time to contribute to the local economy. The main action in town is a ten to fifteen minute street car/trolley ride into the city center. Here we pick up the ever-popular Hop-On-Hop-Off Bus for a perfect overview of Vienna and its volume of unbelievable sites.

A sign on the trolley indicates the cost of the ride to be €2.20 per passenger. However, no one asks for tickets or Euros, so not quick to volunteer for something not requested, we take what must be common place ... a free trolley car ride. We do, however, stay alert and pray the Secret Politzia are not in hot pursuit due to our predictable misbehavior. This becomes our mantra, *"stay alert"* and stay on the lookout for guys in tan trench coats, 1940's broad-brimmed dark grey Fedora hats with two inch black bands, large black rimmed glasses, a newspaper tucked under their left arm and an unfiltered Camel cigarette incessantly dampened by their uneasy lips.

We purchase two, two-day Hop-On-Hop-Off Bus tickets. Today, we opt for the Red Line Bus. The ticket agent has two wireless machines dangling from his forty-six inch waistline. One machine runs the credit card transactions while the other prints the tickets. All quite high-tech with low physical maintenance required.

As with everything we do or with everyone we encounter, *"something happens"*. This time, the ticket machine runs out of paper. Now I ask, what are the odds of this happening? I would suggest 99.9% of the time since the victims happen to be us!

The agent reloads, we miss the Red Bus, the blood pressure rises, the frustration increases and I wonder silently, what's next? With my eyes closed, I suggest privately that, this too shall pass as the agent is now an unofficial member of the Katarina Club.

With the Red Bus gone, we opt for choice #2, the Blue Line Bus and for now all seems at peace; the blood pressure has eased and the frustration level is low. The sun is out. We are off on a fun filled journey.

What I mistook as sunshine is quickly dashed, then replaced by a dark cloud. The customer service lady, who is wearing the official bright red and navy blue Hop-On-Hop-Off Bus Company jacket, announces that we must unload. "Der bus ist kaput," she proclaims. In any language, this means the bus has broken down, and why not?

To make matters worse as well as memorable, while getting up from my seat, I bang my head on the top shelf and for this effort receive a minor concussion. I stagger, briefly feel dizzy, but I *"tough it out"* and do not go down for the count.

We are stepping off the bus when an announcement comes: "Der bus ist fixiert." The bus is fixed. So, we reverse course, return to our seats grateful that we will shortly be on our way despite me banging my head for no apparent reason. And away we finally go to see some Vienna sites and head to the Danube.

Call me old fashioned and I knew I could be treading in nothing more than shallow water, or is it thin ice? But still a profound question is on my mind and I am compelled, to ask it. "Miss young tour bus girl, what were you thinking when you pierced your lower right lip and then decided to be a tour guide?" but I restrain myself as Katarina is poking me in the back and whispering, "Don't you dare say it, Mister." I am telling you she can read my mind all too often and all too clearly I fear.

Since the weather is great and the forecast for Sunday and Monday is not, we decide to head to the Danube to enjoy an hour-and-a-half river cruise. Before arriving at our destination, we get to see many sites in this charming city. Everything is well thus far, but always in the back of our minds lurks a host of potential missteps awaiting us. *"Murphy's Law"* has long become a part of our baggage and laundry.

Our arrival at the Danube River boat departure location is uneventful. I feel safe about asking the tour guide with the pierced lip where we need to go to catch the boat.

"Up steps, turn left." Piece of cake, we follow her simple instructions to the tee. Upon reaching the top of the steps, we see twelve huge *"sweet looking"* river cruise boats. We immediately decide to add a river boat cruise to our bucket list.

We walk what seems to be about a half-mile to the end of the pier but are unable to find the riverboat. We are, however, fortunate to find and ask a bus driver where we catch our designated boat. You guessed it! No more lurking in the background, *"Murphy's Law"* comes into play one more time against us.

The driver points back to where we began our walk. At least, we figure, we got some exercise to help work off last night's dinner, plus it's a nice day for a stroll. I might add: a one-mile along the Danube stroll. Ask Katarina, she's falling way behind. Who could blame her?

We find on open-space where the tour boat docks, but per the posted schedule, we *"missed the boat"* by five minutes. Hang on a moment, others are also waiting for the boat so perhaps the boat has yet to arrive. Surely, the boat is just late.

The rains of the past few days have filled the Danube to the shoreline leaving it swiftly running at twenty-five miles per hour, but no white caps thus granting the appearance of a relative calm. I can assure anyone who may ask about the Blue Danube: it ain't blue . . . looks more like the muddy Mississippi River.

We wait ... still no boat. A sign just ahead of us reading "Ticket Office" offers a glimmer of hope. A quick stroll. We arrive at the ticket office. Behind her desk, we encounter a *"Yankee Doodle Dandy Sailor"* outfitted lady, but with regret, she is anything but a Yankee Doodle anything. We inquire when the next boat will be arriving? She curtly replies: "No boats today. The river is too high," then goes about her business as though we were not potential customers.

I am about to ask about tomorrow's schedule and as I manage no more than half a word she interjects, "Not tomorrow either. Maybe Monday." Ah, she is also, I presumed, a part-time weather reporter and a part of the local Chamber of Commerce Welcoming Committee thus prompting me to ask a one word civil question: "toilet?" "Make left down the walkway." I *"thank"* her in her native tongue. Both of us are very thankful to learn the potty is free.

As you well know, it is rare when I complain about anything. I am often considerate of the faults of others and understand that life and the world is not always perfect. So even I was surprised when I bellowed out: "Hey, Vienna boat people. Ever thought of putting up a red flag or a fricking sign: Boats Not Operating Today!" Now we know to listen to Vienna free 24-hour talk radio for updates on riverboat cruises. Who would have thought to do this? It simply was **NOT** written in the frigging Guide Book.

Heading back to catch another Hop-On-Hop-Off Bus, our path is blocked by a 375 car freight train. Ninety-minutes later we are back on the Red Line bus while this entire fiasco cost us over two-hours of sightseeing time to say absolutely **NOTHING** of the prayer meeting we agreed to hold on deck of the never-arriving boat! Our theme for the assembly was *The Importance of Being Patient."* Unfortunately, ours became a prayer meeting never to be heard and perhaps just as well. Damn. Give me an Amen.

Back on the bus we alert our tour girl to broadcast on Vienna Free Radio, *"No Boats Today"* or hire someone to stand there with a *"No Boats Running"* sign. The look on her face showed excitement and approval. Believing this a good idea, she immediately radios into her boss and announces to everyone who cared to listen that she will be receiving the Employee of the Month Award: A One Week trip to Las Vegas!

Arriving back at the starting point of today's bus ride, the Vienna Opera House, it's time for lunch. We locate a small, intimate outdoor cafe where we stop for a light meal. We pass on the daily special, braised ox cheek and steak of ox (served tough, very tuff or super tuff) settling instead for soup and salad. Our waiter, Peter, is not happy and tries unsuccessfully to *"up-sell us"*. We decline even though he offers the braised ox cheek *"buy one get one fifty percent off"*. My beef soup is to die for. When ordering the soup, you get to select one of three *"add-ons"* to include in your soup. Peter recommends the pancake strips, a favorite, he enjoys pointing out, among many customers. At this point I don't wish to antagonize Peter, relying again on my thoughts about what may go on behind the kitchen doors. We smile joyfully and thank him profusely. "Wonderful choice, Peter, and thank you for your cogent advice." The looks on our faces tells otherwise. I decline, opting instead for the plain egg noodles. His body language instantly conveys, "Stupid choice, Americano." Peter gives up on us and sends the bus boy to bring our salads. When we leave, we get even by taking a monogrammed cloth napkin. When balancing out tonight, Peter will come up one napkin short and, should the gods be on our side, he will be asked to pay for it himself or face the threat of unemployment!

Don't mess with Wolfgang and Katarina, dude! We ask to use the toilet, "€10" we are told (clearly this was *"Highway Robbery"* since we did not order two entries). My loan application for potty funding is declined; cash only and no refunds. We accept Peter's twist on probably upping the toilet fee and cop yet another cloth napkin. We now have a matching set. Regrettably, we shall not be witnesses to the dismay and argument later in the evening over the loss of the napkins, but it will remain fodder for our imaginations. Either way, we win.

We are thinking of going to the opera for some real cultural stuff, something I am lacking big time. What is holding me back from this indulgence in culture is the asking price, €172 per person. All the cheap seats are sold out for Saturday and Sunday, and in my mind, culture can be acquired just as easily from the back row as well as the front. The $400 bucks for two tickets begs the question of importance of culture this late in my life.

Not to prolong the subject, but I will, the money isn't truly the issue even though it is a bit steep for our budget. We decide instead to go to the city square, buy a bottle of wine, sit on the grass and watch the street performers for free!

Capitalism is alive and well in Vienna. You name the retailer and each is here in full-force. Riding the Hop-On-Hop-Off Bus gives us a view of countless parks and walking paths. Vienna has such a calming effect on its citizens and visitors. Why didn't they think of this in America?

We learn that a large percentage of the city is set aside for *"green areas"*. What a great idea! Hang on, folks, I just saw a sign: **ICE FOR SALE!** My lucky night. In a flash, I write down the address and use my IPhone5 to snap a few pictures. Perhaps the owner can franchise this considerate enterprise in Prague and Brussels. Gute idea? He could make a fortune unless there is a black market for ice outside of Austria. Hmmm?

Being the alert tourists that we are, we spot heaven across the street in the form of a Mailbox, Etc.! Now we can buy bubble wrap to secure and pack our souvenirs. Hotel personnel can ship them to Henderson via FedEx.

The sun is still out and it's just past 14:00 hours. However, rain is expected. This is a big holiday time in Vienna. There are many, many people on the streets over the four-day holiday weekend, putting sobriety on the sidelines for a while.

After a strenuous day of touring, spending and napkin-snatching, we head back to our Vienna digs via another free trolley ride. We dine at a local bar recommended by the hotel staff. By our third glass of wine, on an empty stomach I might add, we are enjoying everyone's second-hand smoke. We ask the ladies next to us to "Please blow their smoke our way." We are downwind and enjoying the smell of strong European cigarettes.

Exceptional food and service. I go *"local"*, ordering sauerkraut (surprise) and pork, white potato dumplings and wash it all down with two local beers. For starters, I submerge myself to the bottom of my bowl of liver-dumpling soup . . . another *"to die for"* treat.

A very special treat and surprise, the restaurant owner provides each of us with a sample of their homemade leek soup served in a shot glass. It is superb ... something folks just don't enjoy every day. The owner, a clever and gregarious man, gives us the glasses as souvenirs. What a class act!

People are truly friendly at the restaurant. The staff is treating us more like close friends than patrons. We plan to eat in local bars for the balance of the trip. This is where you really get to know the people. No pretense, no farcical put-ons, just folks being folks. A nice change from what so many of us find ourselves facing as we travel. The *"here today, gone tomorrow"* attitude fades away and replaced with genuine and often grateful memories. You understand, I truly wish to believe all of this even if our readers can't or won't.

Sitting next to us is a young man wearing a hat bearing the word: **OBEY**. I don' know if the message literally means to Obey or an acronym for something else. Katarina says she will own the condo in Maui before she walks next to me wearing a hat making the claim to OBEY! Speaking of *"tribute and alliance"* which we weren't, I continue wearing my UNLV cap and get glances from about every third person in admiration and awe or guessing the cap's meaning. Fair enough. Go Rebels!

Back at the hotel, we go American for 42:17 seconds watching *"The Glades"* season premier downloaded to the iPad. We love a good TV series when one comes along.

Observations from our First Full Day in Vienna

Bungee jumping off a tall tower: Not something I would do even with a gun pointed at my head! All jumpers, leapers and assorted maniacs must sign a waiver so if the wind kicks up, for example, and should the jumper/leaper/maniac hit the building and die, the building owners are not to be held responsible, primarily because the building was there first! Obviously, the owners were smarter than the fun-seekers and employed the services of a California legal firm. As the expression goes: *"It's never the fall that kills you, it's the sudden stop."*

Riders can take dogs on trolley cars and city busses; and per the sign posted in the trolley, you must put a muzzle on the animal. There were times traveling abroad or cross town when muzzles should have been required for certain passengers. But, that's another story.

Billboards, the first we have seen in Europe, are all over the place, a kind of throwback to an era in the States where billboards were essential and part of our lives.

Vienna is big on erotic sex shops. These shops are popular places to visit, schmooze and tinker with the toys. Send your orders to me while I am here, the prices are right, so I am told. Cash only, please.

The roof-top area at our hotel provides a great view of Vienna. The city is amazing and so well defined by lighting and architecture and, in many ways, it is a walk through European history.

We see an amusement park with fifteen rides including something that drops straight down from perhaps 200 meters. Not for the faint of heart or stomach. We decline this ride but opt instead for the Merry-Go-Round.

Lots of new high rise construction going on as well as several renovations. In addition, a new train station is under construction.

This city has so much to see and enjoy. The Viennese style is remarkable and truly a feast for the eyes and the imagination.

Among most of Europe's iconic cities, other than London, Vienna is the most modern city we have visited. Vienna is clean except for what has long been the blight of what can only be claimed as a European invention: The Art of Graffiti. Today a clean wall, tomorrow Graffiti or a mural or worse . . .

The Danube River runs through nine countries covering a range of 2,160 KM in length. It begins in the Vienna woods and, to repeat myself, it is **NOT** Blue. It's the Mississippi with a German/Hungarian accent.

Ah, there's another billboard ad for something . . . I am not sure what. A guy is hugging a girl and whispering in her ear. I can only imagine what he is saying. Let your mind wander for just a moment. The look on her face is difficult to describe; however, she is giving his words some thought ... *"I'll think about it."*

Hold on, I just saw a Marijuana shop. Anyone need a nickel or dime bag? I will have FedEx ship it to you *"collect"*. Make sure your check is payable to a very popular person in the weed trade: Cash.

Many of these streetscapes remind me of the Upper East and West sides of New York City. Now you are asked to use your imagination once again.

While sitting on the top deck of the Hop-On-Hop-Off Bus, we pull up alongside a passing trolley car. Gazing at the trolley's roof, I see a turn-on/turn-off switch. Like a kid just itching for trouble, I wonder what might happen if I reached out and turned that switch to *"Off"*. I considered the consequences and decided my sudden disappearance would be dramatic as I am snatched up by the Secret Politzia. But still, the urge lingers to this day and I still wonder, *"What if ...?"*

Throughout Vienna, people use collapsible bikes. The bikes fold up so you can take them into your office or wherever you may be heading.

"Hi from Katarina! One thing we have mastered, thanks to Wolfgang, is transportation by bus, train and subway. Left to me, I would still be in London trying to find my way out of the Tube. However, at least ten times daily, I ask Wolfgang, "Are you **SURE** you know where we are going? And of course, he rolls his eyes and bends his head ever slightly to the left."

***

Sunday, June 2nd -
Vienna

Wolfgang and Katarina start the day at the awesome and **FREE** breakfast buffet. After doing the obvious (stuffing ourselves), it is time to head off for more sightseeing and contributing to the Vienna economy.

We take another *"free"* trolley car ride. Later, we learn the fine of not paying is €70 if caught. Plus, it's two days in the slammer and solitary confinement. However, we do not fear being caught unless someone in Austria reads this and decides to report us to INTERPOL and end our *"free"* trolley car rides.

Our itinerary today consists of visiting two castles, The Hofburg Palace, home of the modest family of Maria Theresa Walburga Amelia Christina, the only female ruler of the Habsburg dominion and the last of the sovereigns of Austria, Hungary, Croatia, Bohemia, Transylvania, Milan, Lodomeria and Galicia, the Austrian Netherlands and Parma, Italy. This woman was heavily invested in real estate!

The second Palace was the famed Schonbrunn, Austria's showcase! The museum was dwarfed by the Palaces and their histories.

We found an *"Off Vienna"* opera and purchased two tickets for tonight's performance at 20:00. The title, the seating, the planned performance, it didn't matter. It is convenient plus the big one ... the price is acceptable.

I decide to create a back-up public transportation plan to get back to the hotel from the opera tonight. I challenged Katarina to a game of *"who can get back to the hotel first"* (no cabs is the rule). She declines, so I declare myself the Euro *"Get Back to the Hotel First"* winner and take a victory lap around the main Opera House!

If it is Sunday, it must be raining. What else is new? Looking at the architecture and the varied styles from classical to baroque, each seemed perfectly placed in the era of its construction. Newer, more modern buildings were rebuilt after being bombed in WWII close to or between those building that survived. It's all quite remarkable and well worth the tour.

We arrive at castle number one. Katarina asks the tour guide which way to buy tickets. He points to the right. Katarina, based on prior experiences obtaining directions from Europeans, says, "We go left." Wouldn't you know it, this was the first time we get the correct directions, so by going left we waste twelve steps.

Tickets purchased and in hand, guess what determines the next few minutes? Get the Euro change out because *"Wolfie"* must use the gentlemen's lounge. I only have big bills and the price to pee is €.50. I nonchalantly ask the guy behind me if he would treat me to potty. "Are you kidding me, American tourist? You guys have all the money. You pay for yourself." It didn't occur to me to ask if he could make change, it just seemed easier to beg a favor. Do you think the potty money collectors will spot me a free one on a Sunday? No way. I have big bills . . . they make change. For the love of all the saints, not even free potty on Sunday. So I decide to teach the guy behind me a lesson in good potty manners . . . I make a point of paying for the five guys in line **BEHIND** him and all the while my bladder is singing a tune that soon became nearly unrecognizable! You can bum a smoke off anyone but you can't get a free or *"comped"* (Las Vegas talk for a freebee) trip to public potty. It must be a cultural thing, or perhaps a hostile anti-American statement.

Once *"situated"*, I notice a sign clearly stating: **"No refunds!"** Why would anyone want a refund? No logic there so, to get my money's worth, I grabbed a newspaper written in English to browse for nearly half an hour. Time well spent.

I am close to making an executive decision. I shall return to Vienna to study European History from the beginning of time until approximately 15:38 today. I will minor in German and use the rail system to train hop from country to country. I haven't determined why I am considering this but it seems good therapy for the present time.

We are deep within the bowels of a magnificent Austrian Palace, the previously mentioned Hofburg (of which there are many and one more fantastic than the other), and well-placed signs tell us: **"No Pictures in Palace"**. This is subliminal capitalism at work. There is a need, as in most parts of the civilized world, where it is demanded you buy an outrageously priced book at the close of your tour. Capitalism. I love it when I benefit and find resentment when I don't.

In this Austrian showplace, there are 1,400 rooms. A sign is posted in clear view: "Apply Within". It is clear that they desperately need cleaning people. We only get to walk through 943 of the 1,400 rooms due to remodeling.

Upon further scrutiny, here are some observations of our palace tour:

They have a penchant for gold; it is displayed in great abundance. We see carved wood, portraits and landscapes, parquet floors, silk wall paper and a huge billiards table (sweet). Blue and grey are the national colors. They appear everywhere. Opulence is at its highest leaving one to understand the nature of Europe's near-annual rebellions by the oppressed, *"common"* people.

It was abundantly clear, these folks never bought their furniture at IKEA. Tapestries on virtually every wall depict stories with an occasional *"fantasy"* thrown in (spoiler alert: leave your kids at home). The Palace had specific rooms for specific tasks; none are obvious but rather left to one's imagination. Most of these rooms are bigger than our 500-square foot Maui condo!

Well-appointed gardens are an apparent trademark, for they appear everywhere and each in perfect condition and appearance. Who says you must go outside the country for good gardeners? The landscaping here is spectacular and as a special benefit, the servants did not have to commute. Instead, they live on the grounds, kind of like a tale from Masterpiece Theatre on PBS. Nice benefit.

The Imperial Bed is bigger than a California King size bed. This *"crib"* was built in 1741 for Maria Theresa's parents which their daughter soon inherited and had apparent need.

Maria Theresa, it appears was a very busy woman giving birth to sixteen kids in twenty years! Where do you suppose, she and hubby, Francis I, Holy Roman Emperor, spent **MOST** of their time? It sure as hell wasn't on the tennis court, polo field or golf course. She spent half her life in bed giving orders during expectancies.

A note regarding the Palace's knickknacks and things: There are so many objects created just to collect dust. If a vase is broken, the culprit can expect a great chance of never to be seen or heard from again. There are many dungeons within the Empire. That, my friends, is pressure.

Maria Theresa controlled her dominion for a good long while but all good things must come to an end. She reigned from 1740 to 1780. Her husband ... the male factor ... may have had the *"gonads"* to be Emperor, but Maria Theresa was the real boss, holding those male friendly *"gonads"* firmly in her petite yet commanding hands.

King Franz Joseph reigned for sixty-eight years! He died in 1916 at age eighty-six. His benefit package must have been enormous! Curiously, he could have afforded anything and everything but he preferred a leather seat for his loyal and Royal Toilet. It may have been a reminder of horse-riding days in the saddle.

Another feature some folks may have noticed: Jalousie windows and each almost identical to ours in the Maui condo.

They say it took two hours to do Maria Theresa's hair, which fell from her head to her ankles. She really should have gotten out of bed more often.

Just as it will be in my house from now on, there were *"Specially Folded Napkins"* to announce the Monarch was at the table. Franz's napkins, by the way, were one meter by one meter, after all, he was an Emperor.

From our brochures, we learn that:

1740-1780 Maria Theresa, wife of Stephan, was the F.D.R. of her time, an early Democrat instituting Social Security and mandatory education of the nation's youth. She was a very popular ruler. Fifty percent of the girls in Austria bore her name.

Not from our brochures:

Maria was a *"cool chick"*. She liked to drink something stronger than orange juice and iced tea. She smoked, danced, played cards and worked out. Technically, she could not *"rule"* due to her absence of male genitals, but truly she had balls. Her husband, Stefan, was emperor in name only.

Interestingly enough, girls had but two choices in life, either marry or be sent to a nunnery.

Music is huge here. Mozart apparently loved this Palace because he hung out here a lot. He remains very popular.

While on the tour, someone called engineering. There was a bank of lights out along the walls. A gang of repairmen rush to change the bulbs or fix an electrical problem. Upon further inspection, the men discover all the fixtures are working properly; management was trying to cut back on electricity as part of their austerity program. I am guessing someone didn't get the memo. Within moments 300 weekend relief repairmen were sent back to the *"bullpen"*.

The floors creak a lot. Of course, this place is older than dirt, so we hoped to get out just before the floors give out.

Castle stories were derived from notes written by the servants. They received three meals a day for them and their family, a place to live and clothing. Being a servant was a coveted job.

It is difficult to buy gifts at every stop for six grandkids so we commissioned a tee shirt that says: *"Papa and Nana Went to Eight Countries in Europe (with a map of the journey and cities marked) and all I got was this T-Shirt!"* It seemed a good idea at the time but, in recent months it's been hard to look those kids in the eye. We promised Christmas next year was going to be a better selection of "T" shirts.

Maria Theresa, not to forget her, traveled with a 2,000-person entourage. This was one huge posse, my peeps! Surely, she needed name tags, about 1,997 of them. The remaining three were her closest friends, two of whom happened to be paid employees.

Apparently in the early days, they lit the palace with 800 candles. Imagine that task! I wonder if the wax melted on more than the floors and furniture, finding it splotched on gowns, gloves and those silly looking buckle-type shoes.

The ceilings are covered with unbelievable paintings of historical events much like those found at the Vatican, the objects of Michelangelo's endless and sometimes *"bizarre"* imagination.

But for the grace of God and the British army, soldiers preserved the Palace during World War II, not allowing its magnificence to be plundered.

There was mention of a marriage where a ninety-horse driven carriage brought *"someone to the palace to marry another someone"*. We're talking serious horsepower. Details later or buy the overpriced book at the end of the tour. I assume the photos of the wedding never arrived. It was so long ago, who could really remember or care?

Katarina and I are considering commissioning an artist to paint our wedding day, an over-the-counter ceremony at the Santa Ana Courthouse at 5:00 PM. on May 6, 1983. We just got in prior to the office closing for the weekend. We made a subsequent trip to a local 7/11 for cigarettes (what on earth did we just do in that courthouse?) and rice to toss on each other. I had a softball game that night at 7:30 PM soon followed by beer and pizza with the team at Lamppost Pizza in Irvine. This is a true story, and I know what you are about to say, *"That John Turzer is such a romantic!"*

Katarina helps confused tourists seeking to get on the Red Bus. Unfortunately, we are standing at the stop for the Yellow Bus. The Red Bus tours are for other parts of town. Katarina tells the guide to explain to the tourists where to get off the Yellow Bus to catch the Red Bus line. The Guide handles the request. Katarina gets a gold star, two Danka's and a free bus pass for life. She's a delight. She developed outstanding customer service and communication skills while working in the timeshare business when we lived in Maui.

Tour number two was a War Museum housing many armaments and uniforms. It was an interesting short tour paying tribute to Austria's more difficult, episodic history.

Tour number three was the Belvedere Castle which is now an Art Museum. More culture for Wolfgang. I examined closely most of what I could see up-close, and not once did I find a number hidden beneath the paint. Amazing. How do such remarkable things appear on canvas and without numbers? We leave the castle/museum and catch a free subway ride to the main Opera House.

Prior to taking in the *"off Vienna"* opera, we feast on a superior dinner at a high-end (fourth night-in-a-row romantic candles on the table, cloth tablecloth, cloth napkins) whole nine-meters restaurant.

The concert was great. There is nothing else to say on this subject. It's not like: *"Seen one, seen 'em all."* This was a great concert and no other superlatives are necessary.

Jumping on the trolley for another free ride to the hotel, Katarina again for the 100th plus time says, "Are you **SURE** you know where we are going?"

For the longest stretch, I have been aware of her asking this question and always searched for ways of answering her. It is a difficult for me to accept the idea that she believes I am quick to become lost or absent from my widely viewed and discussed keen sense of direction. Clearly, she has zero trust in Eagle Scout Wolfgang.

I am thinking of something smart to say but conclude not to pursue it lest I find myself in grand trouble with the author of my brief consternation, Lady Katarina. I will say this, however; aware of my scouting years, my skills, techniques and innovative thinking, still she asks the same question and yet always continues to look for my merit badges. She has yet to find them but it's a worthy adventure and quietly I thank her.

End of a wonderful thirteen-hour day!

***

Monday, June 3rd -
Vienna

It's a rainy Monday. Cold to the bone and just perfect for laundry and re-charging our batteries.

Katarina is resting. Her *"batteries are plugged in"*, giving her a shot at a new day. Yesterday's thirteen-hour day was brutal for her but she's tough and *"took one for the team"*. Today is our last day in Vienna. Two important chores await us: one, packing and shipping our treasured souvenirs and two, laundry.

The hotel staff directs me to a Mailbox Etc. store nearby. I gather up over 100 KG of meaningless stuff and am grateful that they will pack everything (for an outrageous price of course ... capitalism). I have never said *"Danka"* so often in my life! The owner tells me to return in one hour. The boxes will be securely packed and ready for taking to the Post Office.

Heading back to the hotel I find a lovely candy store operated by a pleasant elderly lady. I strike up a conversation, a sort of pantomime in Anglo/German that remarkably finds its own acceptable level of translation. I think this could be a title for my next book: *How I Mimed Myself Across Germany Without Really Trying*. Frown and smiley faces included.

The candy lady is, as previously described, a *"sweetheart"*; charming, and warmhearted. She reminded me of an elementary school teacher. Wolfgang selects the **PERFECT BOX** of candy for the hotel front-desk ladies. Thus far, this has been the best hotel customer service we've experienced in Europe. I wish I could get them green cards and employment in Vegas!

My note attached to the modest gift read: *Danka Damen. Du bist der beste!* I double checked my English-to-German Dictionary just to be sure I wasn't, you know, writing the wrong words, which could easily start, given my proclivities, a serious diplomatic dilemma. The page's flip as I script my note. Aha! *"Thank you, ladies, you are the best!"* Nailed it!

The women loved the candy and make Katarina and I *"Unofficial Guests of the Week!"* This entitles us to (take a guess): Special **FREE** Potty Pass Cards everywhere in Vienna!

Returning now to the room, the glee of the candy store, the front desk and just feeling good about things, I update Katarina about my day so far.

We head back to the Mailbox Etc. store. Our boxes are packed and ready for the Post Office located about 250 meters down the street. The owner allows me to borrow a handcart but I must leave Katarina behind as collateral. If I am not back in thirty minutes she becomes a part of the company's employ. A fair exchange for the time being.

I could have been in New York City, Las Vegas, Chicago, downtown Los Angeles or Dallas. Dodging cars, cabs, buses and trolleys seems to be something of a sport, but it is not fair when the pedestrian, **ME**, is inundated by a sudden rainstorm, dropping the load of boxes three times and barely missed becoming a hood ornament on a trolley car before finally arriving at my destination: the friendly confines of the local Post Office only to discover the friendship was short lived. The line is out the door and only two, as in **TWO**, clerks are working the windows today. It gets better.

I find myself in my usual spot ... back of the line. Disaster however didn't hide its head somewhere in a back alley; nope, it rose to the occasion only to point its ugly finger my way. Just as I step in line, a whistle blows announcing it is time for lunch. Whose lunch, you ask? The Post Office workers' lunch, of course.

The Post Office will be one clerk short for the next three hours! UG! Don't they believe in brown-bagging it? Where on earth do those postal people go for lunch? Salzburg? Katarina must be rescued or suffer forced labor just because I borrowed a handcart! In my mind's eye, rich in imagination, I see the Secret Politzia ushering Katarina away in a black sedan never to be seen again!

My options are clear. I abide by them regardless of my personal feelings in this matter. I agree to pay the *"go-to-the front of the line"* bribe leading to the only available teller. I cast my fate to the wind, deliver my packages to the trusted mail folks then rush back to meine frau Katarina and save her from her fate. However, rather than finding a desperate woman in distress, I find her smiling at some strapping, good-looking, young scruffy-faced, slicked-back hair Euro who is enjoying the *"cougar"* attention. So much for the heroics and the dramatic rescue. I should have stayed in line and saved the money!

Please do not ask nor estimate the cost to pack and ship stuff with no freaking value beyond sentimental, a value that most likely wears off long before we return home.

If you, the reader, plan to visit us anytime soon, be prepared for an eight-hour video showing 2,831 pictures broken down into eight one-hour segments by country, city, hotels, bars, restaurants, subways, Mailbox Etc. and Post Offices. It would do us good that, should you visit our home, please buy our dinner because we will be broke and possibly in need of having a yard sale.

Next on today's agenda, time to hit the Laundromat. A brief reminder: Laundry is a good thing while traveling. It saves on spending a fortune for new clothes. We gather up the dirty clothes and begin our journey to the Laundromat, which I learned the hard way the other day, is a short nine minute thirty-two second walk from the hotel. On the way, we find a cell phone store. Wolfgang buys an

IPhone5 case with built in backup battery. This is a very un-American retailer. They take cash only. Once more, I put Katarina up as collateral while I hustle to the local bank ATM machine just down the street. Katarina couldn't help herself, "Sure, Wolfie, I will stay here with my new stud-buddy from Turkey." The *"stud"* is complete with scruffy unshaven face and rich, dark black hair. Another Euro seeking a *"cougar"* moment.

I have my ways of getting even. The cell phone guy is convinced we are part of the Embassy Corps. "Yes, I am the Slovakian Ambassador to Austria, the Honorable Wolfgang Turtzer. This is my wife Mrs. Katarina Turtzer. We learned English at Oxford and studied lip-reading at Harvard and M.I.T." He *"buys the story"* and gives us a great deal ... only a 200 percent markup. What a deal!

After paying for the phone case, we are again off to the Laundromat. Katarina has soap powder (white) in a small plastic bag ... do you see where I am heading? The bag falls out of her pocket and onto the sidewalk. Immediately, the Secret Politzia descend upon us from every angle, blocking our path. They demand to inspect our passports and then order up a paddy wagon. We frantically explain **SOAP POWDER, NOT DRUGS** and prove it by swallowing down some of soap powder followed by a bottle of water then belch up soap suds, our mouths foaming like waves crashing along the shores of the Pacific.

They buy our story. After all, who would go so far to prove their innocence when all the cops had to do is add water to the powder in the bag and the truth would be known? It is clear again that the Secret Politzia enjoyed the middle of the day show we put on for them on the sidewalk. Also, curious people walking the streets have their cell phones out and are snapping photos and video taping the incident. I trust this *"event"* will go viral on YouTube.

While still belching soap suds, we take another free trolley ride to the Laundromat. Arriving at our destination, we find a *"dubious"* lady sitting quietly and quite alone. My curiosity considered her doubtless a member of the Secret Politzia establishment. She says nothing, manicures her nails, then *"checks us out"* one last time before leaving. Meanwhile, a plumber-butt-crack character, who is doing his laundry, does his best to entertain Katarina. She is not impressed as she sees enough of this from me at home.

While the clothes are being laundered, I head out to find a coffee shop. Here's what I learned from the nearby merchants as I inquired about the location of the closest coffee shop. Store owners need to get out from behind their cash registers more often and inform other retailers up and down the street what their establishment sells. No one knows where anything is even three doors down! (like where can I buy a cup of takeaway coffee?)

After a short walk up the block, I find a coffee house; however, they do not sell takeaway coffee. "You vill zit down und drink das coffee. Maybe buy das kookies or zumthing?" Translation: "You will sit down and drink the coffee. Maybe buy a cookie or something." My phonetic German is waning. I really should have studied harder in high school.

Anyone seen my gloves? It's raining, plus the wind is blowing fiercely. I am freezing my backside off with faint hopes for a brighter tomorrow! Soon we will be departing for our next location, a two day visit to Slovakia.

I digress for a moment. Through the *"grapevine"*, we learn that there are **NO** laundries in the small tourist village of Sklene Teplice (where one spa offering mineral baths is the extent of the village's economy) in central Slovakia (Google Sklene Teplice for the exact location), our home for the next two nights . . . only a river running through the village with various size rocks located along the shore-line for clothes washing. I suspect we will not be inclined to do our laundry *"Sklene Style"* ... i.e., pounding our clothes against various sizes of river rocks. While we like to *"go local"*, this would be pressing the experience and not good for Katarina's sore knees and lower back!

With the laundry completed and returned to our hotel, we decide to window shop the various retail stores near our hotel. Tomorrow will be a long day.

Time for nourishment. We decide on another quaint *"locals"* restaurant for dinner. Again, great food and great service. As is our custom, we *"tip well"* and earn another beer mug for the collection. As we rise to leave, we notice a group of elderly gentlemen dining in a private room in the rear of the restaurant. We surmise this is either an *"off-the-books"* city council meeting or the place where retired Secret Politzia hang out together and reminisce about the *"good old days"* of Communist rule. It was just one of those moments when I could no longer contain my imagination for mystery and drama; the intrigue provided me a moment of sheer entertainment.

***

Tuesday, June 4th -
Vienna to Sklene, Slovakia

Today, we pick up our rental car and head for Slovakia, my father's family homeland. The purpose of this side trip is to trace his roots and learn about the village and country he came from . . . the who, how and when of one side of my family tree.

We took extra-long showers before leaving Vienna after hearing the showers in Sklene Teplice, a small village in Slovakia, are five-gallon buckets of lukewarm water hung on an oak tree branch, each bucket complete with 1/16th inch holes drilled in the bottom. Should you run out of water someone climbs up the tree and refills the empty bucket. There is, so the story goes, a two-bucket limit per week.

Slovakia at best, has fair electrical power. The systems that make life habitable are thirty-five to forty years old and are getting older by the day. Cell service and Internet could be two borscht soup cans tied together with thin string. So, if you don't hear from us for the next few days, please **DO NOT** call the Slovakian Embassy, KG, Interpol, CIA, NSA or the United Nations in search of us. You **MUST** have the correct Borscht Can SMTP (Simple Mail Transfer Protocol) access.

Should you **NOT** hear from us by Friday. Worry! Call the kids, they have our wills. Please enjoy the Maui condo. While you are at it, cancel the Nevada home refinance with Quicken Loans. Draw straws for the cars, baseball cards and autographed memorabilia. Look for loose change in the couch and chair cushions. Diane gets Tee the cat. One more thing, keep my golf clubs in a safe place, just in case there really is reincarnation.

Leaving the hotel, we take a Mercedes cab (our third this trip; they seem to be in abundance in Europe) and head for the car rental station. Naturally we are being serenaded by the big three on our way out of town: rain, wind and cold! It's June, what's with this weather? What could possibly happen? A phrase that became a question which now haunts me.

Auto Europe uses local brokers to handle their rentals. Our broker *"dude"* is not overly friendly. Must have **SKIPPED** customer service charm school. The first car he offers is a *"stick shift"*. I am stoked. Svetlana, formerly Katarina, is kaput, so we go with the *"stick"* option.

The car has no built-in GPS (as though I was really expecting it) so we, at Svetlana's firm insistence, rent a GPS device for a phenomenal price of €36 a day! That's a lot of borscht!

We provide our destination address to our increasingly unfriendly agent who attempts installing it into the GPS device for us. And, just as I suspected, he, the agent, has difficulty installing our destination address in English. I knew it! I just frigging knew it! Finally, he declares that all is good, it is set up and ready to go. €36 per day ... what a rip off! But wait, there is more insult to injury.

The agent **NOW** informs us that, there is an €18 per day surcharge when taking their car into Slovakia, plus we must buy a driving permit when crossing into Slovakia to access their freeway (note: the only freeway, as in one). The €14 access fee is good for thirty days. We load up the rental, a three-year old, dirty, near-junker VW four-door mini station wagon with a mere 66,000 km on the odometer.

Last, but not least, we are **FORCED** (like no do this, no car, end of story) to put a €2,400 deposit on our credit card for the right to drive in Slovakia! I can only imagine what the roads are like and consider whether I can get my security deposit returned. Brother, they sure know how to treat their guests and visitors! I am still uncertain if our agent is serious or just having fun making up this crap as he goes along. I don't even want to imagine what more he could ask of us or charge to our plastic.

Our journey finally gets underway and, of course, it begins to rain. We miss a few turns in the process. The GPS lady begins screaming at us in both English and Slovak and despite her smug tone, manages to get us back on the right highway.

We enter Slovakia, change our names to Svetlana and Vladislav, find a clean convenience store, acquire our driving permit and load up on munchies, wine, and whatever else caught our fancy. We are apprehensive about the village of Sklene Teplice where no more than 400 people reside. What could we expect the moment word gets out that we have arrived?

Now the *"GOOD"* news ... our very unfriendly car broker and GPS programmer screwed up. The GPS lady, with deft and perseverance, delivers us into Nitro, Slovakia, adding: "You have now arrived at your destination." Not only **"NO WE HAVE NOT, BUT LIKE HELL NO WE HAVE NOT!"**

We drive around the town, their narrow *"roads"* full of potholes and in dire need of repair fifteen years ago. We have *"no fricking idea"* where we are other than we are roaming through a residential area and are being carefully watched by those walking the street.

While fearing the worst, we spot a sign that has a universal meaning for all who can decipher any alphabet including Slovak, German, French, Russian or Italian: Pizza and Coca Cola!

Tired and frustrated, we walk into the only restaurant in Nitro. We met two nice waiters who speak enough English to greet us, chat, take our orders and inquire where we were from in America. The moment we gleefully admitted *"Las Vegas"*, the two were transformed into a couple of fun-loving pals anxious to see *"The Gambling Capital of the World"*, keep whatever they do in Las Vegas a secret, and spend days in Gentlemen's Clubs getting twenty dollar lap dances. Vladislav makes a comment assuring our new found friends that he can arrange the lap dances. Svetlana does not take kindly to Vladislav's offer and whacks him not so gently over the head with her umbrella.

We enjoy our soup and pizza. The boys remain entertaining and attentive. We have made two new *"best friends"*. They bring out their laptop and together show us where we are and where we should be heading. Sklene Teplice is a good hour or so down the freeway. Needless to say, the food is great, the waiters terrific and the directions to Sklene Teplice perfect.

Walking to our car, we meet a local Politzia officer. One of my goals on this trip is to get a fifteen to twenty second recording of a European Politzia car siren *"uga-uga-uga"* that you hear in every European movie Politzia car chase scene. To my chagrin, the Politzia officer looks at me like "You stupid Americana, I will **NOT** turn on the siren for you to record the sound ... just get out of my town **NOW**."

Within an hour, we arrive in Sklene Teplice and decide to drive around the village. The rural roads are like scenes in the back lot of any pre-1950's movie. We are beginning to believe we have found the birthplace of the Turzer family. Now, all we need to do is find the Village Office.

We stop by the only industry in Sklene Teplice, the local spa, and employing lively pantomime communications techniques, we attempt to have the employee we are *"trying"* to communicate with direct us to the local Village Office. Success (we think), she directs us down the street. Unfortunately (i.e. what should we have expected), *"something"* was lost in the translation. So, we stop at a bar close to where the Office is supposed to be located. Of course, none of the town drunks speak English or any language. They are shitfaced at 15:00. Finally, a young, blonde waitress comprehends what we are asking and points to a house two doors down. Off we go.

The Village Office is staffed by two middle age Fräuleins. Neither of course speak English. They call a friend from the village to translate. A very nice gentlemen shows up and, after a brief conversation, proceeds to tells us we are in the **WRONG VILLAGE**. He provides a map printed in Slovak to Sklene (versus Sklene Teplice). One of the ladies calls the Sklene Village office and sure enough, finds out the Sklene Village person is expecting us! We are relieved and say we will be there tomorrow. Not so fast travel fans, the Sklene Teplice lady tells us that the Sklene office will be closed on Wednesday and Thursday, but it will be open on Friday. Holy Shit. We have traveled half way around the world in search of my family roots and the office will not be open until **FRIDAY**. What's up with that? Friday will **NOT** work for us as we will be in Italy! International détente comes up with a solution, the Sklene Village lady offers to wait for us **IF** (a **BIG IF**, like **DON'T** show up at 17:01) we can be there by 17:00 today. Piece of cake. We announce that we **WILL** be there (fingers and toes crossed). The English speaking gentleman provides directions. We head to the freeway for a forty-five minute ride.

After a few miles on the freeway, we exit onto a *"two lane"* winding, narrow, potholes everywhere, and no shoulder *"road"*. Along the way, we encounter transformer-like eighteen wheelers heading in both directions. What is going on? Where are we? Later, we learned that this *"road"* serves as the main route between Slovakia and Poland! Holy guacamole.! Because of the trucks, we are going nowhere fast. Time is clicking down (tic, tic, tic). We need to make it to Sklene by the 17:00 deadline. The directions indicate we should be looking for the *"turn here for Sklene sign"*. All of a sudden, out in the middle of nowhere, we see a twelve-inch square (don't blink or you will miss it and wind up in Poland) sign *"Sklene 4 KM"*. We bear left. Only four KM to go and twenty minutes to find the Village Office. There is no doubt in our minds that we will make it with time to spare. Within minutes, we enter a time warped village. Since the beginning of time, there are no street names, only house numbers. The Village

Office is located at house ninety-seven. We employ pantomime to ask a elderly resident working in his yard where might we find house ninety-seven. We get the typical Euro hand directions and proceed to roam the Village. The houses are numbered; however, we quickly learn they are not in consecutive order. We find ninety-six but no ninety-seven. Pressure is mounting The clock is rapidly approaching the magic hour of 17:00. We *"guess"* and turn right and go another 100 meters. There it is ninety-seven, the Village Office! We arrive with four minutes, twenty-three seconds to spare!

We are greeted by the friendly Village clerk. She speaks no English; however, she has the 1919 Village birth records that are recorded in a very large bound book ready for our inspection. The cursive penmanship used to record each birth is very ornate. With the help of her daughter, Petra, and Petra's boyfriend Adam, we purchase three certified copies of my father's original birth certificate. There is a nominal charge for the certificates. I give her €10 and say "Keep the change." We inquired if there were any Turzers still living in the Village. Unfortunately, there are none. There was a Schwartz (my cousin and godfather's family) and one Antoni (father's mother's maiden name) still living in Sklene. She gave us the house numbers. The Village clerk maintains an 3" x 5" index card for every household in the Village. She also maintains a running Village census . . . 741 people are living in Sklene as of today.

Before leaving, we asked about the 1944 massacre of 187 male residents sixteen years of age and older (including three Turzers) by the Nazis. Petra and Adam offer to show us the Memorial site. We follow. The site is an eerie place as you picture in your mind what terror must have occurred here leaving many widows and fatherless kids. Not just here but all across Europe.

We return to Sklene Teplice taking the narrow, winding, pot hole-filled road all the while being challenged by numerous eighteen wheelers. We check into our ten room hotel, The Sklene Teplice Pension 4587. The balance due must be paid in cash. The front desk closes at 19:00 and the front door locks at 21:00. So, if we are out and about after 21:00 (for the life I me I **CANNOT** comprehend being out that late ... this Village is **NOT** Las Vegas), our room key fits the front door as well as our room. There is no elevator (come on now, did we really expect one) so Vladislav halls luggage up forty-five steep wooden stairs.

Here is a sample of our room *"features"*:

Low to the floor bed (like right on the floor). It is clearly evident by the dusty, musky smell that greets us when we open the door that no one has stayed in the room for at least six months.

No night stands.

There are two wall mounted lights, one with and one without a lamp shade.

The room's one window has shear window coverings . . . so prepare to wake up at 5:00.

The TV is a thirty-five year old, ten inch black and white model offering twenty channels, five repeating four times. None are in English or broadcast world news.

The remote control is missing the battery cover (rubber bands are used to hold the two batteries in place) and would not turn on or turn off the TV. Every time you changed a channel, you had to adjust the volume.

Svetlana asks the front desk lady (owner's daughter who recently graduated from the University of Slovakia) for a hair dryer. She informs Svetlana that this hotel does not provide in-room hair dryers. When Svetlana challenges this policy, she is told, "Lady, this is Slovakia not the United States." Oh well, Svetlana will just have to go with the *"wet hair look"* while here.

We head out for dinner, our choices are pizza, pizza and pizza at the three bars that are open. So, we order a pizza with olive oil and garlic, kielbasa, bacon (really ham), onion and green olives. It is clearly apparent we will be popping Rolaids by the handful tonight to ease the heartburn and chewing breath mints to try to kill the lingering garlic "taste" that will just not go away. No *"swapping spit"* tonight.

The total cost for our dinner of pizza, beer and wine was €7.30. I leave €10 and get to keep the beer glass.

We stroll back to the hotel to watch the *"Bourne Supremacy"* on the iPad. We are frequently brushing our teeth and gargling trying to get rid of the garlic breath.

End of adventurous day one in Slovakia!!

***

Wednesday, June 5th -
Sklene, Slovakia

Good morning world! The sheer window coverings allow the rising sun to stream into our room, awakening us at 5:00. An hour later and, as has been the rule in this town since the invention of the wheel, we are, at precisely 6:00 greeted by the ringing of church bells. The resounding reveille, the sound of clapper against bronze and copper, was the official wake-up call for those who somehow missed the early morning sun shining brightly through their windows. Through it all, and to assure we miss all the early morning excitement, we rolled over and slept until 9:30, or about the time the locals were having their second breakfast or early lunch. We were content not to change either their routine or ours.

Time to fill you in on the shower.

The *"shower"*, about the size of a 1940's phone booth and is **NOT** big enough to turn around in (like NFW). It is **SO** small that one could not extend one's elbows or bend down to reach one's legs to lather and rinse. It was an interesting experience, almost spiritual in many ways.

The towels do not match and are extremely thin. Many are older than we are. Come on now, why should we be surprised. After all, we are **NOT** staying at the Marriott. Some *"towels"* are mono-grammed *"Miami Fontainebleau Hotel"*, souvenirs secured by the owner's daughter and hotel manager during her frequent trips to Miami Beach.

The soap and shampoo. Aha! Nonexistent. There was nothing we could get our hands on or bring home as fond memories of our room in Slovakia. However, being the experienced travelers that we are, we use the soaps and shampoo acquired in Vienna by means of our skilled five-finger techniques, a learned methodology expected of all globetrotting visitors and guests.

Finally, the fixtures on the doors and aging walls of the shower make us feel, let's say, uncomfortable. The hand held shower device, when held, comes loose in your hand. Yours truly, Vladislav, turns around, knocks off both the shower head and wire would-be soap holder basket. Svetlana, the former Katarina, is brushing her teeth at the time and starts laughing so hard that she can't contain herself. Vladislav tries to put the basket back but its twenty-year old suction cups refuse to conduct their duties, failing completely. All we need are four more people to join us to make this a completely tribal activity. Svetlana continues to laugh herself silly for the next four hours understanding the circumstances in which we have so keenly and recognizably found ourselves.

Leaving the room, we find a hair dryer just outside the door. There is no rhyme nor reason why this twentieth century device has been placed or misplaced there; but, Svetlana is relieved to know that, tonight she can and will wash and dry her hair!

Finding something to eat for breakfast is real chore. The *"best"* and only option we can determine as *"food"* is a microwave heated up frozen ham and cheese Panini and two Espressos. The going price: €5.

Sklene Teplice has but one industry: mineral baths. This is how it works. For twenty minutes you soak in a pool heated to 102-degrees, followed by twenty minutes of rest (commando style they tell us) wrapped in warm towels (minus the Fontainebleau monogram) and twenty minutes of sitting in a high-end massage chair. The total cost is a mere €7 each. This turns out to be the best bargain so far on our trip. We tried to schedule a massage; however, the spa is booked until Saturday. We schedule the mineral bath for 16:00 instead.

Another day in Europe, what else, another day of rain. We are heading back to Sklene to look around the Village and get a sense of what the world looked like at the turn of the twentieth century. As we approach the Sklene turnoff, Svetlana sees a man peeing, as in urinating, on the side of the road while smoking a cigarette, not an impossible task but one not worthy of witnessing. At first, she doesn't know if this offends her, then decides to roll down the window and snap a picture of his combined activities. As things often happen, she misses the shot and in retrospective, we asked ourselves if The *"Smoking Urinator"* had done the same thing ... missed his shot.

We arrive in Sklene to search out my family tree. We stop at the main cemetery and read gravestones, hoping to find relatives long departed. Nothing, no Turzers are buried here. Then, we head off to locate the house in which my father lived. After a long drive about the Village, trying to seek advice but without much more than strange looks, we determine the house no longer exists. It is, after all, decades since my father came to America. We finally learn the house was replaced with an apartment building. We stop at the Village Catholic Church and walk through another cemetery. However, the yard and grave stones are not well kept. With the constant rains, the grass is approaching knee high. In my mind, I think, *"Why are people dying to come here?"* The answer is, they apparently stopped some time ago.

Our drive up and down the streets is not in vain as we find a bar and opt for a beer. The only thing on the menu is pizza. However, you guessed it, *"No pizza today"*.

It is not yet noon. Two *"locals"* appear to have had more than enough to drink today. We engage the bartender and her *"patrons"* in pantomime trying to explain that this is the Village where my father was born. Again, looks of inferred ignorance fills their faces, after all, we are in their neck of the woods and not ours.

Vladislav takes a picture of Svetlana with the two old beer guzzling geezers in the bar. One steals a kiss from Svetlana and reveals he is a happy camper. In his native language, he confirms that this *"Happy Camper"* is the **ONLY** man in this Village to have ever kissed an American. I believe this fellow's newest claim is that the Village has an idiot and he resides forever in its Hall of Fame.

Back on our self-created tour of the Village, we notice that wood burning stoves provide heat for the winter months. Each home has large stacks of precisely chopped and uniformly stacked firewood. It seems an obsession that each is the same length and size.

Local women are strong wood choppers and quite possibly strong arm-wrestlers. We take a moment to watch the ladies hoeing and weeding. Svetlana passes on farm labor, preferring instead Starbucks, wine, gourmet meals, reading novels and exploring Europe. No hostels, tents or rooms like we are sharing in Sklene Teplice.

Driving back to Sklene Teplice, we find a small town that, believe it or not, has an ATM and a bakery. We are no longer cashless and we can again assume our roles as *"Filthy Rich Amerikans"*. More than this, we stock up on low cal, no sugar, no fat (right) pastry for breakfast in the morning.

We return to our *"hotel"* and head over to the spa. The mineral bath is *"to die for"*, a must-do before you meet your maker (as the saying goes). On your next trip to Sklene Teplice, please make sure you visit and enjoy the baths.

Svetlana heads back to the room to shower and wash and dry her hair. Vladislav goes to a local's bar for a beer. The bartender pours a shot of whiskey *"on the house"* for me and one for himself. We click our glasses, raise them high and then exchange the local phrase for *"Cheers,"* or *lahime* – *"to life!"* The *"skoals"* are repeated three more times at the bartenders" insistence and suddenly I believe I have a friend forever. A couple of customers enjoy their pub life and fire up their smokes, filling the room with second hand smoke. Oh, how I love that aroma, especially in my hair, clothes and nostrils. The truth is, I do enjoy the smell, it's the rest for which I have little interest or need.

Svetlana has a different need for dinner this evening. Pizza is nice but **NOT** two nights in a row, especially in Sklene! Allowing that I am more, not less, than three sheets to the wind, Svetlana makes like Danica Patrick in our six-speed rental and drives us to a nice restaurant, one with a tablecloth, silverware and a full menu. We enjoy our meal and the view. The sun is out. It has stopped raining. We are in no hurry. We are also the **ONLY** customers left in the restaurant. Unbeknownst to us, after all, we are on vacation, the restaurant closes at 20:00. We get the *"hurry up, shake a leg, we want to go home"* look from the waitress and bartender. The check is paid, the tip left at the table and the silverware intact.

Back at the hotel, we finally get the Internet password **BUT** we must sit on the balcony (large enough for one person at a time) because the signal will not penetrate the two-foot-thick cement walls.

I listen to ESPN 1100 Las Vegas Sports Talk Radio and call in to offer a comment: "Hi, this is Vladislav from Sklene Teplice. Long-time listener and a first-time caller. Love the show. Let's breakdown the Slovak league team handball playoffs." The conversation was brief and pointless. But it helped end my day, a great day on our journey without ado (upheaval may have been a better word).

***

Thursday, June 6th -
Sklene, Slovakia to
Vienna to Como

As anticipated, we awaken to the church bells: 6:00. We somehow slept through the 5:00 sunrise. We bid farewell to Sklene Teplice, most likely never to return but with fond memories. At least two.

Heading back to Vienna to turn in our rental car, we give up on the portable GPS unit and instead do it the old-fashioned way, we use MapQuest and Google Maps on the IPhone5.

Our arrival in Vienna is uneventful with one major, horrific and near-calamitous situation. Google Maps tells us to **TURN NOW** onto another highway. Of course, we miss the turn off. "WRONG!", says our MapQuest lady who then proceeds to tell us, "You are stupid people." As it turns out, we must go ten miles further for the next exit in order to turn around and get back on the right highway to Vienna.

From this point on, it is easy sailing. We turn in the car (by now the rear brakes sound like the pads are gone but we don't say a word for fear they will keep our €2,400 deposit).

The agent takes the deposit off our credit card. We begin to breathe easily once more. It is at this point, we feel safe enough to engage in a bit of anguish regarding the rented GPS that did not function properly. The agent seems distant from my rebuke. I feel better with the knowledge my credit card is safe from his clutches. "I will take this up with Auto Europe," I proclaim as a genuine threat. He doesn't flinch. I did register my complaint as promised, put this fellow in his place, rooted out the proper management of the GPS thingy and was rewarded with a credit I most richly deserved along with the nomination for an Oscar, which I also richly deserved. When all else fails, reach for a handful of B.S. and wave it under their nose. It usually works!

With time to kill, we head to the old stomping grounds by our Vienna hotel. In the offering are two more free trolley rides, and being good customers, we accept the *"invitation"*.

Recall that, among the many responsibilities of world-wide travel there is always the issue of laundry. Dirty, persistent, laundry! Katarina (now that we are once again in Vienna) agrees to do the cleaning while *"Wolfie"* takes more stuff accumulated during our travels to Mail Box, Etc. for packing and then onto the Post Office for mailing home.

With my chores out of the way, I head towards the Laundromat. Along the way, I spot and buy a tan summer Euro cap. Next, I return the IPhone5 battery charger that did not work and get a full forty Euro cash refund (always keep your receipts). I stock up on Euros at the bank and finally arrive at the Laundromat. The rest of the day, Katarina invests in the economy (she shops). I buy two, one-day transit tickets for the trolley ride to the train station. I don't want to push our *"freebee"* luck any further. We enjoy another great dinner at the local restaurant, the one we ate at on our second night in Vienna. Two trolley cars get us to the train station without incident. Securely aboard the train, we get to sit in the First-Class lounge and charge the IPhone5 and iPad. So far, so good until … our overnight train to Zurich and then onto Como, Italy is delayed due to flooding.

We learn that our train is being re-routed to Zurich via Munich. Hence, we will not get to Zurich in time to make our Como connection. We did, however, book a First-Class sleeper car with shower and small sitting area on the top deck of a double-decker train car. We begin our overnight journey to Como, Italy via Zurich, Switzerland. So as we almost always do, we toast one another with champagne as we begin another new adventure. Despite the knowledge we are on board a train, the *"clickity clatter"* of the train's wheels is something best found in the movies when used for sound effects. I get a great night's sleep on the top bunk ... never stirred one bit. However, Antoinette did not enjoy the lower bunk one bit.

At 7:19, the train stops; why this happens is a mystery. My first thought was that the Secret Politzia were looking for us. After all, we had done nothing wrong unless the car rental dude complained that we had threatened to report his poor customer service to Auto Europe. If they were looking for us, our best chance of escaping our imaginary *"run from the law"* is to change our names. Since we are heading to Italy, I am now Giovanni *(aka Gio)* and Leslie becomes the *"alluring"* Antoinette.

The train is rolling again. There is a knock on our cabin door. Our eyes widen and our hearts come to a near halt. We sit quietly, not moving a muscle and barely breathing. Secret Politzia? No, just the conductor with a pleasant "Guten Morgen Herr und Fräulein, this is the wake-up knock on your door." Relieved that it is not the Secret Politzia, air returns to our lungs and the color returns to our cheeks.

I executed a forward flip to get down from the upper bed bunk. Try that while the train is going eighty miles per hour! Perfect landing in a mere two square foot landing area. If you miss your landing spot, you crash into the table and chairs. Glad I am so flexible from working out. Antoinette here, "In his dreams....."

Shortly thereafter, the conductor, good man that he is, brings us breakfast. May I repeat myself just once more: First Class is the *"ONLY way to travel"*.

Let's talk about the train *"shower"*. The water runs for about nineteen seconds and then shuts off. You must press the button again and again. When you've gained its attention, you soak down, lather up and … of course, the train stops, creating a power shut down that lasts for about fifteen minutes, which naturally means no water, no kidding! Of course, Antoinette thinks this is hilarious. She opts for a sponge bath after seeing what Gio is going through.

Finally, the train cranks up. Well, it takes Giovanni one hour to get the dried soap off his body and thick head of hair. But, in the scheme of things, he is clean. One final note about the shower: should you be over six feet tall and weigh more than 225 pounds, forget about the train shower. As for bending over to wash your feet and legs, let that thought pass into a quickly fading memory. Showering on this train is like eating soup with a fork.

At around 9:20, the train enters a long dark tunnel. Where are we? They did not provide us with a map of our journey. We learn through the conductor that we are just a hair more than two hours from Zurich. The tunnel is exciting insofar as it is like a scene out of a James Bond movie.

Why is it there is no satellite TV in First Class train rooms? I am not a complainer, mind you, but as a thought, I am going to slip a note into the train's suggestion box.

We just received word from the conductor, "Two more hours to Zurich". Didn't we hear than almost an hour earlier? The explanation is quite clear, the train is switching tracks and waiting for other trains to pass. "Hey guys, take your time and get it right. We do **NOT** want to meet another train heading our way on the same track! Watch the lights … **RED = STOP, GREEN = GO**". Nothing too hard about that I hope. **UNLESS** (sort of like a **BUT**), the engineer is coming to the end of his shift and needs to get home to the wife and kids. It could be his day to watch the kids and take them to their soccer games. Could be his wife needs to be at work by noon! Gonna be close.

The view from our car is spectacular. Breathtaking scenery of Switzerland: green forests, small towns, farms, rolling hills, quaint villages, waterfalls cascading down the Alps, roaring rivers and the majestic snow covered Alps. I keep waiting for James Bond or Jason Bourne to come running down the train hallway being chased by bad guys!

With all the rain from the past few weeks, the grass is knee high. Landscapers will have a field day catching up, **BUT WAIT!** In this part of the planet, everyone mows or cuts their own grass and trims their own bushes and trees **PLUS NO ROUNDUP** for weed control ... these folks pull weeds by hand!

The sun is now out in full force. It could be in the seventies! Not only shorts and short sleeve shirt weather but sun glasses and tanning lotion could become the new norm. While I am at it, I am looking for my sandals. After twenty-four days, finally **SUNSHINE** and no rain in sight.

We are more than two hours behind schedule with who knows how much longer to reach Zurich. There are however, numerous trains running to Como later today. We **WILL** get to Como for dinner because we have reservations with George Clooney and his 200-fan posse. We don't wish to keep them waiting.

The conductor tells us that since this train is so far behind schedule, it will not *"completely stop"* in Zurich. So, we will have to toss our bags on the platform and jump! I hope the beer glasses don't break and Antoinette's new hip does not fly out of its socket. We practice jumping down into the hallway from our room which is five steps up, so we should be good, but we know we will **ONLY** get one try to stick a landing on the platform or else ...

Finally, we arrive in Zurich. The God's are with us and against us at the same time. We have a three-hour layover allowing us to store our bags in a locker, make a potty stop, grab some lunch and meander about Zurich. Switzerland has its own currency, the Swiss Franc. Potty for ladies is two Francs, for men one and a half Francs. I am not going to try and explain it but it surely must have some anatomical affiliation.

When in Switzerland, we switch names. While it's only for three hours, we become Hanna and Simon.

As the saying goes, *"When in Zurich, do as the Zurichians do"*. Go shopping. We stop at an unbelievable model train store. We buy three model airplanes plus the *"special glue"* for use in assembling them.

To our mutual benefit, I am glad my son has the patience for this kind of *"put stuff together"* skill and can distinguish the do's and don'ts in multiple languages. No worries, there are only 327 pieces per model.

For Jade's oldest son, Christian, we buy a miniature Swiss ambulance helicopter; perfect for him because it is not recommended for kids under thirty-six months. Since he will soon be three, he qualifies to play with it and put it in his mouth. He can also use it for *"Show and Tell"* when he begins pre-school this month.

We grab a few slices of pizza and some beers for a picnic. We head to the canal that runs through the city, a perfect place to just sit and enjoy the weather and the scenery.

The *"new"* Simon character with whom I identify, tosses bits of pizza crust to the pigeons. Swiss Politzia descend upon us from out of nowhere. While not demanding, "Up against the wall," they do ask to see our Passports to check the information against all Internet criminal and terrorist data bases (Interpol, CIA, NSA, FBI, Wal-Mart and the Secret Politzia). Simon and Hanna come up clean. Thank goodness we changed our names at the border.

While sitting on the canal wall, we both notice that very few people are looking at their cell phones. Rather, most read or talk to one another while sitting on the wall or strolling the pathway along the canal. Sometimes, they use hand gestures to make a point during their conversation. What a novel way to communicate. Why don't we do this? Talk, that is. Hand gestures where I am from can get you in a ton of trouble.

While sitting along the canal, we see many James Bond, Jason Bourne type sweet motorcycles. Riders move along like they do in Euro movie chase scenes. It seems to be a favored sport of some kind.

Our trip is now **COMPLETE**. I hear Politzia cars in the distance heading our way with sirens blasting. I am able to record a thirty-second *"uga-uga-uga"* Politzia siren for the movie about *"How We Spent our Summer Vacation in Europe"*.

Time to head back to the station, gather our belongings and hop on the train to Como. Ready or not Lake Como, here we come.

***

Friday, June 7th -
Lake Como

At 19:00, we finally arrive in Como. I call our rental agent/condo owner. "Ciao, my name is Turzer and my wife and I have a reservation ..." His reply is courteous and professional. **PLUS**, he speaks English! "Okay, Mr. Turzer. Your train was probably late. I suggest you take a cab." He provides us with directions to a *"landmark"* where his helper, Muhammad, will meet us. In addition, he tells us he will call the only restaurant near the condo where we will be staying and ask that they stay open for us. Ladies and Gentlemen, this is taking customer service to the next level, what a concept! I hope there is no *"catch"*.

Many people complain about taxi cab rides in New York City, Chicago or Los Angeles. Shoot folks, they don't compare to our *"cab"* experience in Como. What a treat! The *"route"* is complete with hairpin turns and one and a half lane wide roads with traffic in both directions and no place to bail out. It is a game of *"Chicken"* played by all the drivers. Our driver is the Como champion . . . He **NEVER** gives one inch on the roadway or flinches behind the wheel!

As we leave Como, I let the cab driver know I need to stop at a bank ATM machine for some cash. He pulls over in Friday night bumper to bumper traffic and holds up traffic for me. He gets into a verbal Italian battle with an old man standing on the street. They exchange *"choice words"* and a variety of hand gestures. It appears that they are **NOT** exchanging addresses to send Christmas cards to each other.

Thirty minutes later, we arrive at the designated meeting place near the condo, Villetta Felicita Number Four. Through a series of hand gestures, Mohammad communicates he will take our bags to our room and instructs us to walk up the **NARROW** road to the only restaurant open tonight. Well, the *"short walk"* becomes a three-quarter mile hike all uphill and dodging drivers who think they are Formula One professional race car drivers.

Dinner is *"bitchin"*. And ... prepared completely from scratch. We enjoy a terrific view of Lake Como and the surrounding mountains **PLUS** homemade Tiramisu and an after-dinner Lemon Liqueur.

Antoinette is in heaven conversing with the owner/chef. Imagine this, our own private outdoor restaurant with a killer, unobstructed view overlooking Lake Como, enjoying the best service and finest local cuisine. It just doesn't get any better!

Darkness begins to set in as we leave the restaurant. Plus, what else is new . . . just when everything seemed perfect, it begins to rain. We head to the spot where we left our bags with Muhammad; however, being stupid Americanos, we failed to get the address or location of the condo building. Panic sets in. We are high above the Lake but have no clue where the condo is located. Not a hint! There is a house sitting on the roadway with a 180-degree hairpin turn driveway. This cannot be our condo. I spy a set of stone steps descending downward towards the lake. No lights. It is now pitch black. I leave Antoinette at the top of the steps fearing that should the condo not be down the abrupt steps, she will not be able to ascend due to her new hip and its all-too-often barking reaction to physical exhaustion.

Carefully, I descend the uneven, slippery stone steps. About a third of the way down, to the left, I see a small glass elevator built into the hillside. Lacking courage and not feeling adventurous, I do not enter the lift but choose instead to continue my descent by foot.

Low and behold, at the bottom of the steps, Muhammad is patiently waiting for me.

Our condo is on the Lake, front row, seventy-feet from the water, **BUT**, you must walk **DOWN** ten stories of slippery, uneven stone steps to get there! Muhammad offers to retrieve Antoinette and guide her down. He also shows her how the elevator cuts off some of the often-troublesome steps. The fourteen-unit condo complex is exquisite and charming. Upon entering our unit, I look for the bedroom and discover it is on the second floor. The **ONLY** way to get there is to climb up a **NARROW** seventeen-step spiral staircase. Take a guess who got to carry the luggage up the steps? Correct. Gio.

Our view of Lake Como is simply put, **AMAZING**. And wouldn't you know it, George Clooney's estate is just across the Lake. Fortunately for us, he's in Italy during our five night stay. So, we plan to take a boat across the lake and hang out. Fantasy is so much fun!

Recapping our day. Breakfast in Austria on the train in our private sleeper car, lunch in Zurich indulging in beer and pizza while sitting on a wall along the River Walk Park, and finally, dinner in Lake Como, Italy. One day, three meals, three countries. It just doesn't get much better.

Given the number of uneven slippery steps to the narrow main road, we need to plan well and take only one trip up per day. We are in training for the Ultra-Seniors Fitness Competition. Seriously, the stairs are straight **UP**! I'll bet it is easier to climb the steps to heaven. The view of the surrounding area is *"to die for"* ... we just hope and pray we do not die ascending the steps.

***

Saturday, June 8th -
Lake Como

We awake to a sunny morning. What a **GREAT TREAT, NO RAIN!** We open the shutter style windows and look at a breathtaking view of the Lake and the surrounding mountains. What an awesome location for our stay.

Since we arrived late last night, we did not have time to stop at a (like one and only) local grocery store. Most likely at the ungodly hour of 20:00, nothing was open anyway. We did not see a 7-11, AM/PM or any other convenience store on the drive from the train station. Simply, put, we have nothing to eat or drink. After shaving and showering, we dress and make plans for the hike up the 248 steps to enjoy some breakfast.

On our way to the steps, we meet the condo owner, his wife and their eleven-year old daughter. We learn the gentleman is from Oahu, Hawaii and his wife, from Italy. Both have outgoing personalities. During her working years, she was a high-end jewelry designer. He is a businessman who has a touch of class. He and his wife own ten of the fourteen Lake Como condo units. Their daughter was smart, polite, and bubbly, offering us numerous sightseeing suggestions. The key to this family was raising their child in Como. Somehow it all made a good deal of sense. Her parents are essentially internationals and would doubtless take her places most would never visit. She will have the native instincts of a young lady from a village town with a view that is impossible to describe.

Lucky for us, they are heading out. They gave us a ride to the street saving us a 248-step grueling uphill journey and drop us off at the one and only local grocery store.

Before heading out, we notice that the condo complex has a few barbeque grills. We decide to grill and eat in this evening. The local grocery store is something out of the 1940's or 1950's. Intimate and family run, their meat case offers a variety of hand cut meats so plentiful that choosing is hard. Antoinette chose Shish Kabob and augmented our dinner with asparagus, salad, ice cream and wine. This woman is a **GENIUS**. We stocked up on breakfast and lunch items and earned the *"customer of the day"* smile. However, we have one minor dilemma: how do we carry the groceries down the street and then down the 248 steep steps? Using the elevator, we *"save"* about fifty percent of the steps and make it to our new home none the worse off.

Antoinette decides to *"chill"* today and enjoy a good book while sitting lakefront. Gio decides to go exploring. I hike up the 248 steps (no elevator for me, this is my cardio workout today) and grab the local bus to Bellagio. This lakefront area was the vision for the Steve Wynn created Bellagio Hotel in Las Vegas. The bus ride to and from Bellagio travels a narrow road. My bus driver is a former Formula One race car driver. We are *"hauling ass"* in and around cars and motorcycles similar to those in James Bond 007 and Jason Bourne movies. Local passengers seem immune to this and frequently slide across their seats while reading or looking out the window. Nothing out of the ordinary for their journey. I took a seat at the front of the bus. It was astonishing how the driver could squeeze through narrow quarters and avoid people walking on the imaginary space where signs clearly indicate *"there is no shoulder on the right"*.

Upon arriving in Bellagio, of course, it begins to rain. I mosey through the various shops and up and down the steep stone step walkways looking for that *"I just have to have it souvenir"*; however, the journey ends in failure. Nothing grabs my attention. Unfortunately, I missed my bus back to the condo by one minute and had to wait another fifty-nine minutes for the next ride *"home"*. To kill the time, I find an outdoor cafe and nurse a coffee or two. All in all, life is good.

Tonight, we enjoy our first home-cooked meal since May 13th. We fire up the grill, cook our *"out of this world"* shish kabobs, enjoy the asparagus and find tranquility in our one or two or three glasses of Italian wine while watching the sun set over the Lake. It is very romantic and offers a moment of reflection. We have much to be thankful for, including the entertainment committee, a company of local ducks who showed up for treats of scraps and our good wishes.

***

Sunday, June 9th -
Lake Como

Sunday June whatever (and who cares) . . . up a 6:30, put on the head phones so as to not wake Antoinette and watch the Stanley Cup Kings Blackhawks sudden death double overtime game from last night on NHL.com. The Blackhawks win the game and series ... so great to just hear Mike Emrick, the world's **BEST** hockey play-by-play person belt out, **"HE SCORESSSSSS!"** Back-to-back double overtime wins by Chicago. Nothing beats NHL playoffs **NOTHING** period, paragraph, end of story!

A footnote to sports other than the NHL. The Dodgers picked up a rookie from Cuba, #66, Yasiel Puig. The guy has an M-40 rifle for an arm and has hit four *"Jacks"* (home runs) in the last ten games. Vin Scully has found a whole new subject to offer superlatives.

Our day finally begins with Antoinette making coffee and preparing mixed fruit bowls and croissants for breakfast. I am trying to get her back in meal-prep shape for when we return home.

Today, we set our sights on a boat trip to Bellagio and two other super high-end tourist traps. Under lock and key, I am leaving behind all credit cards, rewording the old American Express motto: *"Don't leave home without it"*, reversing their message and their advice; we are now prepared to squander whatever cash we may have on hand.

Antoinette is texting our son-in-law on her iPad. What a world we live in. People in California have not yet gone to bed. We just finished breakfast!

Moments before we set out, we both receive text messages from Steve Wynn and George Clooney asking us to stop by today to *"catch-up"*.

I explain it will be difficult due to our tight schedule, but promise we'll do our best to make time for them. We are confident that, should we not make it later that day, we will definitely catch them tomorrow for cocktails. Sounds good to me. We exchange *"Ciao's"* as good friends always do.

To catch the local ferry, my Ace Wahine Antoinette and I take a five-minute walk along a narrow stone walkway adjacent to large lakefront homes. The weather starts out with a touch of sun. However, as we approach the boat to Bellagio ... what else, it begins raining so hard, the temperature drops dramatically and my eyes roll upward to the heavens asking a very simple question: Why?

Each boat stop has a person hanging out as the official boat-greeter. Part of their duties is to pull the plank from the pier to the boat. We buy an all-day pass for €39 for two passengers. Unfortunately, the first boat that arrives in only going one more stop, a place known as Nesso, a provincial port in the Lombardy district. From there, it will head back to Como. We are faced with choices: a. Stand in the rain, wait thirty minutes for the next boat sailing directly to Bellagio, or b. take the boat to Nesso and discover nothing is there but friendly folks and more rain. We opt for b. rather than stand around and get soaked as there is not a place to hide from the rain.

Disembarking at Nesso, we are greeted by the seventy year old boat boarder/gang plank lady who is fluent only in Italian. Communicating through a series of hand signals, broken Italian and body language, she directs us to the *"wait for the next boat area"*, a sheltered space clear of the rain. We meander to a cave-like passageway and sitting area.

Nearby, we spot five locals fishing, most likely, for their dinner. One dude hits the jackpot and snags an evening meal with perhaps half a sandwich for lunch tomorrow. The remaining four men better catch something soon or, *"no eata tonight"*. The guy who caught the fish is not about to share anything more than its aroma with the others. It's a fish eats fish world in these parts, partner.

As our boat approaches the wharf, the local boat dock lady rushes over to get us. Customer Service! Plus, we are greeted by the departure committee . . . four white swans sail by just for us . . . just like in the movies.

This boat is much larger and is loaded with Italian tourists from Rome. We crisscross the lake and stop a few times allowing people to get on and off the boat.

The view of the expansive hillside homes is magnificent. It's hard to believe that we were standing on this spot and seeing firsthand the progress Europe had made over the few decades since the worst times it had witnessed.

Again, the weather refuses to cooperate. It is cold and rainy. Giovanni is wearing shorts! He feels *"comfortable"* because he is also wearing a light pullover. Tell me, do I look out of place with the others blanketing themselves with jackets, gloves, scarves and winter hats? Well, do I? Stupid Americano.

The *"local"* boat takes a long time to reach our destination. It feels like we have been at sea for three days when we finally arrive in Bellagio. We should not have taken the local boat. Next time *"we taka da express"*. Dammit, I should have called George and Steve back. They must be disappointed. Perhaps I should leave a message on their answering machines.

Famished from all that time freezing on the Lake, we find a nice restaurant located fifty-seven uneven stone steps straight up from the street. The place is very busy. Must have great food. Only one table is open. The table, unfortunately is for four.

The hostess takes our name and tells us, "You come backa in maybe Trento minuti." For my non-Italian speaking friends, she asked us to come back either in thirty minutes or three years. I am not certain but I am banking on the thirty minutes.

Antoinette goes shopping while I wait at the bar for a cherished table. Shortly thereafter, a young couple enters also looking for a table for two. They get the same *"come back later"* message. I quickly spring into action and recruit them to share the table for four. They are *"good"* to share lunch with *"Americanos"*. Everything is hunky dory.

I rush outside to track down Antoinette calling out one of her many nicknames, *"Ace."* Ace, you ask? Simple. 1. Top card on the deck, and 2. How many people use **ACE** as a nickname for their honey? Out of nowhere, she appears. Things are once again looking up, or *"hunky dory"*.

We enjoy a very nice lunch of crepe thin pizza and beer and engage in great conversation with our tablemates. They are in their mid-twenties, unmarried, traveling by car for two weeks on holiday, and most likely living in sin. They live in Switzerland. The young lady is from France and has worked as an emergency room nurse for two years. She works three to four twelve-hour shifts per week. Her male companion/fellow sinner is a commercial mortgage loan officer (double-sinner). She speaks little English. His is better. Despite the language barriers, we understand each other. They give us four or five ideas of what to see and where to eat in Paris. My notebook is jammed. We thank them, pick up the check, implying it would be great if they rented our Maui condo either for a honeymoon or their next holiday. I figured it was a good deal for all of us. Good kids. We enjoyed their company and we trust they enjoyed ours.

Antoinette goes off to do her favorite thing, an odd hobby known as **SHOPPING**! I was here yesterday. So, rather than wander through stores and *"shop"*, I find a sidewalk café and order an eight ounce chocolate shake and a four ounce coffee for seven Euros. What do they think this is, NYC or the Las Vegas strip? I am in a captive tourist area. Good news, the rain has stopped, plus potty is free.

A quick "T.O" (time out) while I say hello to a few friends following us on Facebook.

Humongous shout outs to Patti Crist and Marie Janowick for suggesting our Facebook trip blog and continually requesting more pictures and video. I know they don't get out much, Patti lives in the "tulies" somewhere in upstate New York. I won't divulge the name of her town only because I can't spell it. "Tulies" works fine. Marie Janowick lives on a small volcanic rock in the middle of the Pacific known as Maui in the Hawaiian chain. Patti Christ: "Has it stopped snowing, after all it is mid-June?" Marie, "Are you still wearing those lovely Adam and Eve leaves clothes or did you finish the grass skirts you've been working on for the past two-and-a-half years?" I know I can't control my snarky tone, but it was just great having the chance to sort of reach out and give them both a verbal hug.

Just got word from Patti and Maui Marie that they have de-friended me on Facebook. I must have crossed the line with the above post. Now I am down to my last follower. So, if our other Facebook friend who is following the blogs is tired of the pictures, videos, and stories, tough poopy . . . blame them, not me. We are working tirelessly to please everyone and every request so please be patient. Hold on, I just received a text from Facebook. Unbeknownst to me, there is a three-friend minimum to keep my Facebook account open and active. Wow, you learn something new every day! I really need to start a major Facebook recruiting program for new friends, and pronto. Somehow, I know I can make this happen.

Since Patti and Maui Marie don't get out much, they are living their summer vacation through us. These ladies have already sent us $99.95 for the videos, pictures and autographed first addition of our vacation book and they have made reservations to watch us walk the Red Carpet in Cannes next May as we accept top award for best comedy movie of the year . . . "Sh?#! Happens, Traveling with John and Leslie!"

Now, back to the afternoon in Bellagio. Time to head out. The weather takes a turn for the worse, so we do not get off the boat at the next two tourists traps, deciding instead to head back to the comforts of the condo. Coming home on the last ferry, we meet twenty-two and a half or so drunken Italians heading back to Como after a day of visiting *"something or somewhere"* that also involved lots of beer and wine drinking. 17.2 or so of the people are all talking at the same time, waving their hands in a variety of gestures. It is quite clear that nobody is listening to anyone. One lady begins to strip! I clap and cheer, why should I be a party-pooper? She walks over to me and plants one on my cheek. I smile, wave at everyone, smile again, and say "Thank you for allowing me to participate in your follies."

As we approach the dark, remote boat stop near our condo, we indicate to the boat men that we want to get off here. The boat dudes look at us inquisitively and ask, "You **REALLY** want to get off here? We have not stopped here for years on a Sunday night." They repeat their question three times making us wonder are we really at the right stop? We assure them this is our stop. They are not happy to bring the boat to a halt and are forced to put on rain gear and gloves to come out of the warm boat into the cold and place the gang plank for us to disembark.

Now, catch this, as the boat is approaching the dock, the boat driver blasts the horn three times. A local dude in pajamas and slippers comes racing out of his house down forty-seven steep, slippery steps in the pouring rain and places the plank in place from the dock to the boat. Bewildered, he had to be wondering who is getting off here on a Sunday night?

Today, we fueled the Italian economy . . . the delicious food, the beer and wine, the espressos, and of course, the *"gotta buy"* gifts and souvenirs. The folks we met were good, kind-hearted souls who wanted to share a brief experience with fellow members of society. In return, we received free potty access, and with all the stuff we ate and drank today, we used it frequently. Our total trip cost per potty stop went down big time today. But more than anything, it was simply another day in our lives that we could look at and twirl it about in our minds.

We get back to the condo about 20:00. I am NOT going to walk up the 248 steps to the **ONLY** local store when there is a 99.9% chance it is closed. I am not thrilled with the thought that the local bar, if open, is serving only beer, ice cream and three-day old what-ever's. Beer and ice cream? Really? So, we have a snack consisting of half an orange each, wine, green tea, breadsticks, peanuts (snatched from a bar waiting for the last boat returning home), sparkling water, and a small bag of some funky air chips. Consuming this much nutrition in one sitting could be overwhelming; the need to watch television is not exactly an inspiration but rather a form of mandatory *"can fall asleep"* entertainment. We attempted to turn on the TV and watch a black and white DVD movie. Not the end of the world, but more like a trip back to the 1950s.

How to operate the devices that control the TV and the DVD player are a mystery to us. We have tried everything known to us with zero results. Our next step would be to either put in a late call to the Clooney's (if they will come to the phone) or some prelate at the Vatican, prefer-ably one who has TV savvy or a strong connection to a Higher Source.

We surrender, give up and, as they say, *"just faget about it"*. Outside, it is pouring rain; the Lake is overflowing its banks and is approaching our condo front door. We grab everything and race up the seventeen-step steep spiral staircase to avoid getting our feet wet which eventually could include our knees, hips and all the connected parts. I hope the owner has flood insurance. Standing on our balcony we *"imagine"* our furniture floating out the front door! Remember that part when I said all is fun and good and lovely . . . forget it. It is more like *"what else could go wrong?"*

***

Monday, June 10th -
Lake Como

Monday morning, 6:17, the 8,000-cc pro division motorcycle races begin. We awake to roaring engines as drivers duel around the narrow, winding main road 248 steps high above us. We hear them **SO** clearly even though they are three kilometers away.

Over the weekend, I observed many young studs driving their motorcycles and wearing their leather *"Joe Motorcycle"* body armor riding outfits. Their *"Gina Lollobrigida-Sophia Loren"* look-alike girl-friends hold on tightly while sitting on the Gucci leather padded rear seat. The women are outfitted in the latest Italian designer women's motorcycle fashion body armor riding outfits. Most riders wear multi-colored Rafael Picasso or Michelangelo painted 10" thick padded helmets. Not certain why the guys wear helmets; the way they drive, there cannot be any live functioning brain cells left in their heads. The women, quite a different story, mindless but why mess up their hair?

The bikers and their passengers roar around the hairpin turns swaying from side to side while maintaining perfect balance. Should they fail to maintain their balance, they would fly off a cliff and quite probably into the swimming pool of some unsuspecting owner of a €10,000,000 lakeside five-story villa. Hope they have insurance.

These daredevils fly past other riders going uphill, downhill and around hairpin curves. They pass on one lane stretches of the road.

They pass stopped busses often barely making it back on their side of the road before meeting oncoming traffic. So, sports fans with daughters or granddaughters, keep them **AWAY** from young motorcycling studs who believe themselves to be Jason Bourne and James Bond types. My lesson for the day to each of you.

A footnote to reality: Never think of starting an alarm clock or a designer watch company in Como. You will fail miserably. The church bells ring every hour on the hour ... all you need do is listen and count.

Speaking of strange sounds, the walls of this showplace condo are paper-thin. I swear throughout the night there is a bunny farm residing next door. It begins with what I thought is someone watching a provocative video or Italian program with the sound turned up just a few extra notches when it suddenly occurs to me that what I am hearing is *"live action"*! This guy **MUST** be a stud . . . good night nookie and now breakfast of champions nookie . . . God bless the Euros.

Perhaps I shouldn't share any of my thoughts with you about a person who apparently has a few remarkable talents. But what the hell, why not? I wasn't eavesdropping, mind you, I was ... being imposed upon. Yeah, that's it. The bunny farm guy was imposing upon my sleep. That's my story and I am sticking with it!

By morning I had composed a brief note and slipped it under their door. I wasn't necessarily expecting a reply, but I, at the very least, wanted this fellow and his partner to understand that the evening was entertaining as well as a learning experience.

Where did you learn to do whatever it was you were doing? Can it be found on the Internet or YouTube? Can this DVD be acquired in the back room of a local XXX store?

Is there a great deal of flexibility involved?

How often can a person do what you were doing daily?

Does this *"activity"* require a doctor's approval and/or medications?

When the noises stopped, I bang approval on our shared wall, whistle loudly and give them a standing ovation. I follow by asking Antoinette, "Did you hear that? We must learn those dance steps soon!" By morning, it is apparent that Antoinette is fully aware of what took place last night in the neighboring room. "Giovanni," she says, "Even if I wanted to do whatever they were doing, no fricking way, Bud! Remember, I just had a right hip replacement four months ago and it's going to take more than this short period for my physical therapy to put that kind of a grin on your face." Giovanni's reply was something like: "In addition to improving your health and mine, why do you think I spent the $5,000,000 for the new hip? The doctor assured me that you be better than ever within nine days! It's not like I am looking for a sixty-day money-back guarantee, but before your surgery I could handle *"I have a headache"* much easier than the hip replacement reminder." Although I can't swear to it, but I thought I heard her say, "Not in this lifetime, Mister," or something to that affect.

Every day, I receive at least fifteen emails from various non-English language sites trying to sell me stuff, things like *"sexy women's underwear"*, to the things I would never think about buying regardless of the price. How do these people know I am in Europe? I have never met them and I can't figure out why they think I would be interested in their products. Are the Italian Secret Politzia selling my personal information? Has capitalism invaded the ranks of the KGB? Now I know why the Italian Secret Politzia following us all have the latest high fashion jackets, hats and wearing expensive Italian loafers. The familiar *"Columbo"* look is now passé. No more trench coats and awkward "sorry, just one more thing" replies to their questions. Khrushchev must be rolling over in his grave watching this happen!

Not much planned today. The number one *"Giovanni Honey-Do of the Day"* is to climb the 248 steps and 180-degree driveway to the main road and buy some groceries or, number two, take a fishing pole, walk eight short flat steps, pray for an early catch and then grille it on the outdoor barbeque.

I was satisfied to try the fishing route, but I was out-voted by Antoinette's desire I make that trek up the hill and fetch food like a normal person. I agreed to her *"request"* but with one condition: she must join me in this expedition, claiming with a high degree of sincerity that, her presence would make all the difference in the world to me. It worked. Just hopea da store is open. It is Monday and, as was the Brussels experience, the potential for a disastrous day lingered.

After making it up the hill to the main road, Giovanni and Antoinette meander up the road to Peppo's, a local coffee shop and bar overlooking Lake Como. The view is worth the additional walk. It is a marvelous day. A serene moment while a pondering mind takes root in the sunlight of an enjoyable Italian day!

Giovanni is *"dreaming of creating"* no-overhead business opportunities in Europe. This is not a unique moment in his mind, but the framework for the analysis is grounded not simply in faceless opportunity, but predicated on something far more practical and appealing.

For those of us old enough to remember, on June 26th 1963, John F. Kennedy offered a most inspiring speech to hundreds of thousands of Germans, his argument invoking words of moral courage and inspiration to those imprisoned by the Soviet-backed East German government.

Part of his speech, directed specifically at Khrushchev and the Soviets was, "Lasst sie nach Berlin Kommen", "Let them come to Berlin!" This was a comment the Soviets would scoff at as Western propaganda, but they soon learned that with politicians such as President Kennedy, words have meaning and consequences.

What perhaps has become the most profound statement made during that and subsequent days, were the words that gave rise to a new ambition and view of the future were part of a brief comment that began: "Today, in the world of freedom … all free men wherever they may live, are Citizens of Berlin, and therefore as a free man I take pride in saying, Ich bin ein Berliner!" I am a citizen of Berlin! The German crowd went absolutely nuts, screaming their approval.

Well, sports fans, my dream is to do the same someday in Europe through our new customer service, business opportunity, property management, operational training and marketing company, www.jlt-euro.com.

Antoinette is doing exceptionally well climbing the steep uneven steps with her replaced hip. However, when we get home, she may need some new knees. The good news is that she has mastered the steep steps, and by all accounts is now certified to work as a goat and sheep herder on any steep hill or mountain in Europe with over a forty-five degree angle. I am so proud of her.

The look on her wonderful face offers an occasional sketch of pain and discomfort; however, she is made of tougher stuff and I trust she will bring all her will together to overcome her surgery. I believe we can get jobs locally and stay a bit longer! Giovanni can work as a multi-lingual guide/bartender and DJ Host at Senior Bars. The only restriction: the bar opens at 11:30 for lunch, buy-one, get-one free with coupon but NO AARP discounts. On the other hand, it could be one or the other but, **NO** double-dipping. We close at 19.00. The senior citizen customers will be fine people, but by this time of day, most want to get home to watch Vanna White on Wheel of Fortune or re-runs of Lawrence Welk and M*A*S*H.

Following breakfast, Antoinette and Giovanni decide on a bit of grocery shopping. The two meals in mind include lunch and dinner and decidedly both will be grilled. After buying what seems like one of everything, we again accept *"Customer of the Day"* greetings and receive two small brandy cakes. As a side note, we notice that the stock boy is also the same person who worked as a boat gang plank person yesterday where we boarded the ferry to Bellagio. This guy is a real multi-tasker, part-time stock boy and part-time boat plank person.

Our walk home from shopping again includes the array of obstacles, which by now are a part of our daily ritual. The 248 descending uneven stone steps wait us after managing to maintain our balance down the steep, 180-degree hairpin driveway running from the street to the top of the stairs. We ride the elevator part way saving 117 steps.

Antoinette cooks thinly sliced fresh chicken. We enjoy this along with freshly sliced medium roast beef sandwiches on a roll drizzled with olive oil and accompanied by marinated olives. Ah, the Mediterranean diet, I clearly enjoy every bite! For now, anyway.

While my Ace Wahine, the lovely Antoinette, decides to hang by the Lake, read a book and work on her tan, I decide to once again make the hike up the hill to mail post cards. Instead of following the main road, I choose to be adventurous and start climbing steeper steps leading toward a residential area, knowing that I will eventually (hopefully) arrive at the Post Office.

The uneven stone steps are damp and slippery; I hear and quite clearly see a 209 pound German Shepard who most likely hasn't eaten in days! His eyes are fixed upon me like radar as I ascend the hill. Between his growls, snorts, barks and heavy sniffing, he identifies me as *"fresh meat"* rather than an estranged traveler whose life is dedicated to his wife, children, grandchildren and his cat, Tee, and all things magical, which of course includes staying alive! I desperately search my pockets for anything resembling a snack. This *"heavyweight"* is an intimidating part of my day.

Thank goodness for the fence. I just hope it holds **BUT** (why is there always another **"BUT"** with us), I see what appears to be an **OPEN** gate door where the dog can get out, run down the hill and have me for lunch, snack and dinner! Not needing a new friend today and fearing for the worst, I hastily head up the hill and get the hell outa there! No looka back. Guess there musta be a locked gate I missed or the dog had been trained not to leave the property. Anyway, as I *"beat it out of Dodge"*, I continue to hear him barking and running along fence just dying for a piece of me!

Continuing up the hill, after a mere fifty more steps, I arrive at my originally planned destination, the Post Office and guessa what, the local Post Office is only open 8:00 to 13:30!

Having come this far, my adventurous spirit is alive, intact and well. I am committed to making it to the very top of the hill. My upward journey takes me up narrow, one lane roads and uneven stone pedestrian walkways through residential areas towards a church located at the top of the hill.

I am wearing sunglasses for the first time in four weeks. Along the way, I meet a few locals. We greet one another, them with a nod and a smile and me with "Ciao".

An elderly lady approaches. I give her one of my cheeriest Buongiornos. She thinka she knows me and begins a tirade like "Was that your grandson Joey who spray-painted my housa the other day, the little shit?" She continues rattling off verbs, nouns, adjectives and whatevers in rapid fire fashion while thrashing her bony finger in my face. I sense her anger and say, "No kapeesh, mio Americano, no understand-o."

I get an *"uh"* and disgusted wave of her right hand. We each go about our way. Musta be my Euro hat make me look like a local!

Would you believe it was 320 steps straight UP to the church including the last 117 at a 100-degree angle? Finally, exhausted and out of breath, I reach the church. Built in 1744, the ecclesiastical structure had numerous altars. The interior is well-maintained. The 180-degree view of the lake is spectacular. I look up and see more houses and two more churches 200 or more feet up; however, I am out of gas and running on fumes. I do not have the mental or physical energy to go any further. So, I decide to start my journey downhill. Hope I make it back. Pray for me, my legs, knees, back and lungs.

On the way down, I see a *"shortcut"* down seventy-six steep, uneven steps and say, "What the heck, you only live once". Since I said my prayers in the church, I am ready to roll the dice. I proceed down. The *"steps"* are **SO** steep I must shuffle down sideways lest I lose my balance and roll uncontrollably down the rocky terrain. I don't believe anyone in their right mind has used these steps in years. When I reach bottom, looking back up the hill, I discover why.

Drawing on every ounce of energy left in my body, I finally make it back to the main road and need liquid refreshment. The local grocery store is closed so better yet, I head to Peppo's bar for a few cold ones. Aliana, the owner's wife, do it all one and only employee, says to me, "You wifa Antoinette, she leava her sweater at breakfast." It was kind of her to tell me. Later we discovered she also called the condo owner. What great customer service! Before heading back, I stock up on *"Caramelle Italiano"* (Italian Candy) for the grandkids.

After 248 steps, downhill (no elevator ride for me, I am in training), I return to the condo and head to the lakefront beach to *"veg"* until 18:45. Antoinette and Gio spend two hours with the condo owner and his wife . . . super nice customer-oriented people. We talk shop and the JLT Euro ideas.

Time to grill the kabobs, sausage and zucchini. Antoinette makes a great salad and opens a bottle of vino. It is a superb dinner capped off with coffee and Italian ice cream, AKA gelato, for dessert.

Before you know it, it is time for bed. Tomorrow, our last day, we plan to rise early and take the boat into the town of Como.

***

Tuesday, June 11th -
Final Day in Lake Como

We awaken to a sunny day (two days in a row, a record for this trip). Today is the end of week four. Only seven more days abroad. It seems as though we've just got here. Giovanni, no wanna leaveo … no go home, not just yet.

We take the ferry to the town of Como for a day of sightseeing and other chores. First stop, the train station. Reviewing the schedules, we decide to take a later train to Paris on Wednesday. Mr. Train Person inspects our tickets and informs us that they are good for all day tomorrow, "justa get ona whenever you likea".

"What about the First Class upgrade we have, can you change it?"

"Not issued by our company, do it on train. Thanks, goodbye, good luck, arrivederci. I go back to my nap." He disappears! I can't wait for tomorrow! I just *"feel"* another great story will unfold and engulf us!

Our second stop today is to find an office supply store to buy boxes and bubble wrap for obvious reasons. Why, pray tell, did we buy all of these Italian souvenirs? I drop my Ace Wahine off at an outdoor food and coffee shack complete with outdoor seating in the shade. The weather is getting toasty. With no trouble, I locate the office supply store where a very pleasant store clerk walks me into their receiving department and says, "helpa youselfa to the open boxes and all da bubble wrap you wanna takea." These boxes previously contained various merchandise items they received. Thus they are available for me to, so to speak, help them get rid of. I find three sturdy boxes and tons of bubble wrap. I go to pay her but she says, "No charge. We no sella da boxes, we give em to you. Taka da bubbles too. They not for sale. Gift to you." I can't believe it! I am getting something for free. Christmas in June and in Italy at that!

I haul the boxes and packing material back to the outdoor café. Antoinette and Gio pack our *"worthless"* junk. Next, I gather everything together and march to the Post Office located three blocks down. To my surprise, the Post Office doubles as a bank. Unfortunately, or as things simply happen to us, I get in the wrong line.

The bank clerk directs me to Window Five, *"International Shipments"*. Please note, there is no sign over Window Five. I guess everyone in Como knows that Window Five at the Post Office is exclusively for international shipments. Now the *"fun"* begins.

Let's start with the fun and ignore the rest. I meet a real *"Antoinette"*, a lady in her late fifties or early sixties. I place the two boxes on the counter and after a two second inspection, she proceeds to tell me that I have used the **WRONG** packing tape. I wasn't aware of the difference between domestic and international packing tape. "Screw it," I say, "Just ship it." She must have gotten the drift of my comments. She gave me the international shipping forms to complete. These forms include *"from and to"* shipping address boxes. Customs inspectors need these forms completed. So far, so good. I ask for shipping labels to place on the boxes. (like I got at every other Post Office in Europe). "No havea, justa writea on boxas." Unfortunately for me, there were no Mailboxes, Etc. in Como. Aha, another business opportunity.

When filling out the international shipping forms and placing the address information on the boxes, I use our home address in the *"from and to"* areas. Next, she has me list the stuff inside both boxes including the quantity and price of each item. "Lady, it's just junkie cheap shit souvenirs! The postage will cost more that the stuff inside the box. Just ship it!" Now she checks the forms and boxes and sees the same address for *"from and to"*. "You cannota do this!" I tell her that I have done this more times than I care to remember in every European country we've visited. She calls time out and asks other clerks if this is acceptable. The answer comes back the same, "Rules is rules. We can no shippa d'boxes witt'a same *"here et there"* addresses!" Except for my growing frustration, the entire conversation was being conducted in one-sided Italian! I can see this is going nowhere and should I raise my voice once more, I am convinced she will call the Politzia. I make every effort to seek her assistance. I even go so far as asking if I could use **HER** home address as the *"from"* portion of the shipping label knowing this request was headed straight to the toilet. The shipping process is as they say, dead in the water.

Fast as lightening, I remember that **MY** Antoinette has the condo owner's name and address. I gather my boxes and my wits and head down the street with **NEW** blank custom forms to find my favorite person in the whole world, the one with the addresses, and like magic there she was sitting in the shade reading and enjoying a cup of coffee. It takes little time for me to explain the dilemma. Immediately, or *"quick as a bunny"*, we fill out the forms. Next, confidently feeling that this process is close to coming to an end, I head back to the Post Office and their Antoinette.

When I return, I am second in line behind a guy cashing paychecks for his **TWENTY-FRIGGING-SEVEN** employees! And I thought Window Five was **JUST** for International Shipments. Antoinette, I guess, was promoted to check cashing bank clerk during the short time I was away in addition to her duties as the one and only International Shipping clerk in Como.

Now, as everyone knows I never, if rarely complain about anything. But why didn't she direct the check cashing dude to a bank clerk or me to another mail person? Antoinette is a loyal government worker who gets paid by the hour and not the transaction. Ideas such as these occasionally whirl about in my head and every so often they find the release valve which allows me to articulate my frustration. To further accelerate my increasing blood pressure (which, until this day, was never much of a problem), I discover the guy cashing the checks also wants to ship a large envelope to Milan. She has to go find the special *"To Milan Only"* shipping form! More time goes by as he fills out the special *"To Milan Only"* shipping form! All the while, I am growing a nice two day beard waiting for them to finish!

Knowing I also need to change some money, I hold my place in line at Window Five by leaving the boxes on the floor and I mosey over to a bank teller and ask him to break two €50 notes. He informs me he can only break one! Am I not in a bank? Does he really say that he can **ONLY** break one €50 note? Does he ask fellow tellers for help? No? God, I hope Window Five does **NOT** closea for lunch soon!!

The Italian Antoinette completes the check cashing and mailing of the Milan envelope. Finally, she decides to finish my transaction. With gross efficiency, she examines and reviews each damn block on the customs shipping forms, asking me questions in Italian. She no *"speaka da English"*, which was obvious. Does she ask one of the twenty-two clerks standing around doing nothing to help her? Well. Does she? **NO!**

Let me get this straight. She is working the **ONLY** counter for international shipping. Based on her actions and questions, it appears that she has never ever processed **ONE** international shipment before!

Italian postal worker Antoinette appears **NOT** to be *"the sharpest knife in the drawer"*. In my humble opinion, (yes at times I **CAN** be humble) she is at least *"three Paninis short of a picnic"*! Am I her first international customer? Finally, it appears that we are almost done. The forms are correctly completed, the boxes are weighed and my breathing returns to normal. She pulls apart the six-part form. "Wait. Signori, you no pressa hard with da pen. I can no reada last e' piu importenta di copia." My interpretation of her English matched very well with her interpretation of English. "No, I am **NOT** going to fill out the forms all over again! Can't you make copies of the top readable forms?" You think I discovered a cure for Alzheimer's! Finally, it sank in. She scurried off to make copies of each form, twice, as in two-trips! Again, I am NOT a complainer, dammit, but anyone would think this maiden of confusion would look at the second set of customs shipping forms to see if the sixth part is legible. No, she doesn't. Hence, two trips to make copies. I often wonder what this world would do without my insight. I almost give her the stuff and say, *"Keep it. Just take them home to the kids or use for Xmas presents!!"* You can't make this shit up! This is real . . . she must have been trained and put in twenty years at the USPS or Kmart!

Finally, after a good ninety minutes, the shipping process is completed. But, I have one more question for her . . . I need sixteen international postcard stamps to mail our post cards home to family and friends (another Gio traveling tradition). Makes sense to me, she is the only international shipping counter clerk, so she must sell stamps to the USA! Wrong sports fans! She directs me to Window Seven across the room. So, off I go, no line and no clerk! Finally, someone looks up from reading a celebrity magazine and says **"WHATA U WANT??"**

"Sixteen international postcard stamps please."

"No havea."

"Dude, see that lady over there (my girl Antoinette!)? She sent me here to Window Seven to buy international post card stamps!"

He reiterates, "We no gotta international stamps here. You gotta see lady at Window Five." Antoinette was suddenly thrust back into my waning life. As I step away and head back to Window Five, a fellow standing near the end of one of the lingering window lines speaks perfect English, or, more specifically, he is no doubt a transplant from a borough of New York when he says to me, "Hey, bud, try the guy over there who is selling non-postage items and miscellaneous stuff. He's your ticket out of here." The guy doesn't look like he is an Italian Post Office employee. No uniform, I.D. badge and clean hands. Guess what? It turns out he **IS** the guy who sells the international postage card stamps. Why in hell didn't I figure this out an hour before? Walking out, I high fived my new friend and thanked him. As I was leaving the building, I briefly thought of giving the postal and bank clerks the *"internationally recognized single-digit salut"*. However, I decide not to. I may **NEVER** see my two boxes of worthless stuff again!

Time for a beer and a sandwich! Calm the nerves and recharge the batteries. After lunch, Gio and Antoinette head to a tram that runs up the side of a mountain to a small remote village.

The tram takes about eight minutes to reach the top. Eight minutes of uninterrupted peace and quiet. We are standing in the first car and take in the awesome views.

As the tram climbs the steep mountainside, we see tram repair-men expertly balancing on high wires fixing lights. At first, I thought they are either tram stowaways jumping off to avoid the conductor and payment for the ride or part of a high wire act much like the Wallenda's rehearsing for an upcoming performance.

We wander about the small village and head to a local outdoor pub to enjoy the spectacular 180 degree view of Como below and the magnificent day. Here we meet a very nice couple from Surrey, England. They, too, are world travelers. We exchange email addresses. They offer to put us up the next time we visit London and we recip-rocate should they visit Maui.

Time to return to sea level. We wait for the tramcar to take us down the hill. Also waiting are forty or more seventh grade school boys and girls returning home from a class field trip. Like pre-teen kids everywhere, they are making lots of noise. Suddenly, a female teacher belts out in Italian, "Shut up and act like you have been in public before. Don't embarrass yourselves or the school. Respect other people waiting in the 100-degree heat and 200-degree humidity!" or something to that affect. Whatever she said worked! They listened, what a novel concept. It was so quiet one could *"hear a Panini drop"*.

Antoinette and Gio jam into the last car. Here, I meet three young boys from the school group. We *"converse"* in hand signals and broken English/Italian. I discover they like soccer/football. They ask the name of my favorite players. I chime in Messi and Ronaldo! Well, some boys like Messi and others prefer Ronaldo. So, being a true Euro, I join in their rhythmic and blaring chants. "Messi, Messi and Ronaldo, Ronaldo", much to the chagrin of the other passengers and teachers. Antoinette is also not the least bit happy with Gio's behavior. Her eyes are rolling like a Vegas slot machine. "Gio, act your age", she bellows. "I am Antoinette, I am."

As we leave the tram, the chants continue all the way to the street. More kids join in, booing and waving hands in disgust at the name of the player they happen not to like. We have a mini-soccer riot going on. The teachers are not happy at all with Giovanni, but *"who cares"*? I am on vacation plus, these kids are really into this. As we walk down the street, I take a few photos and make a video. The boys are all responding like my grandson, Hunter, a true leader and showman! The leader of the pack asks if I am going to post the video on YouTube. I give him my email address. "Just email me and I will email you a copy." He beams like a beacon in the night. I am not certain if I am pleased or confused about this whole circumstance. Emails, YouTube, Viral? Did I just become an American Rock Star or an international nuisance? Only time will tell.

By now it is fair to say that, Antoinette is not happy with Giovanni and his childish ways. As we and the school boys go our separate ways, the boys continue to chant "John, John, Ronaldo, Ronaldo, Messi, Messi" all the while waving and calling out "Arrivederci" to me.

I am a cult hero in Como. Best feeling in the world is having fun with the kids while their teachers seek out the Secret Politzia to haul my ass away! I miss the students already. No matter the language barrier, we were having fun and truly communicating. I hope the young boy can sneak onto a computer at school or home and email me so I can send him the video and pictures he asked for. The boys were just fired up and not for a moment did they mean any harm. I am still hoping the teachers think the same of me. Amen.

Nana Antoinette is wilting in the oppressive heat and humidity. We *"crawl"* to the ferry. She finds three inches of shade and attempts to gather her strength. The ferry arrives but we, quite naturally, are at the wrong pier. *"Murphy's Law"* is in high gear!

A ferry person directs us two piers to the left. We walk as fast as we can and catch the local ferry home. This ferry makes frequent stops on both sides of the Lake so now it's just a matter of minutes before we can leave *"Murphy"* and his laws of probability behind.

We are so glad we had a super warm and clear day. The bright side of nearly frying in the heat of an Italian lakeside day is, despite the warm weather (remember for most of our trip it has been unseasonably cold and raining), seeing all the sights and hillside homes.

Dinner at 19:00 at the best (and only) restaurant in the village. This is our second night eating here. We now consider ourselves regulars. Chatting with the new waitress, we learned she lives 300 steps up past the church I climbed to. The same steps I climbed and nearly died the other day!

Another super meal topped off by the best homemade Tiramisu and personally churned homemade low calorie, low-fat whipped cream. We lick the bowls . . . what a treat for our last Como dinner.

The restaurant is struggling to make ends meet. The owner is a great chef but lacks what the business schools call marketing skills. Chefs work long hours and rely heavily on the quality of their food and their service. Listening to his story, he invited our review. Antoinette and I gave him a few suggestions on how to develop relationships with local tour bus companies. Adding frequent tourist bus lunch stops at the restaurant would greatly benefit the bottom line. We spoke of creating brunch/lunch one or two-item menus and working to have the tour busses stop on their way back from places such as Bellagio. Do the first one or two at near-cost to develop trust and show the tour companies the benefit of doing business with him. He needs more business to survive.

This is **NOT** Las Vegas nor is it Maui, but customer relationships are a premium regardless of where you *"pitch your tent"*. There are many small restaurants throughout the world that day after day, year after year, rely upon local and tourist traffic. In every case, the key ingredients to their success is customer service, location, food quality, food prices, customer satisfaction and the management of all the above. Take great care of the customers, it goes a long way!

Sitting next to us at dinner is a young couple traveling by car with their eight month old son, Johan. The infant goes about twenty-seven inches, seventy-two and a half pounds and has cheeks to match his body size ... very pinchable! Johan immediately develops a relationship with Nana Antoinette, something I also have enjoyed over the years. During our conversation, we ask why young German citizens want to travel to the USA? We learn they come to America not for employment but rather for the *"Glitz"*; i.e. what is portrayed by the large multi-national fashion and entertainment companies: the movies, Broadway, New York, the lights of Vegas and the fog of San Francisco. It's a very enlightening conversation.

On our final walk down the narrow street toward our condo, we must use hand signs to communicate with drivers where there is no shoulder or sidewalk, which is most of the way to our rented dwelling. We are sitting ducks and, with one false step, Giovanni and Antoinette can easily become hood ornaments. Italian drivers, I suppose, get points for plucking American tourists.

We stop by Peppo's to say goodbye to Aliana. She introduces us to her husband Luka, who is old enough to be her father. Luka is a burly, barrel-chested guy who, at the drop of a hat, looks as though he could redecorate a bar room in a matter of minutes. The locals are out in full force tonight. Most are *"two sheets to the wind"* and high five us on our way out. Who says *"Gio is a dumb Panini?"*

Back to the condo for our final Lake Como evening. We decide to pack in the morning.

One final note from today: We got free boxes, free bubble wrap and **FREE POTTY** privileges. However, as I almost learned the hard way, there was no toilet paper in any of the twenty-six public men's stalls. To enter any establishment in Europe without *"tissue paper"*, either for the nose or other venues of ordinary use, could be detrimental. As the Gods of fate would have it, this day we forgot to bring along our *"reserve"*, leaving the near newspaper quality tissue in our condo. Stupid us. "Ah, Antoinette, you havea any Kleenex in youra baga?" **YES**, my lucky day! Problem solved! If Antoinette have to blow her noisea, she will have to use her shirt or jacket sleeve. Life is series of choices.

Most European potties do not stock paper towels. Rather, they are very environmentally conscious. Europeans prefer hot air dryers to dry their hands. It can get a bit noisy on a busy day, but I get their point.

***

Wednesday, June 12th -
Leaving Como for Paris

Question of the moment: How do we get our suitcases down the seventeen narrow spiral steps? You would think we would have asked this long before having to carry anything anywhere! Conclusion: Plan ahead, that's my motto. Expect some weird things to happen, and when things get tough, the tough get going. Here are the choices we came up and the odds for success:

Pack and carry: odds of surviving walking down the steps with the suitcases: 9.2%.

Have Muhammad carry the luggage down. But, what if he is not on duty today? Too risky, too many unknowns, so zero odds on board.

Carry down empty suitcases then separate and pack clothes on the first floor. Odds of success: 56.4%.

Since we have Samsonite luggage we can do like the gorilla in their commercial and toss each bag over the second-story balcony to the lawn or toss them down the seventeen-step narrow spiral staircase. Odds, still not too perfect: 34.4%.

What would you choose and of equal importance, what, from the above, did we choose? Take a guess.

We now need new luggage. We purchased trip insurance. All we need do is turn in our claim. In Paris, we will buy the most expensive designer leather matching suitcases and there you have it: *"All's well that ends well."* However, Antoinette adds, "NOT"!

There remains one twenty-four ounce Italian beer undisturbed and cooling in the fridge. Anyone need a brew this early in the morning? Oh, heck, I will drink it. It is, after all, past 8:00 and the local boys at Peppo's are probably absorbed in their third round of drinks while attempting to solve the world's problems. Bottoms up.

Can't wait for Paris. Before retiring last night, I send the usual email *"We are on our way to your hotel, but we have a few "need-to-knows"*:

1. What is the best way to get to the hotel?

2. Directions to the nearest Post Office?

3. Location of the closest self-service Laundromat?"

Now, catch this. This morning I check my email. I received a terse note back from our Paris Hotel: "Sorry, no reservations under TURZER!" No what? No Reservations? This single near-sentence via email causes us to enter panic mode. Antoinette immediately calls Hotels.com. Our reservations are confirmed by this web site and the evidence is both on our iPad and in our travel folder. Antoinette is relieved to hear that Hotels.com contacted our Paris hotel and learned that they found our reservation under ... now, get this ... Leslie D. Turzer! Cannot wait to meet these Frenchie rocket scientists later tonight! Can't they understand that we go by one name, as does Madonna, Messi or Ronaldo! We are Turzer.

Getting dressed this morning, I quickly realize my luck is running out. I am wearing the last piece of clean clothing I brought . . . a pair of shorts. Doubling this dilemma, I am out of underwear for Thursday. What to do? I guess I can go *"commando"* or wear one of Antoinette's more fashionable under garments. The temptation is strong, but I am not so sure the style meets the requirements. Tough call.

Packed and ready to head to the train station. Today is our lucky day. The owner of the condo complex is heading to Como and graciously gives us a ride to the train station. One last time to watch the crazy Italian Grand Prix want-to-be drivers do their thing. We bid adieu and say like MacArthur, "We shall return some day."

We climb the steps to the train station and enter the platform area. We are waiting for the 11:45 train to Zurich. At 11:41 a train arrives. Good, it's early. We're ready to go. No problem. We ask a local person, "train to Zurich?" He gives us a yes *"head-nod"*. We thank him and board the train. It takes no more than a few heartbeats before recognizing that the train car we are occupying doesn't resemble any other long distance train cars we have traveled in. The local guy should have said in any frigging language, "I don't speak a word of English!" I would have thanked him and now I cannot forgive him.

Antoinette is getting worried. "We are on the **WRONG** train," she belt out, "heading to who knows where? Think about it Giovanni, we are going to disappear and never see the grandkids or, my God, we won't see our cat Tee ever again." I am staring at her in disbelief until she adds, "Okay, Putz, now what?" I feel my head do a double-take and realize she was not concerned but **REALLY** pissed!

A large tour group of seniors follow our lead and hop on the train (perhaps *"hop"* may not be the best description). I try to find a conductor. None in sight. Suddenly the train pulls out with Antoinette, myself and the grey-haired crowd. My eyes find a route map on the train's wall. This is a fricking locals train! Nana Antoinette is peppering me with a barrage of *"colorful"* four letter words and if she could, she would have tossed the preverbal kitchen sink at me. And, should we ever get home she promises to take away the Maui Condo and run away never to see me again. It was something to consider and however brief it was, I thought first of our close relationship, the condo, our years together, the condo and decided to remain calm, cool and collected. Let the condo be my guide.

I look around for a local dude who is still sober. I find one; he apparently hadn't finished reading his morning newspaper. I am not at all certain what to do to get back on the right train. Without hesitation, he tells me to just "get off at the next stop" which happened to be the last stop for this train, "then find the correct track for the right train to Zurich." Simple enough. What could possibly go wrong? We arrive at the next town, grab our suitcases, disembark, locate the correct track for the train to Zurich and guess what, the right train shows up a few minutes later for us and the seventy-nine old people on the group tour! Nana Antoinette owes me one big time! I took a bullet that I did not have to. Now, I have one extra bullet in my chamber.

The conductor stops by our first class accommodations (no free-bee's, not even peanuts) and tells us that this train will reach Zurich at approximately 15:38 and **OUR** train to Paris departs at 15:27. Do the math! The other shoe again dropped ... what could go wrong? Am I crazy? Everything could go wrong.

I try to rationalize and consider that, in addition to ourselves there are twenty-seven other passengers who are also transferring to the Paris bound train. If only one or two people are late for their connection, I am sure that they would just leave, or as they say in Poland in such a situation: *"Tuffshitski. Catch the train next week!"*

But then I again try to rationalize that, due to the large number of people potentially missing their connection, the railway higher-ups will decide to hold the Paris bound train and wait the few minutes required. Sayonara to lunch in Zurich! The conductor tells us that the engineer will try to bring our train into the Zurich station on the track next to the train heading for Paris or else we will have a three kilometer run to the connection. The old folks group would simply not make it. I look at our circumstances and consider the plight of the others. I consider the train schedules, the engineers and all that is required to bring it all together for a satisfactory conclusion. There is nothing more I can concern myself with so I sit with Antoinette and watch through the window as the world beyond simply passes on by.

The scenery is so pretty and so difficult to describe. I will, however, try, or more reasonably, *"give it a shot"*. Hold your breath . . . one hellava sentence is coming up.

The snow-capped, jagged peaked Alps overshadowing small, neatly manicured homesites, farms, vineyards and pastures with sheep, goats and cows safely balancing themselves as they eat the organic grasses and foodstuffs that will produce organic milk and organic meats for the dinner tables of the hard working families living on the steep slopes in the high pitched roofed homes sur-rounded by a variety of multi-colored flowers and shrubs, homes colorfully painted and built by the family with the strongest lumber grown right on the mountains at the tree lines just below the snow lines accessible only by horse-drawn wagons or ski chair lifts used to also transport goods and materials not available in the village and take the kids to and from school each day after they get up a sunrise 4:45 to milk cows, feed the animals, cut the grass, put the sheep, cows and goats out to pasture and finish their homework as the elec-tricity ran out last night when the hamsters went on strike protest-ing the working conditions in the twenty-four year old wheels that leave their tiny pink feet sore and blistered plus an occasional case of athletes foot fungus and ingrown toe nails (front feet only) and the back-up generators failed because grandpa ran over the extension cord running from the utility pole over the barn and (loosely hanging from a 193 year old pole that was splitting in three) to the house and grandma filled the gas back-up generator with 100% virgin olive oil instead of unleaded regular gas stored behind the barn in five gallon red canisters away from the dried out hay that the animals sleep on dreaming of better days, automatic milking machines that have foam covered inserts where the cows tender nipples are placed to suck out every last drop of milk so dad can sell the milk and can pay the bank the mortgage payment which is three months behind and the bank is threatening to foreclose on the .33 acre farm and house where mom, dad, grandpa, grandma and nine brothers and sisters live in their three bedroom 1,327 square foot house without indoor plumbing, but has a fireplace for heating and cooking that vents out the little kids bedroom and a fifty-nine gallon Hawaiian style cooler to keep the cow's milk and other perishable items free from spoiling and contamination (last summer all were sick as dogs for a few days with food poisoning for eating spoiled meat and drinking sour milk, dad's fault, there has to be exceptions to the clean your plate or sleep with the animals for two weeks rule; he is a real black and white no nonsense old fart but he loves all of us especially when we are good and do well in school) when grandma forgot to get ice from town and it was 103 outside with ninety-five percent humidity and the washing machine broke so we had to carry our dirty clothes seven kilometers to the river straight down a steep 125 degree hill to wash them on the rough rocks collected specifically one day in case the washer broke as these rocks really get the stains out especially with lots of elbow grease. I hope this clearly describes the scenery we're looking at.

What an incredible history I see before me. How I wish I could find a way to share it with others. My narrative takes vivid imagination, but still it isn't enough. Seeing these rural people and witnessing their land and their busy day is both exciting and humbling.

We will soon be coming into the Zurich time zone and will need to get off and bolt to catch the train to Paris. An update from our conductor doesn't somehow surprise me. The Paris bound train engineer decided on his own **NOT** to wait for us or the twenty-seven others, claiming our train is too far behind schedule. My cynicism again raises its ugly head begging for sensible replies.

"Are we on Amtrak along the Boston to Washington, D.C. corridor?" The announcement informs us that we are thirty-five minutes behind schedule. In an instant, a decision is made to put twenty-nine lives on hold while an engineer elects to promote himself to

a decision-making executive member of the board. We passengers have paid for this transportation and clearly our obligation has been met. Now it is their turn to man up and get us to Paris!

Another announcement is made while our train has stopped waiting for the light to change from red to green over a one lane bridge. I hope the engineer is **NOT** color blind. Now, this is where it gets a little fuzzy, so pay attention and perhaps we can both figure it out. Anyway, a very professional conductor (obviously **NOT** Amtrak trained) informs us that we will have two choices upon arriving in Zurich:

Option 1. Catch train #1534, get off at Basel and catch the train that left Zurich *before* we arrive. "Are you saying that #1534 will leave later but will BEAT train TGV 9226 to Basel?" "Yes," he confidently replies.

Option 2. Hang in Zurich, eat an overpriced lunch and change our ticket to TVG 9230 at 17:25 hours, a train direct to Paris.

Extremely tough choices. My cynicism is now at full capacity, and after weighing both options carefully, including a cost/benefit analysis in an Excel Spreadsheet, we take 2.3 seconds to choose option 2, not believing that the train to Basel will leave later but will beat the high-speed train to Basel, a factor that just did not compute. Reminds me of those math teaser questions: if a train leaves Chicago at 8:00 traveling west a 100 miles per hour, will it get to Omaha faster than the train leaving Milwaukee at 8:15 traveling southwest at 125 miles per hour? Moreover, our luck thus far sucks, especially when it comes to trains and close connections. Once on this trip, we made a train connection by twenty-three seconds with Antoinette having to toss her suitcase and jump on a moving train! How is that for sacrifice?

Arriving in Zurich, we wait in line to change tickets to Paris as per the conductor's instruction. Wrong line. Need I say more?

The customer service representative tells us to go to *"Guest Services"* to re-issue our First Class tickets. We oblige him and enter the Guest

Services area, a large and *"must take-a-ticket-and-wait"* room. We are at the Nevada DMV again! At least this is a nice waiting room. Only thirteen people with an "A" ticket ahead of us. We hope to get out of here, First Class ticket or not! Only eleven more numbers to call. In the back of my mind, I am praying that it is not approaching some employee's afternoon beer and pretzel one-hour break. My anxiety may increase a need for a potty call. Not now!

While we wait for our number to be called, we learn that the train we are trying to get on is sold out due to an air traffic controllers walk-out/work stoppage throughout Europe that started today. Time is ticking away. I offer €10 for the next ticket to be called in exchange for our ticket. No takers. How dumb am I, in Zurich they use Swiss Francs as currency, Euros are *"dirty money"* to them. Even when I increase the bid to €15, still no takers. These snooty people. We wait in line like dutiful socialists rather than hardcore capitalists always *"willing to buy"* our way to the front of the line.

At last our number is called. That's the goooood news. A very professional, pleasant and multi-lingual customer service agent listens to my story about train delays from Como, etc. (reluctant to state that we simply decided to sleep in and take a later train). Well, travel fans, the travel gods caught up with us.

The agent excuses herself and steps away to speak with her boss. I am expecting the "You didn't have train delay Herr Buddy, you flat missed the 7:45 train from Como. It's your fault so you must pay for the First Class upgrade." I could have handled that, no *"biggie"* just another €35 wasted. Well, this is **NOT** what she said. Were the Secret Politzia onto us? Will we be taken away never to be heard from again? Bad news and good news. The bad news is that this train to Paris is **SOLD OUT** in both First and Second Class! The almost good news is, we can mosey on over to the train and plead our case with the conductor, something perhaps he has never heard before but is yet naïve enough to believe whatever we may choose to tell him. Worst case, we stand between the cars for the five hour ride to

Paris. My mind begins to spin, searching for some reasonable excuse why we should find accommodations in Zurich, get a good night's sleep and take a train to Paris in the morning versus heading to the train with a solid *"story"* for the conductor. After all, this is *"the last train to Clarksville"* today. So, we do the obvious, *"flip a coin"* (it comes up *"Heads"*), opt to get on this train and in doing so, tell our *"sad story"*.

"My aunt Marcella, a fourth cousin on my mother's side, suddenly fell ill. She has lived in Paris for several years, she even helped the restoration of the French government by volunteering as a both a librarian and part-time English teacher for underprivileged children." No, that wouldn't work. I have never been good at this.

Okay. This is what I am going with and it must be told with rapid-fire confidence. "My mother's cousin, a post-world war aid worker, who left her farm and her studies as a nun in Pennsylvania to help establish an orphanage for Malaysian refugees in Marseille is gravely ill. We received an email from the Vatican advising we get to Paris ASAP ..." No. That won't get it. I am just no good with making things up and trying to fool someone. Perhaps I can ask Katrina/Svetlana/Antoinette to whip something up and make it look like cherry pie? Ain't happening.

Finally, I just say, "May I be perfectly honest with you, sir?" He says, "I understand your predicament; we will find a place for you and your much younger sister. Be sure to see me before you board the train."

That was easy! I was bowled over by his English and his notice of my *"much younger sister"*. A typical Frenchman. But for his doing us a favor and being something of a gentleman, I will allow the *"much younger sister"* thing to slide. At least for the moment.

Antoinette is not the happiest camper in Zurich. I read body language well. To settle things down, I propose we eat an overpriced and forgettable dinner in the train station. She spills a €10 glass of cheap red wine. It justa missa Gio. The food was okay, similar to

economy section airplane food. We are a captive audience so I just
enjoy the homemade veal sausage in brown gravy with some type
of over-buttered fried potatoes (cholesterol count just shot up to
moon). Antoinette is having mother's homemade baseballs disguised
as meat balls (we can play catch) and risotto.

The train to Paris is to arrive and depart from platform number
sixteen. This, therefore, was a good reason to wait on platform
sixteen. Just in case we never see our cultured conductor from our
previous encounter, we go over a few ideas that may land us either in
First or Second Class. This is how well we've planned, organized, and
expected this entire adventure to proceed. Yeah, sure.

Which of our tales would be the most believable or sympathetic?
We run through a brief list of ideas, many of which were lifted from
films, Internet stories or fantasies and we settle on *"fourth cousin,
sudden demise scenario"*.

We can't help but notice the heavy presence of security people
in the station. Big burly guys with guns and walkie-talkies. So, you
ask, what do I do? I do what comes natural in such a circumstance,
I take their picture! Now, you would think that someone may take
exception to our taking photos of security personnel, but nothing.
Not a "Halt!", not a "Your papers, please." Nothing nadda. Later I
was convinced it was because they had already checked us out and
concluded we were beyond harmless. Pathetic comes to mind.

The train arrives. We get on board and explain the *"family fourth
cousin demise scenario"* to the conductor. He tears up, does a double
cheek kiss on Antoinette, gives me a Super Chicago Bears hug
(good lord, this guy, Otto: Big guy, no doubt a former NFL ten
year All-Pro defensive tackle with the Bears and 2013 Hall of Fame
Nominee incognito on the last train to Paris) then welcomes us into
the First Class section.

The story I could not convey to one conductor took hold on the
other. Perhaps, and I am only speculating, but it could have had
something to do with Antoinette flirting with the conductor.

There are only two stops before Paris. The odds are in our favor, worst case, club car where the conductor tell us drinks are on him! Wouldn't you know it, our First Class stowaway seats are claimed at the last stop before Paris which is two-and a half hours away. Our choices are:

1. Scour the train for empty seats anywhere.

2. Sit in the bathroom that has an odor riper than a porta potty sitting in the 100 degree Las Vegas sun all day.

3. Stand in the club car looking super cool drinking sparkling water and making idle conversation with the French-only speaking crowd.

4. Jump from the train, walk to the highway and hitchhike to the Paris train station early enough to retrieve our luggage.

The options are clear: we eliminate 2 and 4, and roll with 1 and hold 3 as backup.

We find two seats in the Second Class section and then pretend we are working stiffs just to make the others feel at ease. Being *"different"* ain't easy.

Antoinette takes a seat and sits comfortably with that special flair of hers. A second seat is open, but when I attempt to rest my weary backside, some dude across the aisle speaks up and says, "Taken." Not wanting to start an international incident, I make an executive decision and head to the club car. What the heck . . . I will just stand there *"looking Euro"* especially since I am wearing my new summer Euro hat. I am the only guy on train 2371 wearing a Euro summer hat . . . you think they would look at me and see a stud Euro or . . . just another Euro wanna-be stupid Americano.

Shortly thereafter, I head back to check on Antoinette. I discover an unoccupied jump seat between two rail cars right over the coupling connecting both cars. I take it and set up shop. There is an exit door to my left. I am sitting facing West. Everywhere, there are signs clearly printed in French … in **FRENCH**! It is apparent that each sign warns of the danger of pushing **ANY** buttons. To do this may create a very difficult incident in one's life ... ending it, for example, when train cars uncouple and sucks one under the train wheels when the train is going 159 KPH. Instantly if not sooner, one becomes shredded fresh bird food for starving pigeons and oversized retired black birds who, because they are so fat, cannot fly any more. Despite the warnings in French, I get the message. However, should I push the correct button ... just the correct one, would I become either James Bond or Jason Bourne? Double clicking the button may allow me to *"flip"* my rival then snatch the now unoccupied First Class seat. I weigh this option and look for the smallest guy in the First Class car to challenge to an all-out *"rock 'em sock 'em fight"* to the end between the cars! Bad luck, every male in the First Class car plus the two heavily armed train Politzia Marshals decked out in full uniform (unlike in the USA, they do not have their train/airplane security marshals incognito in street clothes; they are decked out in full uniform with guns clearly displayed and wearing shirts two sizes too small to accent their 18.7 inch biceps and there 51.8 inch chests on six foot, seven and three quarters inch body frames). They look like Otto the conductor, ex All-Pro NFL offensive and defensive linemen! A battle to the finish for a First Class seat is just **NOT** going to happen. Thus, I either stay on the jump seat or head back to the club car to play Mr. Cool Joe Euro.

FINALLY, we arrive in Paris. Otto, our super nice train conductor, comps us two bottles of water (one still, the other *"with gas"*, the sparkling kind for the uneducated among our readers and one Coke Zero). We bid farewells, double cheek kiss-kiss plus a bear hug for Antoinette and a firm handshake for me. His hand shake almost takes off my hand! Otto has the biggest set of paws I have ever seen. I am still shaking my hand trying to restore normal blood flow. I think it may be broken!

Disembarking from the train, we employ the famous Polish strategy for finding a taxi stand. We follow the largest herd of people and play follow the leader. Again, it works like a charm.

Another day, another country. We leave Antoinette and Giovanni behind and assume our new identities: Fifi and Claude.

We are in a cab and heading for the city otherwise known as the gateway to Europe's museums, nightlife, and culture. Paris. Our hotel, Hotel Les Jardins d Eiffel, is located down a dark, narrow one way *"street"* loaded with ladies dressed *elaborately* and showing lots of cleavage and extra-long legs, wearing 7.3 inch platform high heels, silk fishnet stockings and ultra-expensive Channel Number Five perfume. Must be a school teachers' convention staying at our flop house 5.4 star hotel. Shout out to Maui Marie for recommending we **MUST** stay here. Anyway, I meet some of the ladies and tell them my mother and two sisters are school teachers in the USA.

Since it is late at night when we check in, I decide not to start an international incident about the hotel not having/then having our reservation. Save that card for another day when we may need something from the front desk. Our room is but one floor above the lobby and **NOT** at the end of the hall . . . they must have upgraded us! The room is the size of a twelve-inch square box but has a big screen TV, street view, a safe and particle board furnishings. The potty is the more valued room of interest, and surprisingly, includes soap and shampoo. However, what makes our room special . . . we can clearly see the Eiffel Tower from our bedroom window.

After settling in, we head out into the alley. I wave at the ladies in response to their claims that I look *"cute"* outfitted in my stud-like summer Euro hat, three-day old scruffy, unshaven Euro look, and my flowing grey locks dancing across, not the pale but rather the sultry tan beneath my hat, and highlighted by my Oakley shades. Yes, I wear my sunglasses at night and I do still catch the eye of the lovelies. What did I say earlier? "When you got it, flaunt it!" I am flaunting it! Fifi, aka Leslie, hits me **HARD** on the top of my skull and says, "Stop dreaming, Claude, they just want your Euros and have zero interest in a man who can remember both Howdy Doody and Captain Kangaroo! They are **NOT** interested in a sixty-four year old, half dead, worn out Americano wearing plaid madras shorts, knee high, multi colored argyle socks and white velcro strapped K-Mart $6.95 blue light special sneaks that you **JUST** had to buy for this trip along with a cheap, multi-colored, tropical flowers 250% polyester Hawaiian shirt purchased seventeen years ago for $5.99 at Hilo Hatties in Oahu, HI while on the shirt factory tour (a Tom Selleck Magnum PI style Hawaiian shirt). Claude, you even tried to grow a bushy black mustache like Tom but wound up buying one at the ABC store by the Sheraton Waikiki on a trip funded by you winning the jackpot trip to Hawaii on The Price is Right!"

Good news, the Laundromat is right across the street from the hotel entrance. Fifi does not have to haul dirty clothes on a subway and bus to get to the river to wash our clothes. Right around corner from the hotel, there it is in its full grandeur all lit up . . . The Eiffel Tower. Our hotel appears to be in a great area of town. We don't have to go far to see and enjoy the many familiar trademarks of Paris.

We also benefit from being steps away from a neighborhood grocery store. The store is open from 7:00 to 23:00. At home we call them 7-11 stores. However, this one is much larger and clean and not owned and staffed by guys who shave three times a day. We meet a very pleasant checkout girl in her early twenties who looks just like my knee surgery rehab lady Danielle Mollett. My Fifi-Angelic-Wahine is in Starbucks heaven simply because one is just two blocks from our hotel.

Europeans like to eat, drink and stay out late. Spirited conversation supersedes staying home to watch TV or play games or spend time on various social media platforms with one's cell phone. So when in Paris, we do as the Parisians. We find a small, intimate outdoor cafe nearby. It is Parisian in style and in price. We share an €19 club sandwich (add €2 for get **BOTH** chicken and bacon on white toast only, forget the wheat or multi-grain breads). The food prep team cuts off the bread crusts; thus most French people who eat these sandwiches do not have curly hair (old wives tale).

McDonald's style french fries accompany the sandwich. Our beverages, €5 for an 8oz beer and €8 for a glass of red grape juice disguised as expensive French Bordeaux wine, are just OK. Holy Guacamole, Paris is **EXPENSIVE**!

Wednesday turns out be another three country meal day. We started with breakfast in Como, Italy, a late lunch in Zurich followed by a late snack in Paris. We are just **"WAY TOO COOL"**!

***

Thursday, June 13th -
Paris

Tired from yesterday's adventurous (to say the least) long travel day, I got up late, and much to my chagrin, I noticed I missed a triple OT hockey game! The Chicago Blackhawks win four to three, twelve minutes into the third overtime! Game must have just ended. I quickly logged onto NHL.com to watch the highlights. They have not yet been posted.

It is raining and cold. What else is new? Along the way, we meet Tiff, the ultimate souvenirs shop salesman, who says, "I make you good deal today. Twenty percent off!" He then called her *"Juliette"*. How quaint. Immediately, if not sooner, Fifi wants to change her name to *"Juliette"*. I suppose the *"wild"* Fifi found a need to upgrade her name after Tiff's sultry advances. We originally chose Fifi but later realized only French poodles are destined for that kind of personalized identification. Juliette, she wants, then it's Juliette she will be.

We catch a ride on the Hop-On-Hop-Off Bus to begin our *"see what Paris is all about"* quickie introduction. Our tickets are only valid for today and are **NOT** on a twenty-four hour *"clock"* as every other Hop-On-Hop-Off Bus in Europe is. Is it viva la France or *"leave it to the French?"* Anyway, we quickly determine that a two-day pass, coupled with a river boat cruise or an evening city lights bus tour **PLUS** a day trip to Versailles needs to be added to the itinerary.

Unfortunately, the tour bus lady, the one with the power to make these changes, *"disappears"* from the bus. We ask the bus driver where can we go to upgrade our passes. He drops us off near the main ticket office, a ten-minute walk in the rain.

We arrive at *"world tour company headquarters"* and explain to a service representative precisely what we want, including upgrading our one-day bus pass to two-days. Simple enough, you would think.

The customer service rep informs us she cannot upgrade our €21 per person one day pass to a €30 two day pass! Her company only sells tours and is not affiliated with the Red Bus Company! She tells us to make the change **ON** the Red Bus. We explain to her we tried but the bus driver directed us to this location after the Red Bus lady disappeared! After a few calls up the chain of command, she **FINALLY** finds the one person who is available to make an executive decision that allows her to sell us **NEW** two-day Hop-On-Hop-Off Bus passes (we **MUST** use on consecutive days only, **NO** Exceptions!). Therefore, should any of our many readers find yourselves in Paris and decide to go to Versailles on Saturday and begin your two-day pass on Friday, which was our plan, you **CANNOT** use your **SECOND DAY** Red Bus pass on Sunday! However, and believe me there is always a *"however"*, just as there is always a *"BUT"*, the Chief and Absolute Decision Maker required the booking number of the **ORIGINAL** one-day Hop-On-Hop-Off Bus Internet purchase! Something I always carry with me . . . right?

"Well, we **HAD** it, but the bus lady who disappeared took our confirmation order receipt which **HAD** the booking number on it!" So I calmly ask her, "Can you do a search using our last name (like how many Turzers booked the Hop-On-Hop-Off Bus in Paris like **EVER**)?"

"No, Mr. Turzer, c'est impossible," she replies. "We can only look up orders by date of purchase. When did you buy?" she asks. Exasperation was getting to me. I was wearing thin trying to recall and offer a calm reply.

"Lady, please. I believe it was sometime after April 20th and before May 13th." Hold your hats, here we go. You guessed it, she starts a day-by-day search for our order.

It then hits me. The Red Bus Company emailed me a link to print the tickets. I never delete emails for *"stuff"* purchased on-line for our trip. Hold the presses, just give me a few seconds to search my old emails on my IPhone5 (remember her super computer had only one search option). A few seconds later, I find it!

I was anticipating music, confetti, a small party, anything! Without looking up at me, she officiously finds our original order, and without saying a word, manages to declare *"the world has been saved and only with her involvement and guidance"*. She orders our two-day bus pass, plus evening riverboat cruise, saving us a lot of Euros, maybe as much as … a bunch? Then, we decide to purchase the Versailles *"All Day Package"* and schedule the trip for Saturday. Talk about making it flexible and easy for people to do business with you. Geez! Did I even get a simple, *"Merci"* in French or English? No.

The other shoe dropped the minute we scheduled Versailles on Saturday. I repeat, I am not a grump nor a complainer, but I am a stickler for getting things done correctly.

"Lady, if I buy a two-day pass, I want to **USE** it for **TWO** days! Plus, the two-day pass Hop-On-Hop-Off Bus includes a terrific discount on the **SECOND** day versus buying **TWO SEPARATE DAY** passes! Plus, we get the night boat city lights cruise at a big discount with the two-day bus purchase! Plus, you suggested we go to Versailles on Saturday!" Wait, where is all of this going? I am now so confused I can't begin to explain anything beyond it being a really tiring and strange day. I ask if this is some kind of a scam or timeshare presentation? She has no response. To ease your reading, I will make a long story come to an end. We switch our Versailles trip to Sunday. Everything is now cool.

All of this back and forth between us, her phone calls up the corporate ladder and calls to the French President Francois Hollande take over an hour! Meanwhile, a few people stop in and leave as we take up all her time. Naturally I came within a breath or two of *"losing it and going off on her,"* but I did the smart thing and simply kept my big, speak first, think second mouth shut. Did not even need prodding from Juliette. Why pray tell did I exhibit such patience given the circumstances? Well, Ms. Customer Service Sales Agent brandishes her Magnum .357 and says "Go ahead Americano shit head, just make my day!; how about it, will you punk?"

Finally, we have all of our required tickets. All the drama disappears. There is no further need for anxiety, arguments, reasoning or playing *"friendly, good natured American tourists".* Besides, we had to get to the Post Office to buy post card stamps.

Finding the Post Office should be no problemo. A sign mounted on a street light pole indicated that it should be *"close by".* We do the smart thing in the rain (by the way, we are now on umbrellas four and five for the trip; they keep breaking in the wind . . . that's what you get for €4, €5), we ask for **AND** get correct directions ("Cross street at the traffic light and go up that little street over there twenty meters"). We find the Post Office on the very first try! What a country!

Based on our past experiences, we conclude this should now be a rather simple process; buying stamps is internationally commonplace. We anticipate the lines, the slow public servants and the weather. All we have to do is ask for *"international post card stamps",* pay, throw out a *"Merci"* and leave. What could possibly go wrong trying to purchase post card stamps? Well, sports fans, here it comes and it is true: *"Shit always rolls downhill!"* And, by Jove, we could see it coming. Could there be another Italian-like postal worker (think Antoinette) about to enter our lives? When we enter the Post Office, we are greeted by a 157-lb. welterweight boxer-type guy who asks what we do we need. After we say "international post card stamps", he proceeds to tell us . . . buckle up now. . . "Postal workers are on **STRIKE TODAY**!" Wisely, I choose not to get into the whys and wherefores about the strike. Rather, I say to him, "I notice those machines over there sell post card stamps. Any chance of me buying some from those metal boxes?" He understands and advises he will be happy to help instruct me on their use. I give him more of a *"mercy"* than a *"merci"* and he replies in kind with, "Think nothing of it!" We have an understanding. I reach into my wallet for my MasterCard. "Our machine will **NOT TAKE YOUR** MasterCard, only French issued Mastercards! OR . . . only coins (no paper money). This is how the system works here." We only have one € 1coin. He continues to show me how to use the machine and then tells me where I can find a bank and obtain some coins. So off I go to find the bank. Around the corner, I locate a money exchange store where I ask for €20 in €1 and €2 coins. There is a young girl behind the eight inch thick bulletproof window. I can barely make her out. I slide my €20 through the magic drawer and what do I get . . . €10 in coins and €10 bill. Recognizing that something was *"lost in the translation"*, I hold up the €10 bill and pantomime I need € coins. Even though her cash tray was loaded with €1 and €2 coins, she gives me the *"no, no"* index finger shake . . . *"€10 coin limit per day"*! Whatever! So back to the Post Office I go to buy the stamps. So far today, nothing has been straightforward and *"easy"*.

It is clear we have wasted more time than we have put into our sightseeing and all for the sake of changing our bus tickets and buying a few postage stamps. Who would have known that we would encounter a customer service agent unwilling to quickly change our tickets? How were we to know that a national labor strike at the Post Office was scheduled for today? And finally, who would have guessed that there is a daily limit on the number of Euros you can exchange for coins? Our postage stamp issues now behind us, we decide our time would be better spent window shopping. It is a great idea, believe me.

After a three block stroll, we find the most *"awesome"* cookie store ever, and to our satisfaction and theirs, we buy them out! They are ecstatic. We then get the *"double cheek kiss-kiss"* routine.

They turn off their store lights then post a sign on their door proclaiming: "Closed. Come back next week."

Our next stop finds us browsing through a fancy liquor store. We eagerly splurge on one expensive bottle of French red wine and a bottle of Champagne.

When we get home, one of our first objectives, other than saying hello to our cat and a few friends, will be to enter alcohol rehab just to *"dry out"*. Juliette, however, keeps reminding me that, "Claude, we are on vacation."

We continue to wander casually about downtown Paris. The clock strikes 14:00; it's time to recharge the batteries with a late lunch. Studying our restaurant guide, we decide on *Le Grand Café Capucines,* located at Four Boulevard des Capucines, quite naturally.

This is truly a very posh, high-end, up-scale, expensive, place! Judging by the look on the maître d's face, we appear suspiciously common, two drowned rats dressed way down for his taste . . . so he seats us at a **SMALL**, out of the way table next to an ornately decorated support beam. At the adjoining table, three Russian adults and a young girl and boy are dining. Over a relaxing dinner with someone truly special, I need to let what little hair I have left down and simply talk. Juliette was amenable to listening. I went on for a couple of silly moments saying nothing at all. Then, I wanted her to know that the day wasn't really wasted because we spent it together. Enough of the romance! Let's get back to the story.

The three Russian adults are nursing a bottle of Dom Perignon and eating *"perfectly grilled"* steaks. The two kids are hard at work playing on their handheld electric game thingies. The little girl, age seven, is celebrating her birthday. The parents order her medium-rare, thinly sliced fillet mignon. She crosses her arms and does not eat it! The father eats three slices. There are three slices still left on the plate. The mother cuts up one slice. The girl just picks at it. **DUDE** this is the best looking piece of meat I have ever seen!!! Just send it over here . . . I will eat it, don't waste it!! Juliette knows exactly what I am thinking and is kicking me **HARD**. *"STOP IT, Claude, they are* **NOT** *going to give it to you. Just stop it!!"* As a side note, on the way back to our hotel, I have the leg X-rayed ... not broken but severely bruised. Hospital emergency room staff ask how it happened . . . given their experience, it looked like an obvious case of wife abuse. To avoid Juliette spending ten years in the slammer, I tell the staff and hospital Politzia I just slipped on the wet curb and landed the wrong way on the outside of my left leg. Success, they *"buy"* my story.

Back at restaurant the family sings happy birthday in Russian. The waiter brings an ice cream sundae loaded with whipped cream and cookies. With a smile on her face, the birthday girl devours it in 4.8 seconds, a new restaurant record! She gets a standing "O" from 374 other restaurant guests who then proceed to shower her with luxurious gifts and Euros. Not a bad deal for a kid who would not eat her supper! Those enabling Russian parents!

Juliette and Claude enjoy a wonderful three course meal, for appetizers, oysters on the half shell for me, goat cheese for Juliette followed by a fresh salad and for our entree, salmon with veggies is *"to die for"* . . . moist, perfecto. I enjoy the meal with two cold ones. Juliette opts for a nice French red wine. Of course we leave room for dessert; we are on vacation! Our desserts, an apricot parfait for Juliette and chocolate cake with warm fudge in the middle and ice cream for me **PLUS** cappuccinos. I go the *"piggy"* route and ask the waiter to bring us a large cup of whipped cream. He obliges. When I get the bill, I ask the waiter if I can buy the awesome beer glass. I get a *"No, not for sale"* nod. So I leave a €20 tip and sneak the glass into my backpack, toss in my IPhone5, break the glass and bolt, leaving Juliette behind to create a diversion. When we assemble outside, I get *"super stink eye"* and a chastising from Juliette for leaving her behind. Juliette says "The waiter came back with a bag to give you the glass."

I guess €20 tip changed his mind. I tell her that the glass I pilfered broke; however, what the heck, I go back in and get another glass.

On the way out after retrieving a new beer glass, I attempt some Russian/USA détente. I wish the girl happy birthday in English and extend my left hand for a fist bump American style. She looks at me awkwardly, like *"go away Americano, I no touch fists with you!"* She glances at her grandfather. He gives her a three head shake up and down, i.e. *"okay"*. She extends her hand to bump fists. I also fist bump her older brother. After I leave the restaurant, I immediately send an email and text to the state department, CIA, KGB, NSA, CNN, Fox News, Congress and the White House letting them know international relations with Russia are now at an all-time high; they have switched policy and now support the USA arming Syrian rebels against the vicious dictator and his supporters. They email and text back that I am a nominee for the Noble Peace Prize and the cover of Time magazine. CNN, Fox, BBC and other major US and international TV networks are flying in camera crews for tomorrow's 10:00 press conference. Today is sending Savannah Guthrie. Barbara Walters is also coming along with Ellen, Jim Rome, Chris *"back back back gone"* Berman, Dr. Phil, Dan Patrick, Bill O'Reilly, Wolf Blitzer, Megyn Kelley and, of course, how can I forget, Rush Limbaugh!! Obama is sending father of year, Bill Clinton to represent him. Please watch the news tomorrow for full coverage. Claude is an international relations rock star!

After lunch, we continue our window shopping and lucky for me, we buy nothing. Time to head home. While walking to the subway, we realize that we left the huge bag of cookies, wine, champagne and umbrellas at the restaurant. "No brainer. Claude, **YOU** go back and get them; I took the last bullet."

"No problem Juliette, I will go back but please stay put so I can find you when I return." Arriving at the restaurant, the hostess takes me to the coat check room where our treasures are sitting on the floor waiting for me to come back for them.

To return to our hotel, we decide to take the subway. Since we are not sure where to go or which train to take, we seek out and find a great customer service agent. She provides directions on which trains to take to our destination. To summarize, we go one stop on one line, change to another line and go three stops. We get off the subway at station X and walk up and over to the platform for the next train to the hotel. We start out on the right foot, as we find our way to the right platform for the train that is going in the right direction. Piece of cake. The day is **NOT** done, however, without a *"brilliant"* statement from Juliette. She looks at the station sign and says, "Didn't we just get **OFF** the subway here?"

"Yes, my Ace Wahine Juliette, we did about five minutes ago. We are on a different platform catching a different train!!"

"Oh!"

For one of the few times on this trip, we obtain the correct directions, find the hotel and retire for the night. That's all for today folks!

Two final tidbits from today:

Tonight in the juniors rugby tournament, South Africa beat the Frenchies.

With the Paris high temperature of ninety-three today and high eighties for the rest of the week, does anyone want to buy two jackets, some scarves, gloves, long sleeve shirts and pants and two sock hats? I make you a great deal!

***

Friday, June 14th -
Paris

Up and at 'em, it is Friday and we are in Paris! Off we go to get on the Red Hop-On-Hop-Off Bus to continue our quest to learn all about the *"must see"* touristy places. But first, we stop at Starbucks for a **LARGE** cup of coffee. I guess Starbucks has *bought **ALL*** of the **LARGE** take away coffee cups in Europe. Why do I say this? Easy, every coffee shop, restaurant or pastry shop we have patronized since day one of this trip did not have **LARGE** take away cups for coffee. It must be either a conspiracy or a brilliant marketing move.

Moving on, as we head up the street to catch the bus, we pass by a butcher shop that has roasting ducks proudly on display in their front window. The heads are still on the little critters. It would be tough enough to eat the guy under normal circumstances, but this poor guy is looking back at us asking, *"Why me? What did I ever do to you?"* I would rather feed these guys than devour them. Let's move on.

We continue up the street two blocks and stop by the souvenir store to see our *"new best friend"*, Tiff, the *"I give you a great deal"* hustler dude. He is multi-tasking, washing windows and minding the empty store. We exchange hello's and claim we'll be back later to take full advantage of his *"great deals"*.

Paris is like New York City when it comes to crowds, traffic, and most especially, souvenir stores. It's a fact that Macy's, Bloomingdales and Saks Fifth Avenue compete with an array of quality merchandise; but souvenir shops, it's always the same stuff. How many different replicas of the Eiffel Tower do you think you can find in the junk shops of Paris? Try the number, *"endless"*. They never run out of key chains, ties, T-shirts, ashtrays, glasses, cups, dog and cat dishes and even vaguely crafted sun glasses with the image of the Tower painted somewhere in the lens. Look closely and you may well find the words, *"made in China"*. Welcome to the merchandise mart called Paris.

By now you know me all too well. I can't just pass up an opportunity to mention a humorous situation or make a smart ass comment under my breath. So, after another smartass *"Claude remark"*, Juliette breaks the French record for saying "**CLAUDE** stop it now, shut up and behave yourself!" We still have 3+ days in Paris. Juliette has a real great chance of reaching the century mark!

Real slow *"shit happens"* story day. I see a middle aged lady on the Red Hop-On-Hop-Off Bus wearing black high top Chuck Taylor Converse sneaks just like the ones I wore as a kid.

Music is playing on the bus. So, I decide to play band conductor. Someone needs to be the leader. Juliette does not think the same way as I do. She grabs me by the arm (leaving a bruise) and says, "**STOP IT**, just sit down and enjoy the sites!" Of course, she is right, but still, the temptation to lead the band remains.

Imagine this picture. As we get off the Red Bus at Notre Dame church, I see a lady getting on the bus wearing skin-tight yellow, gold and burnt orange pants with fox faces on the pant legs. It must be a new fashion trend to let people know that you are a fox/cougar. I want to take a picture but the guy she is with is way too big for me, so no picture, just a memory.

Notre Dame is a phenomenal Cathedral. We stroll through, looking at the many distinctive objects and artwork, and most particularly the French gothic architecture, stained glass windows, the naturalism of their statues and its numerous altars. We listen to the splendid singing of the boys' choir. Before heading out, we light a few candles and offer our prayers. It is easy to feel the power of prayer and the untold millions who have offered them in this tribute to the human mind, faith and soul, to say nothing of centuries of genuflecting that continues daily.

Lunch time. We work hard to make certain we have three high calorie, high fat meals every day. We find a sidewalk café and split a quiche washed down with a beer and a cappuccino.

Prior to getting back on the Red Hop-On-Hop-Off Bus, we invest in the French economy and purchase more *"stuff"* from the street vendors. We can never get enough, it seems.

While getting back on the bus, we meet young ladies on holiday from Australia. We mention that we've been to their lovely country.

Our destination is Galleries Lafayette. We are 100% certain that most of our readers are aware that Galleries Lafayette is a famous, very high-end block-long department store much like London's Harrods at Knightsbridge.

Uniquely, the seventh floor rooftop area of Lafayette provides an amazing 360 degree view of Paris.

A huge *"shout out"* again to Maui Marie for this tourist tip. This store is very *chic*, high-end, and elegant, precluding our spending too much time beyond window shopping. Unfortunately, (or better yet fortunately) we did not bring our tax returns to take out a second mortgage to fund purchases at Galleries Lafayette.

Back on the Red Hop-On-Hop-Off Bus, our next *"have to stop and see site"* is stop seven. Everyone is familiar with stop seven, the famous ending place of the Tour de France, the Champs Elysees archway created by Napoleon as a monument for kicking the Austrians' asses in early 1800's. As hard as we try, we cannot find any Lance Armstrong *"Seven-Time Tour de France Championship"* T-shirts. We learn that all of Lance's merchandise is *"no longer available, discontinued"* and that "We mustn't look for any of his merchandise to return in the near future." Google *"Lance Armstrong, bike racer"*, if you do not understand the last sentence.

The Archway is closed today. La Police, or, as I prefer to call them, La Politzia (giving them a more intriguing title), seemed to be in full force. We observe several old guys in full regalia police uniforms, each bearing numerous medals. Must be a parade day; however, we decide not to hang around. Seen one parade, seen them all.

Opting to remain anonymous, you know, blending in, we climb back onto the bus and are driven along *Avenue des Champs-Elysees*. There are many interesting aspects of this world famous street, including several high-end retailers, perhaps the most expensive and elaborate in the world. For a moment, I thought we were slumming along Rodeo Drive in Beverly Hills, but on a much grander scale. Our bus tour terminates at the base of the Eiffel Tower, which we both found appropriate, tucking these moments securely in our fondest memories.

On our walk back to the hotel, we stop at Tiffs store and buy lots of *"I can make you a great deal"* stuff. We also grab as much bubble wrap and boxes as we can carry.

Next, we stop by a Rugby clothing store. The sales clerk wants *"an arm and a leg"* for anything in the store. Being *"low on arms and legs"*, we decide not to be a Rugby store supporter. But, no fears! I remain an *"athletic supporter"* and my reputation precedes me.

Tonight, we decide to take the 22:00 evening Seine River riverboat cruise. As you may or not recall, these tickets are part of the one hour negotiations yesterday to upgrade our Red Hop-On-Hop-Off Bus passes. But first, we head back to the room to recharge the IPhone5, the iPad and most important, our bodies.

Our electronic devices and our bodies are fully charged for our night out on the town. We walk over to the Eiffel Tower to catch the boat. Along the way, we grab a snack to "take the edge off". The weather is outstanding (i.e. no rain). At this time of the year, the sun sets around 22:30. Buildings along both sides of the river are magnificently lit. Locals gather along various shoreline walkways and sitting areas to enjoy the pleasant evening. This was our best night out on the town so far on our trip. Disembarking at the Eiffel Tower, we head back to the hotel. Along the way, we stop at a local outdoor cafe and split an €18 bacon cheeseburger, fries and adult beverages. This late night evening outing carries into the wee hours of June 15. Juliette staying out past midnight? She is now in training to take advantage of the Las Vegas casinos coffee shop graveyard dining specials when we return home. Anyone up for biscuits and gravy for $1.99?

***

Saturday, June 15th -
Paris

Time to recharge the human batteries. Juliette sleeps in, and well-deservedly so. We decide to pack up our *"souvenirs"* and mail them today only because we **KNOW** that the Post Office is **OPEN** from 10:00 until 12:00 on Saturday. What a concept . . . a European Post Office open on Saturday!

On the way to our chores, we discover a new individual and/or team sport called: *"Little Kids on Two and Three Wheeled Scooters Playing Chicken Using Tourists as Freaking Targets."* Not wanting to create an international incident by chasing the little kids off the sidewalks, we let them win. However, I choose not to move for an older (fifteen year old) kid and I win. I teach him a lesson! We also learn that Frenchies **DO NOT** get out of the way when walking the other direction on the sidewalk. You better move or they will simply bump into you and allow you to believe it is your fault.

The Parisian postal experience was easy and carefree. I am still not certain why nothing went wrong! The clerk knew what he was doing and he didn't budge when I gave him a triple kiss, kiss, kiss and a quadruple merci.

The aroma and decadence of fine chocolates in a window display draws us into a *"to die for"* culinary shop. We each gain seven kilograms just passing through the door; the aroma alone is rich and tasty to the imagination. We tell the owner we shall return on Monday to buy her out!

The owner seems pleased by our intentions and immediately calls Euro Rail, purchases an unlimited use Rail Pass, then clicks on Hotels.Com and books thirty-nine days across Europe. Next, she gives me a double cheek kiss-kiss. Juliette gets a big hug, but only one kiss-kiss.

It's past 12:00, time for brunch at Café Gustavo. We have a partial view of the Eiffel Tower and clearly, we have become as obsessive of this landmark as any true Frenchman.

Juliette and I pass on the duck foie gras with stewed onion on white toast! We opt for a great omelet, an okay quiche and two coffees (another no free refills place). Maybe, just maybe, the next coffee shop or restaurant we stop at in Europe will be the first place to offer free coffee refills.

Our table is so small that our plates do not fit, so we take up two tables. I hope Philippe, our waiter, does not charge us for using two tables. Out of necessity, we have reduced his seating area and potential customers. When we get the bill, we learn that a two-table charge is built into the price! So, Juliette starts washing dishes. I will be waiting tables! If you thought New York City or Las Vegas strip restaurant prices are expensive, they are **NOTHING** compared to Paris prices!! I call Quicken Loans for a second mortgage or line of credit.

I can't vouch for what I am about to share with you, but we receive a text from our house sitter who is babysitting our spoiled rotten cat Tee. Apparently, our scatter-brain cat saw a picture of Juliette (Leslie) petting a kitty owned by an organ grinder and all kitty-cat hell broke out. Using Diane's cell phone, Tee sends us a threatening text promising to move out of our house and move in with Diane. Knowing this little beast, he will make demands for daily extra treats rations as compensation for pain, suffering and mental anguish. Hope he is not getting a lawyer.

*Friend Dale: Handyman Special. Please explain to the maintenance and repairmen at our Paris hotel that, if they moved the towel rack located inside the bathtub/shower to the **BACK** of the tub instead of hanging it in **FRONT** of the tub, they could mount a bracket to hold the hand-held showerhead higher thus creating a "real" shower. Dale, there is a great need and opportunity for you here. Plus, they use mobile home skirting for the bathroom ceiling. You will feel right at home. Begin studying French ASAP.*

We jump on the Red Hop-On-Hop-Off Bus and exit at a stop with a pedestrian walkway over the Seine River. This is a romantic bridge where couples write their names on a lock, the type you would use to bolt a door or a bicycle chain, hang the lock on the side of the bridge, and then toss the key to the lock into the river, symbolizing their true love forever. I ask Juliette to buy a €10 lock and write our names and date on it to commemorate our thirtieth wedding anniversary.

To demonstrate what a romantic I am, we hang the lock on the fence sixteen planks from the second lamppost on the left side of the bridge as one walks away from the Louvre on the top row next to a hot pink lock linked to someone whose romantic inclinations are like ours. Written on this anniversary lock is: *"Keoni and Leslie, 2013"*. We expect to see this lock on our sixtieth anniversary.

We stroll along the riverbank and head towards a museum, but first, we stop for a drink at a nice bar/café. For the price of a cappuccino and a beer, we get free potty privileges. Who could not possibly take advantage of this perk?

Without drawing the attention of anyone, I casually walk over to the shelf of clean beer glasses, take one and tuck it into my back pack. I have more than eighteen beer mugs in my tourist collection and now I can claim number nineteen!

Our first choice for museum viewing is Musee d'Orsay; however, there is a big time wait causing us to move along the Seine looking for the next available art showcase.

We check out a palace visit but unfortunately it is closed during repairs. Just across from where we are meandering, we happened to find a *"petite museum"*. There is no line to view the exhibits and Slovenian impressionists' work.

Juliette realizes she left her *"must have"* one-of-a-kind scarf at the all-inclusive potty-café bar. Claude volunteers to walk the mile and a half back to look for the scarf in lieu of visiting the museum. I am *"disappointed"* (not) but happy to take one for the team.

My Euro hat aids in my swagger when approached by French tourists asking *me,* stud Euro, in broken English for directions to the subway. I check their map, find where we are standing, stick up finger and conclude that they should keep going in the same direction to find the subway! Great guess by Claude. Just hope I was right. I find two landmarks, point them out to them thus installing total confidence that they are heading in the right direction! Claude the Euro Man does his good deed for the day . . . Mr. Boy Scout.

Killing two birds with one stone, I find Juliette's scarf left at the bar then celebrate my direction-giving with a drink. Make that two beers with french fries while engaging in small talk with the waitress and bartender. Admittedly, I was not anxious to rush back to the museum.

It didn't take long to make my way back to the museum where Juliette was waiting for me. Pleased to have her scarf, I decide to move along and visit the Rodin Museum to see the famed Tim Tebow statue, *"The Thinker"*. Juliette decides to sit this one out. I start walking. There are many sites worth taking a picture of. I reach into my backpack for the IPhone5 but alas, it is nowhere to be found. I know I had it at the steps of the museum. I rush back to the museum, hoping I may have left it somewhere at that location. I retrace my steps and tear apart the backpack. I find nothing. The building is about to close. I ask other tourists sitting or standing in my general area if they have seen it. Much to my relief, a couple tells me they found it and gave it to security. My breathing returns to normal as I seek out the *"rent a cop/security guard"*. He says he has my phone and returns in a matter of minutes.

My phone and I are re-united. I am relieved big time and offer a modest reward. The guard is a man of integrity and declines my offer. Sometimes we just get lucky in life. From this surely is a measure of lessons to be learned. Where would I begin? How about, "Hey, stupid, be careful where you put your IPhone5. Got a pocket?"

I start out again to the Rodin Museum, a good fifteen-minute walk. When I arrive, I quickly learn that they are closing at 17:00! I sneak into the gift shop and buy virtually one of everything written in English.

With purchases in hand, I head back to meet up with Juliette. We cross the busy six-lane street and wait for the next Red Hop-On-Hop-Off Bus. Suddenly, a parade of Politzia vans with sirens blaring *"uga-uga-uga"* come out of nowhere! Are they looking for Juliette? She has been wearing an electronic stimulator to help blood flow and aid in the healing process of her new right hip.

It is something of an explanation when describing this electronic apparatus; the Tens machine is the same size as an iPod. People often ask why she "plugs the earphones into her pants?" Good question, but the answer is simple enough.

The wiring that connects the Tens machine pads to the Tens machine stimulator sticks out of her pants at the waist. Perhaps someone noticed the wires and reported her to the Politzia as a possible suicide bomber! We breathe a sigh of relief as they pass by and keep on rolling to their destination.

While walking back to our hotel, Juliette finds an intimate restaurant *"just begging us"* to step inside for dinner. Our order includes the finest delicacies from their menu. Shortly thereafter, another waiter shows up with two long-stemmed glasses of champagne. We are more than impressed with the complimentary drinks. Obviously, I am recognized as Claude Euro without a disguise but wearing my famed Euro hat. To brighten up the table even more, the waiter returns with a full bottle of chilled water. At this point I am convinced that, although I am a celebrity, the glamour girl on my arm, Juliette, has to be the person who set the fire gaining everyone's attention.

We toast. Suddenly after just two sips in, out of nowhere, the greeter/receptionist runs over, grabs the champagne glasses from our hands, apologizes and steps over to the next table to give **OUR** glasses of champagne to a couple sitting to our right.

"Uh, scuzzi, madam," attempting to get the young lady's attention in broken French. "We took two sips," I said. The greeter puts the glasses back on our table. We say "thanks"! After a great meal including breast of Donald Duck (head removed) we receive the bill, pay and add the tip. I then ask myself, "Why is our bill SO high?" If you've been paying attention from the moment we sat down to eat, you would have surmised that they charged us for their mistake about the champagne. Snapping my fingers to call the waiter over and offer more than my credit card, I wish now to take the air out of his tires with a few choice words. Juliette, suddenly the arbiter, looks warmly at me and says, "Drop it, Claude. We both enjoyed it." Twice tonight she was right on.

Meandering five blocks to our hotel, we both comment about the evening air, the meal and the horror story regarding the champagne ... how silly it was ... but pleased it was the restaurant's fault and not ours.

We decide to hit the sack early. We have to be out the door by 6:30 to get to the rendezvous place to catch an early bus for a day trip to Versailles! Viva la France!

***

Sunday, June 16th -
Paris

After experiencing the most wonderful time traveling across Europe, our five-week vacation (aka holiday) is coming to an end. Never have we enjoyed ourselves so much. From Laundromats to train stations, to Post Offices, restaurants, car rental agencies, you name it, we did it and will no doubt do it again.

We rise at 5:45, shower, dress and take the subway to the gathering place to catch the bus for our day trip to *Versailles*. In one day, we will visit a Palace that took thousands of workers to build and countless praises from the millions who have witnessed its splendor.

Planning, as we are quite aware, is everything. Arriving early, we allow enough time to enjoy a nice breakfast at a local establishment. Then, the unbelievable happens ... finally, after over thirty-five days abroad, we get **FREE** coffee refills, and on top of that, what all tourists enjoy most, free restroom services!

This is going to be a tour long remembered. *Versailles* is a Palace ... literally. The weather is great and helps make the day additionally enjoyable. A day without sunshine unfortunately has been the norm for us on this journey.

The Palace was first built as a hunting lodge in 1623 by King Louis XII. I can't imagine what they may have been hunting back then by the size of this joint. King Louis XIV enlarged the complex, creating the current royal Palace. The major expansion took fifty-four years to complete and served as the principal residence of the King and the seat of France's government.

At its peak, 2,000 people worked with impeccable skill and energy to serve the King and Queen while maintaining the Palace's 700 room complex. It is not difficult to imagine the Palace was large enough to handle up to 20,000 people including staff, their families, visitors and others.

Opulently decorated, the Palace is complete with the most exquisite artwork adorning the walls and ceilings. Handmade tapestries line the parapets and windows. The walls in most gathering rooms are covered with extremely large paintings depicting French battle scenes, all of which, I am certain, were victories. The precision and detail in each painting is unbelievable, especially given the timeframe during which each was created.

A *"summer"* home and other buildings are part of the vast complex. The grounds are meticulously groomed. Statutes and water fountains accent the landscape. *"Stunning"* is as good a word as I can use to explain this exquisite area.

It has been a great day to close our fantastic trip. Today was more than special, it was significantly more. Versailles is unlike anything we have ever seen before. The Palaces and museums across Europe are treasures beyond their magnificence. Each are tributes to the artistry and care of humanity. Versailles has its own moral compass, as do many of these wonderful wonders of the world.

We head back to Paris in Sunday night traffic. Fortunately, we find a *"hole-in-the-wall"* bar where we enjoy our *"last dinner in Paris"*. Interesting name for a possible movie, you think?

Around the corner, we visit an ice cream store where one French Scoop equals one American sized teaspoon. Their price for the teaspoon size ice cream is three times the price of one large U.S.A. scoop! We finish the day with a bottle of French Champagne and?? *Bonne nuit et au Revoir de Paris.*

***

Monday, June 17th -
Paris

We awaken to, you guessed it, the thunderous serenade of rain. Our departure may be delayed due to the international heaven world bowling finals! Just got the report, Jesus beat his Father 247 to 239. The Father missed the beer pin (number five) to lose, or did he throw the match so his son could win? Checking with the Holy Ghost and saints for their opinion.

Another day and another great breakfast featuring scrambled eggs so fluffy they had to have been made with cream of goat mother's milk. Our servers went so far as to butter our French bread. Apparently, word is out that we never do well with knives.

Off now in the pouring rain to the dreaded Post Office and to whatever harangue that surely must await us. The last of the useless Euro souvenirs must be mailed today. Our saving grace is we will stop and buy out the *"to die for"* candy store.

Within moments of finally reaching the doorsteps of Tiff's souvenir emporium, the curse again returns. The skies are as dark midnight. It begins to **POUR**. I really don't wish to understate the downfall but I am talking *"end of the world rain"*! Where is Noah and the Ark when you need him?

Naturally Tiff is pleased to see us. He wasn't the least put out when I asked only a favor of him rather than fork over a few extra Euros for more touristy stuff.

I needed a box large enough to ship our useless souvenirs to the States. He hasn't anything but eagerly volunteers to shoot across the street and ask a fellow retailer to provide one for us. His friend *"delivers"*! Tiff may be a hustler, but he's a good kind of fellow and a genuine character.

Walking through the driving rainstorm, we arrive at the Post Office at 9:53. Do the God's give a rat's nose about us? No. It took virtually all we had to get there only to learn the Post Office is freaking closed! Is it a holiday? No. Is it a postal strike? No. The Paris Air Show starts today. Does this count as a Holiday? There is a reprieve. All we need to do is read the sign on the damn door! The sign informs us they open at 10:00 giving us a couple of options to kill seven minutes.

We can:

wait the few minutes in a downpour and become drenched until we squeak or,

rush to a nearby coffee shop and enjoy coffee, pastries, rolls or whatever on earth they are pushing today!

This is a no brainer. We opt to use up our remaining Euros for coffee and an éclair.

The Post Office experience was again easy. They accepted our package, placed a huge label and stamp across it and took it from our view into the back room. Whatever goes on from that point, I couldn't care less.

We agree 100 percent that buying out the candy store will be our last official Parisian purchasing act. We also realize that the chocolates may never make it back to the States and possibly not even past the train station. We'll see.

Either we are at odds with the gods or they are doing their level best to keep us in Paris. The rain persists. We have but one option. Get the hell to the hotel and get out of our wet clothes.

Sheets of rain make it all but impossible to cross the street. Without a doubt, this is the hardest rain of the trip. A clerk in a dry-cleaning store sees our plight and invites us to step in from out of the rain. Watching from the dry-cleaner's window, we can see the water gushing over the sidewalks. No point in trying to navigate through this tidal wave; our umbrellas are useless and as is our patience leaving us official members of the Paris Duck Club. Claude and Juliette are soaked head to toe.

The clock is ticking down (tic, tic, tic) . . . time is running short. We need to get back to the hotel, grab our belongings and catch a cab to the train station. There are no more options. We thank our host and bolt out into the deluge. Adding insult to injury, a Mercedes rushes by sending *"rain roosters"* along the curbs in our direction. Thanks Frenchie for the unexpected shower. Juliette and Claude both give him the American one finger *"salute"*.

The hotel is a fortress against the enemy from the gods. We are soaking wet. Our clothes, socks, sneakers and back packs are all drenched. Only one option, strip and change clothes. Claude runs across the street to the Laundromat and tosses our wet clothing into a dryer. The cab is scheduled to pick us up at 12:00. Juliette pushes our cab back to a more reasonable pick up time. Now, we have a fifteen-minute window to dry our clothes and sneakers, get the hell out of our room, the hotel and town!

I fondle the drying clothes to assess their dampness, checked my watch and proclaim, "Close enough!" Two ladies sitting the Laundromat look at me with a *"what the hell is that crazy Americano man doing running in and out of the Laundromat?"* "No time to explain ladies." I beat a path back to the hotel and my Juliette.

Our clothes are reasonably dry. Our sneakers are squeaky but comfy. We get to the train station at 12:45 for what Claude believes is the 13:39 train to London. Claude kills time taking pictures and incurs another Juliette moment. "Find out what track our train is on and one more thing, genius, our train to London is scheduled to leave at 13:13 (mumbling dumb Schmitt under her breath) **NOT** 13:39 dumb shit!"

Claude is still *"chilling"*, buying a takeaway train lunch and waiting for the track number to post on the mammoth departure board. Juliette is now fuming at Claude. Time is ticking down but no track number. Suddenly I see a tiny note on the wall, *"Train to London Leaving From Upstairs Level One"*.

Would it be fair to add that we bolt upstairs where we find out we must fill out *"Entry to England"* forms and then go through security and customs? At the same moment, train personnel are yelling out, "Hurry up, Americanos. The train is leaving. We are **NOT** waiting for you two dummies!" I believe that's what I heard (or something close to that).

We answered all seventy-seven questions on the customs forms and rush through security like two crazed Americano tourists. We make it to our seats with five minutes to spare. Juliette puts Claude on the *"do not touch me list"*. She calls ahead to the London Doubletree Hotel and asks for a sofa bed for Claude.

The bullet train from Paris gets to London in one hour's time. Upon arrival, Claude and Juliette again become Paul and Elizabeth, aka Betty.

Disembarking the train, we follow the herd and descend to the Tube for a twenty-four-stop local subway ride to the airport area followed by a fifteen minute free bus ride to the Doubletree at Heathrow Airport. The sofa bed is made up and waiting for yours truly, Paul, the clown taking the magnum .357 and its entire eight rounds!

The hotel is *"Americanized"* complete with an in-room coffee pot, shampoo and conditioner in separate bottles, a real plus for Her Majesty, Elizabeth. Included in this royal treatment, we find ice as well as large coffee cups and free refills complete with a nice bar and restaurant.

One last shopping trip. The *"Big Guy"* (Paul) needs a Cricket shirt. We take a double-decker city bus to a local shopping area. The neighborhood is a bit *"rough"*. Every store closes at 18:00. We get to the sporting goods store a few minutes past the deadline at 18:03.

However, despite pleading and showing a few bucks in my hand, the clerk refuses to open the gated door.

We enjoy an adult beverage in a *"locals"* bar while waiting for the double-decker bus to take us back to the hotel. As anticipated by Betty, I illegally obtain my last souvenir beer mug.

Tonight, we keep it simple and eat at the hotel. We download an episode of *"Burn Notice"* and watch it on the iPad. The countdown is on. Our trip is nearing its end. We have both remorse and a bit of relief. Despite all the missteps and plain foolishness, we have had a great time filled with pleasing memories and a host of stories . . . some of them are for real! Add to this, an array of photographs and videos just to support whatever happens to come to my mind.

***

Tuesday, June 18th -
London

Today is our last day on vacation. Europe is now behind us as we begin our return to the States.

We awake to the weather lady on TV informing us and the United Kingdom, to "expect drizzles today". It doesn't affect us. It follows us around like a bad habit.

Our final meal before departing for the airport and home is the hotel breakfast buffet. We can choose from baked beans, sautéed mushrooms, grilled tomatoes, ham, seven-minute and soft boiled eggs, fresh breads and pastries. Included are an array of cereals, freshly squeezed juices and English "Bangers".

To get to the airport, we chose a cab over the free shuttle bus. The cab is clean. Our driver is very professional. He informs us that he was born in Bulgaria and later moved to Sweden. Her Majesty, Elizabeth (Betty to some), comments on the car's cleanliness, allowing Giorgi, the driver, to reply with, "This is what customers expect!" Obviously, Giorgi has **NEVER** been to New York City where taking a cab ride is more an *"adventure"* than a customer's *"expectation"*!

When you appreciate the services of someone's helping hand, you find an interest in taking good care of them as well. We enjoyed the brief conversation with Giorgi. He left us by recommending we visit Sweden, a beautiful, peace-loving nation ... one that will not break the travel budget.

Because we are flying First Class, we manage our way through the airport check-in rather quickly. Paul (who will soon become John once again) has no problem going through the security screening. Elizabeth (still Betty to some), however, sets off the bells and whistles. Security personnel *"wand"* her. The alarms continue to blare, frightening some folks seen clutching their hearts and making the hairs on the back of my neck stand straight out.

She gets the full-body treatment, a real pat-down! I am almost certain she is beginning to enjoy this. Why you ask? A young man was personally investigating the situation. Her Majesty continues to return to the back of the line at least three times! Clearly, she is enjoying this moment in the spotlight and is moving along with a smile on her cute face.

The journey may be coming to an end; however, the shopping has not. Her Majesty cannot pass up a new watch at the Duty-Free (**NOT** free) shop.

Ah, the advantages of First Class. We leisurely wait to board our plane in the private American Airlines waiting lounge. What's more, we have access to free food and drink. We toast to the finish of our trip with mimosas. We just **LOVE** those frequent flyer miles that gets us this luxury and *"free stuff"*.

Time to board the big bird. We quickly learn that there is First Class and then there is **FIRST CLASS**! We each have our own seating pod complete with Bose headsets and individual TV's with access to numerous first run movies. Each seating pod converts to a full length bed. PJ's, sleeping masks, socks and blankets were available for our use. Now catch this ... the food and drink choices ... appetizers, salad, salmon or chateaubriand, bananas Foster or chocolate fruit sundaes with, of course, fresh whipped cream and nuts.

We are offered a variety of fine wines, imported beers and cocktails of choice ... enough to choose your own poison or simply dabble. A purser and two stewards are there to meet our every need.

We are absolutely spoiled! This is a once in a lifetime **FIRST CLASS** experience not to be forgotten.

Arriving on time in Miami, we have no room for as much as a conversation regarding food. Our plane leaves for Las Vegas in forty-five minutes. We are pleased to again be on American soil and known simply as John and Leslie.

My Ace Wahine clears all the security checkpoints without setting off a single alarm. However, she asks for and is granted three personal *"hands-on pat-downs"*. The woman is incorrigible. Time to catch the plane.

There was one more unanswered question that, without asking Leslie, I managed to figure out for myself as I simply gazed at her while she was sound asleep in the comfort of the First Class cabin. It was one of those moments when all was silent, even the sound of the jet engines somehow no more than a whisper. She was extremely happy.

Thanks for reading about our travel adventures. Most of you know I cannot say anything in less than 63,000+ words.

***

Traveling With John and Leslie

September 25th to
October 6th 2016

Sunday, September 25th -
Henderson, Nevada to Twin Falls, ID

Well, Travel Fans, without equivocation we just set a Turzer family traveling record and something to be proud of: twenty-four hours **WITHOUT** a calamity. Certainly, nothing near that *"stuff"* that happened on our 2013 European Trip including:

Leslie getting left on the subway platform when the doors closed before she boarded. (London)

Bank cards not working in Germany.

No seats on the train to Paris (unlike the adventures of the Orient Express. But that's another story).

Going to the wrong village in Slovakia where English was *"Greek"* to them.

But, I digress.

We make our way to Twin Falls, Idaho and find our hotel; our reservation is confirmed and our credit cards are eagerly accepted. We eat at a great restaurant, took a quick spin around town, return to the hotel, watch some TV and go to bed. After just one day, it is again confirmed that, we are a boring, slightly past *"middle age"* couple. With twelve days remaining, surely we would have plenty of opportunity for adventure or, to embrace a well stated *Leslie-ism,*

"When adventure and good times finds us, we'll be ready for it!" Wish us well.

PS: Leslie Turzer did spill coffee on her shirt as we were pulling out of the driveway. Plus, after driving one block, we return home to get my sun glasses. So the first day is not 100 percent without incident.

***

Monday September 26th -
Idaho Falls, ID

Today's adventure begins with a trip to Shoshone Falls, considered *"one of the top seven wonders of the world"* (perhaps more a suggestion from their Chamber of Commerce and, rightfully so). If the reference to Wonders included Idaho's cattle, potatoes, fishing, hiking, farming, friendly "natives" and the bonus of snowy windy winters, then all would agree, The Falls are indeed a *"wonderland"* for the eye and the spirit.

If you Google this *"landmark"* and check out the pictures, Shoshone Falls remains quite the site, a **MUST** place to visit. Don, the entrance greeter and money collector, gladly took our three dollars, smiled and **THEN** points to the sign that reads, **"Falls Dry"**. We take that to mean someone turned off the faucet. The gatekeeper offers to refund our daily site seeing allowance; we decide not to accept his offer preferring instead to carry on. There is **NO** adventure in a refund.

We proceed down a windy, narrow one lane *"road"*. If you could only see it today, the *"Falls"* are underwhelming. So be it. We learn that when the river is running at its best, we can only imagine how spectacular the Falls are, and often properly referred to as *"The Niagara of the West"*. There is so much to learn about this sanctuary for national pride.

After a fifteen minute stay, we leave and begin our journey to Baker City, OR to see our good friends The Millers.

Leslie and I found Twin Falls to be a very friendly city. We enjoyed our short stay.

PS. Enjoying the great weather. Leslie is at the wheel and going bonkers throwing caution to the wind with the eighty miles per hour Interstate 84 speed limit. You go girl, I've had a great life.

***

Monday Afternoon, September 26th - Baker City, OR

We arrive safe and sound in Baker City, OR. First stop, time to catch up with Jack and Vickie Miller, a great couple who worked for me many moons ago in the mobile home park management business. These hard-working people taught me a lot and came through for me on more than one occasion.

We check into our accommodations at the Blue Door B&B. It was easy to find . . . just look for the **BLUE** front door. This charming home was designed and built in the 1940's by a local architect. We are greeted by the owner and offered wine, crackers and cheese. Our oversized room is tastefully decorated. Not having a shower, just a bath tub, will most likely present a challenge that I will talk about later.

We decide to slow this adventure down, grab some take-out food from the local Safeway and dine with the Millers during the TV presidential debate. The *"debate"* is poorly managed by the moderator and left many of the real issues on the sidelines. Today was a long day; however, we are just grateful to share it with good friends and the libations from Safeway.

***

Tuesday, September 27th -
Baker City to Phoenix, OR

I don't wish to paint a lasting picture of what I am about to tell you, so be prepared to ignore the visuals and simply imagine yourselves *"stuck"* in the same dilemma I am suddenly facing.

Our morning began with numerous attempts to climb into the bathtub without falling, slipping, banging one's head or breaking a leg or an arm or both. On the third try, I determine that getting into the tub backwards and executing a 180-degree body turn is the only safe way to proceed. The next challenge . . . you guessed it . . . removing my mortal frame from the porcelain cache without injury. On the count of three, I could balance my body on both hands, throw both feet over the side of the tub, turn my upper body ninety degrees to the left and flip myself out, sticking the landing with gymnastic precision. Now, for your own sake, please remove any pictures from your mind that you may have needed to better understand this most difficult bathing experience. Thank you.

Prior to hitting the road, we enjoy our homemade breakfast and conversation with a couple from Washington state.

Next stop, Phoenix, Oregon to visit our good friend Jennifer. There are no main highways on this leg of the journey, plus my co-driver is under the weather, leaving me to drive the 450 miles on two-lane state roads over numerous hills and valleys and, as the song suggests, *"over the river and through the woods ...".*

Occasionally we slow down to twenty-five miles per hour driving through small towns located in the middle of nowhere and accompanied by doubtless speed traps and radar. One of the larger towns we pass through is John Day. This quaint city of mid-19th Century local lore is located about two miles north of Canyon City (the county seat) at the intersections of U.S. 26 and 395. We noticed that this town has **EVERYTHING** one needs to survive including True Value and Ace Hardware, Napa Auto Parts, Dairy Queen, Les Schwab Tires and a tractor and farm equipment sales and service dealer.

Believe me, John Day is more than it appears and with one heck of a history.

"The Squeeze Inn" (I love that name), a local watering hole, with deer hunting season quickly approaching, proudly displays a sign **"Hunters Welcome"**. Not exactly a breathtaking marketing scheme, but their message is clear enough.

Before enjoying my breakfast earlier today, I noticed the local Baker City daily newspaper had a sixteen page special section covering everything hunters need to know about the upcoming deer hunting season. I am getting the impression we are entering a sort of members only social club for those packing long rifles, scopes and ammunition. Best we move along to presumably safer ground.

We drive through several National Parks. The tree leaves are beginning to turn into their fall colors. We pass numerous farms where the cattle and horses feast on green pastures, relaxing with fellow animals or roaming freely. In addition, hay bales are neatly stacked and covered for the upcoming winter. Periodically, we see the sunlight sparkle across lakes, rivers and brooks.

We are amused and entertained by roadside signs including: **"Do Not Pass Snowplows on the Right," "Deer Migration Crossing," "Chain Up Area 1/2 Mile Ahead," "Chain Removal Area," "Wildlife Crossing," "Elk"** and **"Snowmobile Crossing"**. Yes, I am by now convinced we are in the wilds of today's American Frontier. It feels great.

Half-way through our journey, we stop in Bend, Oregon for a tasty lunch with Danna. She is a long-time member of our adopted family and our daughter's best friend. Her boyfriend took time from work to join us.

Catching up was probably the best part of this day. We had to leave far too early to keep with our schedule and subsequent meetings with friends.

Tonight, we are meeting our friend Jennifer, for dinner in Jacksonville, a quaint village consisting of a three block *"downtown"* and designated as a National Landmark. This distinctive community is punctuated with local boutiques, bars and restaurants. Curiously, this small town is a view of the past and a revelation of how well we can preserve the best of what we have in this country. Leslie and Jennifer "catch up" while eating dinner. I chose to watch *"Sports Center"* on the TV located over the bar in lieu of listening to and participating in *"girl talk"*.

After dinner and closing the bar, we head to Jennifer's home located in Phoenix, Oregon. Her house has a fantastic view overlooking the lush landscapes and mountains of Medford. Jennifer has put her heart and soul into remodeling the home. In fact, she did most of the work herself! She owns all the tools of a master craftsman while I am proud to say I have a screw driver and hammer but no shovel. Household repairs to me means calling a repairman. Leslie and Jennifer continue *"catching up"* and *"icing their jaws"* while I settle in for a much-needed good night's sleep.

Can't wait to see what day three brings us.

***

Wednesday, September 28th -
Phoenix, OR to Calistoga, CA

We arise after a good night's sleep, give Jennifer hugs and head out. Today we head south to the California wine country and all that it offers. It is Leslie's turn to drive. She is alive and well thanks to the miracle of modern western medicine and a good night's sleep.

Snowcapped mountains, lakes, hills, farmland and herds of cattle dot the landscape along Interstate 5 as we head south.

It suddenly dawns on us that we have no place to stay tonight. After many failed attempts, I finally get an Internet connection and search for last minute hotel deals near Calistoga. Three come up.

1. A $400 per night stay for two that includes mud baths and other spa treatments

2. A hotel with good ratings and

3. A bed and breakfast with *"only one room available"*.

After serious discussion of the pros and cons of mud baths and spa treatments, we unanimously vote **NO** choosing instead to save our *"fun money"* for the matching tattoos we just know we will get in a drunken stupor after drinking too much wine. The hotel sounds like a great option, the tattoos yet to be determined.

Leslie likes bed and breakfasts; however, I question if the *"last room available"* is nothing more than a pull-out couch in the living room with community shared bathrooms or a single bed tucked in the utility room closet. So, I call the B&B, speak to Max, the *"concierge"* (he is probably a desk clerk but I just have to put this word to good use) and learn that the one remaining room has a queen size bed, bathroom and shower plus free breakfast. He quoted the same price with fees as <u>Hotels.com</u>. We need two more nights booked through <u>Hotels.com</u> for a free night (seniors are always looking for a deal . . . we have lots of time on our hands), thus I apply logic and reason to parlay both into a constructive decision. I inform Max that I will book through <u>Hotels.com</u> and look forward to arriving before 6:00 pm.

We exit I-5 and head off on a two-lane country road for the final seventy-five miles of today's journey. About ten miles in, I just happen to glance at the gas gauge and the *"remaining miles to empty"* display. Fifty-two (as in 52) miles to our destination and Forty-two (as in 42) miles until empty. **"Houston, we have a problem."** Not only are we running low on fuel but we are out in the middle of nowhere with no Internet or phone connections! As the miles-to-empty tick down and communications are nonexistent, we go into *"conserve fuel mode"*, slowing to fifty-five miles per hour and turning off the AC even though the temperature outside is 100 degrees. We **KNOW** there is a town *"somewhere"* on this route as we have traveled this road years ago; we just don't know the name of the town or how far it is! I continually reassure Leslie *"everything will be good . . . we will make it"* all the while saying to myself, *"what the hell is going on? Please God, tonight I do not want to sleep in the car along the side of the road."* Memories of our European trip creep into my mind with awesome clarity.

Every time I'm behind the wheel, Leslie frequently leans over to check the gas gauge; however, while she is driving she **NEVER** glances down to check anything! Go figure. Kind of like Slovakia. No?

Further down the road to parts unknown, the low fuel *"idiot"* light comes on. This dramatically increases the tension and stress. But alas, and with just twenty-four miles from *"empty"*, we enter a small town, spot the first gas station and fill up. Tragedy is averted and, as promised, *"all is well, Leslie"*.

With the threat of running out of gas no longer an issue and our collective blood pressures returned to normal levels, we are confident we will at least survive the day. This fearless couple can now mosey on down the remaining thirty-six miles to Calistoga and an eight-room B&B not so curiously named **"The Wine Way Inn"**.

Our host, Max, warmly greets us, gives us the three dollar tour and recommends a restaurant for dinner. Before we head out, however, we avail ourselves to the complimentary Merlot red wine and relax. Tired we may be; crazy we are not.

We stroll the half mile through downtown Calistoga to Sam's Social Club for what else, dinner. Our evening starts out with a glass of wine for Leslie, and a house made India Pale Ale for John. We share a typical Northern California overpriced *"fu-fu salad"* (where's the lettuce?) complete with pork belly deep fried croutons and natural yogurt. To be honest, I could have eaten about three or four but, I would have exceeded our dinner meal budget. We follow the shared salad with a traditional pepperoni and mushroom pizza. So if any of our limited number of friends and Facebook followers ever travel to this area, we highly recommend that you stop by Sam's Social Club for great food, service and ambiance.

The walk back to the B&B barely burns off ten calories of tonight's dinner, especially when Ms. Ace Wahine Leslie just **HAS TO** stop for Dryers ice cream. Remember her favorite slogan, *"We are on vacation!"* I, however, show restraint and discipline and pass on the dessert. After all, I am in training for something.

An interesting day to say the least.

The question of the day: We noticed something quite odd about two road signs . . . both seemed normal until faced with the following dilemma and proverbial double take:

1. Falling Rocks

2. Fallen Rocks

Do we travel with baseball gloves and strong push brooms or simply put the signs out of our minds? I am going with *"Put them out of our minds"*.

***

Thursday, September 29th -
Calistoga to Mill Valley, CA

Rise and shine in downtown Calistoga. The eight-room B&B is full. The smell of fried bacon provides more than enough incentive to rise and shine, shower and head down the steep, narrow steps to the first-floor breakfast room. The place is abuzz with laughter and small talk among a group of eight ladies celebrating someone's fiftieth birthday.

The breakfast buffet is located under a glass enclosed patio and is loaded with goodies including granola, fresh fruit, freshly squeezed juice, freshly baked (and **NOT** the low calorie, fat free variety) homemade scones, thick, perfectly cooked bacon and a *"to die for"* baked egg casserole that included the plumpest yellow raisins, a hint of maple syrup and topped with small slices of French bread.

I won't lie to you; I am proud to say that I grossly over ate or more specifically, *"pigged out"*. Multiple helpings (i.e., more than three) of bacon and the egg casserole raised my cholesterol count to an all-time high over 300 with the bad cholesterol count off the charts. What a way to go, smugly reminding myself it was a good idea I passed on the ice cream the night before.

We are joined at our table by Mark, a young gentleman who tells us he is a Senator in Thailand. Obviously, this part of his traveling resume seemed not made up following a short and introductory discussion. He sounds knowledgeable about Thai politics and the U.S. party system; however, he didn't have a business card. Not surprisingly, I could not find him in the online list of Thai Senators. Maybe he is a CIA operative or perhaps Thailand has a semi-pro baseball team known as the Bangkok Senators. He is tall enough to play first base or least center field. Well, why not? Who am I to judge? Time will tell if he emails me his info.

Before we leave Calistoga, Leslie makes one last romp through the downtown shopping district while I hang out on the porch catching up on the happenings in Las Vegas and around the world. Before long, I am sharing the porch with eight ladies waiting for a stretch limo to take them on their Thursday tour of the local wineries. I make their day with small talk and tell them they all look great and their perfume smells wonderful. For these accolades, I am rewarded with smiles and high fives. No hugs or kisses, eh, better than nothing.

When Ace Wahine Leslie returns, we head south to the Frank Family winery. Leslie invests in four bottles of their very finest.

Our next stop is Schaumburg where we are card-carrying, dues-paying members of their *"exclusive"* club of 5,374 winos. It is here we enjoy a taste of a new vintage wine and a smooth champagne, and with grand old American initiative and imagination, make a meal out of their breadsticks and pick up our next quarterly shipment of wine and champagne. Leslie adds a few bottles of wine to the order. I treat myself to a new Panama Jack hat.

The last stop today is one of our favorite wineries, Sattui. This award-winning family winery only sells their wines at this location. We are members of their club; however, since we do not buy a case of wine, we do not get preferential treatment or discounts. On our way out the door, we avoid the *"to die for"* gourmet deli. Trust me their food and desserts are outstanding.

As we are leaving the wine country, Leslie gets a text from the Schaumburg Winery office saying she was chosen *"customer of the day"* in the sixty-six to seventy female age group. I thought to myself, should I ever receive such a text proclaiming my *"age group"*, I would refuse to accept both the message and the award, after all, there are so few of us *"never-over-fifty-ish"* remaining.

For the past four evenings, a series of one night stands, reality was catching up with me. Tough on the body and worse on the mind. Further, we violate the basic car traveling rule: return everything back in the same place. Hence, every day begins with *"Where the heck did I put that?"* By the way, I was right about Max. He was the concierge and not simply the bell-boy. His managed the B&B for his parents.

The traffic on the country roads and CA Highway 101 heading north it is bumper to bumper with the occasional gridlock stops and potential for road rage. Thankfully, we are heading south.

We check into the Holiday Inn Express in Mill Valley, located across the Bay from San Francisco and close to Sausalito. My body is screaming for a workout so I head to the gym to answer the call.

Leslie is fighting a nasty cold. We find an organic, gluten free (oxymoron??) Mexican restaurant. She recharges the batteries with a bowl of chicken soup. I opt for the chicken tacos.

The night alone is calling us to get a full night's sleep requiring no reminders from anything or anyone. We are pooped!

***

Friday, September 30th -
Mill Valley, CA

Leslie is still not feeling great. Therefore, we decide to take a semi-rest day. She is on ginger ale and saltine crackers while I eat the typical Holiday Inn Express free breakfast: instant oatmeal, sweet rolls, toast, powdered eggs, cold turkey sausage (the food warmer lights are out) and coffee. Lots of fat and calories to *"nourish"* the body. At this point, who am I to complain? Life is good and the *"meal"* is **FREE**.

We head out on a driving tour of the surrounding scenic area. The two-lane serpentine road takes us *"over the river and through the woods to grandmother's house we go"*. The ten miles up and down steep roadway presents physical and mental challenges for numerous studly male and female bike riders. Steve Worthy: please note, I was thinking of you. Needless to say, this is your kind of challenge.

We stop at Muir Woods, home of the Redwood Trees. The walking tour is **"OUT"** for Leslie. So, back on the road, we admire spectacular long-range ocean views.

The next stop on today's journey is Stinson Beach, the ultimate Northern California beach town, population 456. The weather is perfect, cool, sunny and breezy.

Lunch is *"to die for"* at Parkside Cafe, an organic beachside eatery. Everything is made from scratch and is healthy. What a novel concept. I cannot pronounce, let alone tell you about the various spices, sauces and condiments but they all look and smell great. I thoroughly enjoy every bite of my homemade finger-licking-good veggie burger. Leslie is still doing the soup thing. Before heading back to Sausalito, we take a *"brief"* twenty-step walk onto the breezy beach.

Littering is discouraged with a $1,000 fine. Think at least twice before tossing something out the window.

In Sausalito, Leslie window shops while I sit near the water enjoying the distant San Francisco city skyline and the Bay and Golden Gate bridges. I **NEVER** get tired of this view!

I need *"something to do tonight"* while Leslie stays back at the hotel and recharges her batteries. The San Francisco Giants are playing their hated rival Los Angeles Dodgers tonight at AT&T Park. MadBum Madison Bumgarner, is pitching a *"must win"* game for the Giants as they battle the Cardinals and Mets for the two wildcard playoff spots as the season ticks down to the final three games.

I know I can fight the traffic and drive to the game with little to zero difficulty. However, a *"little bird"* coaches me to check out alternative options to get to the game. Alas, there is a ferry from Larkspur, just eight miles up the road, directly to AT&T Park. After securing the go ahead blessing from Leslie, I book the round-trip ferry ride. We hustle back to the hotel. I change into four layers of long sleeve shirts and jackets. AT&T Park is situated on the bay. At night, the wind blows and the temperatures drop. Trust me, fans gear up with multiple layers of clothing, scarves, hats and blankets. You would think they are heading to a football game in December in NYC. Wearing ten pounds of clothing, I head out to the ferry station. The seven mile trip takes forty-five minutes in mostly stop and go and stop again traffic on Highway 101 North. Rush hour Bay Area traffic is a nightmare. Why anyone would endure this daily commute is beyond me.

The ferry is packed with Giants fans decked out in their multiple layers of black and orange team gear. Many carry heavy blankets. If you want a winter vacation in the summer or fall, head to a night game at AT&T Park. I am surprised to see some brave souls decked out in Dodgers gear, apparently unaware of the circumstances in which they find themselves. Perhaps these are simply die-hard (no pun intended) Dodger fans who have survived this type of intrigue in the past and are willing to face the many possibilities again. Hey, it's only a game. Right?

The ferry calmly maneuvers across the bay for the one-hour voyage. I engage in conversation with Giants fans and learn about a great place to stop for lunch on our Saturday drive to Carmel.

Thirty minutes before the first pitch, the ferry docks at the stadium. The game is a sellout. I set out to find the local entrepreneur scalpers. Finding a single ticket has proven to be easy many times. An independent *"businessman"* asks me what I am looking for . . . *"Box seat, downstairs between the bases"*. While he does not possess the ticket I want, he calls out to his *"associates"*. One of his guys has just the ticket I want for only $150 and no taxes or service and handling fees. Negotiations to reduce the price prove fruitless so I fork over the cash knowing full well a few hours earlier the best remaining tickets at the ticket office were less desirable seats and priced over $250 with fees and handling charges.

The seat is great! The avid Giant fans endure a quick two run Dodger lead; however, the home team ties it up in the bottom of the first. A pitching duel continues until the Dodgers breakthrough for a run in the top of the sixth. Dodgers manager Dave Roberts makes a pitching change that proves to be fatal. The Giants erupt for seven runs highlighted by a two run double by *"MadBum"* (Madison Bumgarner) and a three run homer by Brandon Belt. The Giant crazies are all standing up, going bonkers and waving tonight's giveaway rally towels. On multiple occasions, my face is towel whipped by the lady sitting in front of me. While she left a bruise or two, she did not draw blood or apologize.

For the present, all is well for the Giants and their fans. They remain in playoff contention with a hard fought nine to three win. What could possibly go wrong?

The ferry heads back to Larkspur thirty minutes after the last out. By the time I get on, all indoor seats are spoken for. Outdoor seating in mid-fifty degree weather is not an option for this near-senior citizen, ahem. So, I secure a spot indoors, on the floor. A few minutes later, a young lady offers me her seat. She must be a former Girl Scout or was raised to properly respect her elders. I regret, however, that my appearance of related age was so obvious. I guess there are a few good people left in this world.

After taking fifteen minutes to dock the boat, I disembark and drive the seven miles south to the hotel on an empty Highway 101.

A long but great day comes to an end around 12:45 AM Saturday.

***

Saturday, October 1st -
Mill Valley to Carmel, CA

We bid ado to Mill Valley and start our journey south towards Carmel. Leslie is *"back in the game"* and feeling much better. Our Aussie in-car navigation person directs us to take the main roadways; however, we want to saunter down CA Highway 1 along the coast. After four or five commands to turn around and get back on the route he mapped for us, the Aussie is thoroughly frustrated. He throws his hands up, tells us to go to hell and displays the fickle finger of fate on the navigation system screen. He also sends a series of unkind emojis to Leslie's cell phone prompting the good and grand lady to say, "Sorry, you are fired, **CANCEL ROUTE**." That's telling him!

Since this is Saturday, the drive is slow; but, the weather is great . . . fall-like temperatures with a nip of fresh air in the cloudless sky. The views are breathtaking and spectacular. We use turnout areas to stop, admire the view and take more pictures that we will never look at again.

The route we chose is along the coast, hence the Tsunami Evacuation Route signs. In one of the small beach towns, we sit through what seems like an eternity of traffic light changes as we inch, and I mean inch, our way south.

If you recall Friday night's ferry ride to AT&T Park, I shared a sitting area with Giants fans. A middle-aged lady, who, upon listening to our trip itinerary for Saturday, recommended we stop at Gayle's in Capitola for lunch. She promised we would not be disappointed. You know how people often offer suggestions for this and that. Ninety-nine percent of the time we politely reply *"great"* or acknowledge with a *"thanks, we will try it"* but never do.

Well, this was the one percent-er! We stop and are amazed at the variety of hot and cold food choices from salads to sandwiches to everything one could want, plus ... the numerous bakery selections are just *"to die for"*.

Once you decide what you want, you take a number and wait your turn. The large staff is very efficient. Numbers are quickly called, so quickly in fact, that we must go back three times to get a new number being that we were not paying attention. You snooze, you lose. I order a small veggie wrap and a side of quinoa salad while Leslie selects a chicken tarragon walnut salad on a fresh croissant. As I am waiting in the cafeteria style line to pay, Eve (from Adam and Eve) Leslie reminds me to get the small key lime pie for dessert. The checkout person offers two choices, a small parfait cup or a small five-inch pie. Eve said *"small"* so I made an executive decision and buy the five-inch **SMALL** pie. Lunch is all the Giants fan promised it would be. Fresh and tasty, nutritious and filling. We now attack the pie. I never knew a five-inch pie was **SO BIG**! The delicious and *"sinful"* key lime pie filling is topped with a generous, make that a very generous, mound of homemade whipped cream. We believe it is a sin to waste food, so we finish the whole thing save for a few graham cracker crust crumbs at the bottom of the tin pie holder. Our glucose count is off the charts. We are close to going into shock. We are *"stuffed like pigs"* ready for slaughter. But, oh, what a way to go! Gayle's was without a doubt, an over the top recommendation. So, if any of you are ever near (say 100 miles near) Capitola, you **MUST** stop at Gayle's for lunch. My best advice: go on an empty stomach.

We waddle thirty-five steps back to the car, groaning the entire way. It wasn't a bad groan, but rather a groan of good taste and expanding waistlines.

Back on the road, we stop at the lighthouse at Pigeon Point. We take many pictures again that we will never look at after the trip but at least paid homage that it was a trip well taken.

We arrive at our two-night retreat in Carmel and decide to check in but not unload the car. Since Leslie is driving, she makes an executive *"her way or the highway"* decision to take the ten-dollar, seventeen-mile drive through some of the most expensive real estate in California. Executive style one and two story homes dot the wooded hillsides. Many have panoramic views of the Pacific Ocean and the many local public and private golf courses including Pebble Beach, Spy Glass, Spanish Bay and Poppy Hills.

When we reach the coast, we stop to admire the views and continue to take those *"we just have to have"* photos and videos. Like we have never seen the Pacific Ocean up close and personal or heard waves crashing the shoreline. It is simply the moment and the truth is, it is worth watching, feeling and experiencing.

We stop at the Spyglass and Poppy Hills clubhouses to pay homage and admire the pristine, well-manicured golf courses and invest in some *"gotta have"* golf hats and ball markers.

Pebble Beach Golf Course and Resort is the final stop before heading to the hotel. We stand by the eighteenth green admiring the coastline that borders the left side of this spectacular par five finishing hole from tee-to-green. We watch well-intentioned golf shots into the postage stamp small green find the conveniently placed sand traps, fly by the green stopping just short of the water or sucked up by the thick, unrelenting rough guarding the front and right sides. One golfer, however, sticks his third shot within a foot of the cup for a pick-up birdie. Before leaving, we stop by the bar for a cold beverage and continue to admire the million dollar views. On the way to the car, we make a quick stop at the pro shop and buy more golf souvenirs and holiday gifts. More homage, but well worth having evidence we were there!

Our Carmel based hotel is just minutes away. We are both tired after a long day of driving, sightseeing, shopping and gorging ourselves at Gayle's. Parking at the hotel is *"tight"*. Finding no parking spots in the hotel parking lot and adjoining street, Leslie pulls in next to the office. I unload the bags and ask Leslie to stay put, I will be **RIGHT** back. Thirty-three seconds later, I return to where I left her only to find that Leslie and the car are nowhere to be found. That's okay, she probably just drove around the block. No worries as I head to the street corner anticipating her eminent arrival. I also find an overnight parking spot that will be just perfect. I play centurion guarding the precious parking spot from would be parking spot thieves. Five minutes pass, then ten. The night air is cold and breezy. My light weight jacket provides little warmth. Where the hell did she go? Shopping, perhaps? And for what?

After fifteen minutes, I am ready to give up and head to the room. Let her find a parking spot on her own. Just then, a couple hears my loud bellows **"LESLIE"** and informs me that a tall woman is knocking on room doors looking for her husband. I streak around the corner, and let out another **"LESLIE, WHERE ARE YOU?"** (in my best French) and hear a faint reply, "Over here."

"Where the *"French"* have you been? I told you to stay put. I found a nearby parking spot."

Leslie says, "I found one three blocks down."

So I say in no uncertain terms, "Go get the car and bring it here." Five minutes later the car and Leslie arrive. Does she pull into the on-street overnight parking spot that I have risked my life to prevent three other would-be cars from parking in? **NO**. She pulls into a spot adjoining a small strip shopping area. "Read the sign Leslie, it says **NO** overnight parking." Not to be outdone, she parks the car and heads to the liquor store.

Moments pass as Leslie returns with really good news: "The lady in the liquor store said I could park here. I will go check with her again." She returns and says with a sense of pride: "Yes, the ten dollar an hour part-time weekend clerk said it was okay to park here" proclaiming with a great sense of pride.

"Overnight?" I bellow and by now having lost the last ounce of *"be calm and cool"* I had left in me.

Leslie says, "I will go back and ask that." Having *"had enough"* of this fiasco, I start the car and move it into the spot I have now been protecting for thirty minutes. May I suggest and with all due respect, I was 200 percent right again.

All the while, Leslie is laughing her *arriere* ... definitely French ... off at me warning "you are going to have a heart attack if you don't **STOP YELLING**". In her mind, she is saying quietly to herself, "If he keeps this up, I am going to get the Maui oceanfront condo." I could almost hear rosary beads fumbling in the background. It was a long day, after all.

You guessed it, the love and romance mood has evaporated/ gone far away. Feeling emotionally abandoned, I am resigned to a lonesome trail created by the earlier ordeal. That hope is dashed in an instant. (Leslie here, "he can be such a schmuck ... but he is all mine!") At least there is a great college football game on TV. My takeout dinner is terrible and brings on Montezuma's revenge, possibly the gods are simply against me. I feel humbled. Tomorrow just has to be a better day and have a better ending. Again, pictures of anger and unrequited love race across my haggard mind. Please indulge me. I am weak and really need to win an argument at times (especially after again being 200 percent correct!).

***

Sunday, October 2nd -
Carmel, CA

Sunday becomes a sleep-in day. We need to recover from all the tonnage we ate yesterday. I cannot wait to get home and start a thirty-day juice cleanse.

Our route to breakfast takes us down the main touristy shopping street. Each overpriced shop plays soft *"come in and buy music"* like the magical seafaring sirens lure unassuming pirates into a seductive trap. We methodically avoid the temptations to buy stuff we have no use for. Our breakfast destination, a quaint cafe, offers multiple breakfast options. Leslie opts for the toast with avocado and egg. I go full bore healthy: steel cut oatmeal, raisins, coffee and cucumber water. All organic fans. The cleansing of the temple of John has a long way to go; however, you must start somewhere. The task is underway the moment I completed a morning belch.

After fueling our gastronomical tanks, we head to the beach. It's a cloudless, sunny, high sixties, just a perfect Northern California fall day. The walk is considered easy and all downhill. However, remember what goes down must eventually come up. More later.

We find a spot on the soft, sandy beach, park ourselves and spend thirty minutes allowing the brisk ocean breezes to lick our faces as we sit and listen to the strong waves crash along the shoreline. My cell phone is connected to the Ryder Cup live broadcast. I watch and listen to amazing shot after shot by American and European players.

This has got to be the year we bring that Ryder Cup home. What a week thus far, food, wine, good company, the Dodgers getting whipped by the Giants and now the Ryder Cup. Say Hallelujah!

Fellow beachgoers today include children frolicking and energetic dogs of all shapes and sizes playfully chasing balls tossed up and down the beach and sometimes into the cold Pacific. The dogs are getting plenty of exercise while enjoying themselves.

It's time for us to get some well-needed exercise. So, we take off and stroll the soft, sandy beach. A group of energetic young ladies, wearing two-piece summer bathing suits, are thoroughly enjoying themselves jumping, running and taking group pictures. Possibly, they may never have seen the Pacific Ocean. While some of the girls are *"game"*, I unsuccessfully challenge the group to run into the icy cold ocean. I promise a video and pictures. No dice, so we move on.

Time to start the dreaded Bataan death march ascent up the loose sand hill. We spot a local's pathway that gradually leads us up the hill to the main roadway. Breathless but still alive, we reach our summit. Leslie stops at an open house while I listen to the exciting victorious American Ryder Cup finish.

Our journey back to the hotel, however, is far from over. Eight blocks straight uphill at a seventy-degree angle. Slowly, we start out and challenge the hill making sure never to look back for fear of retreating or giving up. Park benches are strategically placed at intersections for out of breath tourists to stop and rest. On the eight-block walk, we stop at six. There is no dramatic regret of my endless and adventurous trips to countless café's, restaurants, deli's and hotel food bars. It is simply a long freaking walk. Both of us are tiring rapidly.

Alas, we make it. We reward ourselves with a snack at a local eatery that takes the pre-dinner hunger edge off. After ascending one more hill, we arrive none the worse, ready for a cat nap before dinner. We watch the second half of the 49ers loss to *"Jerra"* Jerry Jones and his Dallas *"Cowgirls"* and head out for an enjoyable seafood (versus see food) dinner.

Sitting at the bar, we engage in lively conversation with a local *"Carmelian"* and a newlywed (like yesterday) couple.

Time to head back to the ranch to rest up for a new adventure on Monday.

***

Monday, October 3rd -
Carmel to Los Osos, CA

It's time to bid goodbye to Carmel and continue our journey south to the Morro Bay Area. First, we take advantage of the free Comfort Inn breakfast (free and breakfast, neither are new to my vocabulary if you hadn't noticed). Next, we need to find a Laundromat and wash our well-worn clothes versus going commando for the remaining four days of our adventure. We stop at the Post Office to mail postcards to our friends not on Facebook. In this quaint town, the Post Office is only open 10:00 AM to 4:00 PM even though the government guarantees all full time postal workers eight hours per day pay. Only in America.

A small spa located next to the Post Office offers a *"pumpkin enzyme peel"*. Not sure what that is; however, maybe we try it next time we are in Carmel around Halloween.

Our second stop is the bank where we load up on quarters. We drive around the block to the local Laundromat and feed the washers with quarters just like a Las Vegas slot machine. Being an experienced house husband, I stay behind while Leslie makes one final pass through town looking for that *"we just have to have something"* thing. She returns with an ornate wind chime that will drive our Henderson neighbor, Alyne, *"bonkers"* every time the winds kick up. This could be an interesting purchase after all.

The clothes are now dry. Leslie forces me to actively participate in the folding and packing process.

As we head out of town, Leslie, not wanting to have another potential run out of gas scare, cuts off a car for the one remaining open pump at a local gas station. Not cool. Four gallons of gas later, we pull out and take California Highway 1 South.

The first road sign informs us **"Hills and Curves Next 63 Miles"**. As we soon find out, this is no understatement. We traverse numerous hills and look down on waves violently crashing against sheer cliffs, spraying water up in all directions. Mother Nature at her finest. Reminds us of driving the north road in Maui.

Today, the weather is overcast and slightly humid. My silver locks turn super wavy and curly. I am a senior surfer dude.

Although we are clipping along at fifty-plus miles per hour, Leslie is both driving and directing, constantly prodding me to *"take pictures"*. To get the best pictures without guardrails in the photos, I unbuckle my seat belt and hang out the narrow sunroof. This is insane, plus I almost lose my new Panama Jack hat.

I am freezing in the fifty degree cloudy weather but continue to take pictures as Leslie calls out, "Take a picture, take a picture." Like, how many waves crashing on the rocks pictures do we *really* need? Meanwhile, I continue to hang out of the sun roof like an inept and underdeveloped high school kid on prom or graduation night.

The sixty-three-mile drive takes us through the area known as Big Sur. The steep hillsides on both sides of the roadway are covered with many deciduous and non-deciduous trees including oak, redwood, eucalyptus and cypress. Occasionally, we see hillside homes built on a 150-degree angle.

This stretch of highway is **NOT** the road to take my mother and sister for a drive. I can see and hear them in the back seat, rosary beads in hand, imploring the Lord, *"I will **NEVER** do x and y again, I promise"*. I would have to break out duct tape, blindfolds and sleeping pills after constantly hearing, "Watch out, Johnny, oh my God, Jesus, Mary and Joseph. Oy vey, be careful, watch out, slow down!"

Meanwhile, standing in the brush along the side of the road, we see a local painter with an easel set up and brush in hand, painting the local landscape. Is that you, Thom Metcalf?

Occasionally, we pull off into one of the many photo taking parking areas. We must keep documenting the trip with more ocean waves crashing against the rocks or shoreline pictures. Why? I cannot tell you. I just follow orders.

For a fleeting moment, a very fast fleeting moment, we thought about hiking down the quarter mile *"pathway"* to the ocean below but thought better of it.

As Leslie attempts to reenter the highway, an approaching car does not slow down to let her merge in. She mutters some unkind remarks, punctuated with profanity regarding the rude driver. Then fifty feet later, she cuts off a mini-van trying to get back on the road, perhaps believing she evened some mythical score.

This narrow stretch of two lane hilly highway, complete with hairpin turns, would make a great movie set location for a Jason Bourne *"The Bourne Identity"*, Tom Cruise *"Mission Impossible"* or Daniel Craig *"007"* sports car/motorcycle chase scene.

Male and female bicyclists, some with bags strapped to their front and rear tires, traverse the twisting, narrow, hilly roadway that makes the Tour de France roadways through the Alps look like a Saturday afternoon ride in Central Park. It's a wonder that Tour de France bike riders don't come here to train. On the other hand, perhaps they do or should or can't. Too much on my mind today.

As the roadway narrows and is right up against the rocky hillside, appropriately placed signage warns us of **"Rock Slide Ahead"**. A few feet further, we observe **SERIOUS** falling rock fencing protecting the roadway and passing cars from severe damage due to extremely large falling rocks.

As time passes, blue sky begins poking out of the clouds as the sun burns off the morning clouds and haze.

A few days earlier when Leslie was *"under the weather"*, she cancelled our hotel reservations in Los Osos, CA, a small community next to Morro Bay. I attempt to search for last minute hotel deals; however, there is no cell or Internet service along this stretch of coastline. Thus, searching for accommodations is on hold.

As we descend closer to sea level, cattle and horses roam freely and enjoy the grassy hillsides clearly unaware of the million-dollar long-range spectacular ocean views.

The cold Pacific Ocean is clear blue just like the blue waters one sees in Hawaii, Florida and the Caribbean.

We pass through a few small towns and stop for lunch in Ragged Point, CA at you guessed it, the Ragged Point Inn. We each enjoy a small Cobb salad, no blue cheese, that hits the spot. A short while later, we come across a beach where hundreds of female seals lie in the sand. Most appear to be resting and working on their tans. A few snuggle up and communicate through a series of sounds they appear to understand. Others use their flaps to throw the sand and dig in. Close your eyes and imagine that single sight. The aesthetics alone are staggering.

One of our goals on this trip is to find interesting pieces of driftwood for our backyard. I spot a beach with various sizes and shapes of driftwood. After pulling over and parking, I head down to look for *"just the right piece"*. Securing one was easy, but carrying the forty-pound piece of wood from the soft sandy beach up the soft sandy hill challenged my cardiovascular system to the nth degree. Unfortunately, the piece of wood was too long to place in the car.

Leslie joins me as we make our way back to the beach. A quarter mile walk later, we both agree on two *"perfect"* pieces of driftwood that will immensely enhance the value of our desert landscaped back yard. The trick will be how to get the heavy pieces of wood up the steps to the parking lot. I luck out by perfectly balancing the heavy, lopsided piece of wood and climbing the twenty steps. Leslie drags the second piece over to the steps for you guessed it, me to carry up to the car. Both pieces of wood fit perfectly in the SUV's back seat. An elderly lady observes us loading the wood and asks, "Is it legal to take wood off the beach?" I reply, "Well, I see fire pits on the beach where people burn wood so we are saving these two pieces of wood from a painful death." I was anticipating yet another single digit wave, this time from a protesting granny.

The last hour of the day's journey is appallingly uneventful. We finally establish connection with the outside world and rebook our two-night stay at the Back-Bay Inn. This establishment is owned by Bill Lee, the founder of Lee & Associates, a large, highly successful Southern California commercial real estate brokerage firm. Leslie worked as Bill's assistant for two years in the mid 1980's. After checking in, we meander across the parking lot to listen to the Monday Night 5 PM - 7 PM weekly home-grown band performance. The locals stand out, enjoy an adult beverage or two, and rhythmically sway, clap or dance to New Orleans jazz music. Many people bring their dogs.

Leslie finds Bill Lee and reintroduces herself. They spend time catching up and inquiring about the whereabouts of former employees. Bill retired from the business, left the rat race known as Orange County, California and purchased a home here about ten years ago. He invited us to stop by and see his place late morning, Tuesday. We graciously accepted the invitation and mutually agreed to be there around 11:00 AM.

Before settling in the watch the second half of the Monday Night Football game between the Vikings and Giants, we order a takeout pizza and stop for a six-pack.

A long day ends in anticipation of a great Tuesday.

***

Tuesday, October 4th -
Los Osos, CA

This morning, we wake up to a magnificent view of the Back Bay. Leslie opens the French doors to our private balcony. We gaze at the cloudless sky over the tranquil water and breath in the crisp, invigorating, fresh fall morning air. A million-dollar photo is right before our eyes.

We get the day started off on the right foot. A homemade breakfast, which is included with our Inn stay, is served at the adjoining cafe. Steel cut organic oatmeal with fresh bananas and strawberries is my choice while Leslie opts for the two farm-fresh scrambled eggs, thick and crisp *"to die for"* bacon and a homemade scone. It is just as good as the Calistoga Winery Inn bed and breakfast bacon.

After finishing breakfast, we drive to Bill Lee's hillside five-acre home. Bill is at the vet's dealing with an injury to his cat; however, his daughter-in-law invites us to walk the grounds. Bill has created a farm that will serve his soon to open Farm to Table 100 percent organic restaurant. We walk the grounds and see a variety of fruit trees and vegetables including grapes, blueberries, raspberries, lettuce, onions, pumpkin, potatoes, brussels sprouts, radishes, tomatoes, papaya and avocados. A large chicken coop is home to the fifty to one hundred chickens that lay the eggs served at the breakfast cafe. Greenhouses protect a lettuce patch, where the lettuce looks perfect and ready to eat. It is also home to winter vegetables in their early stages of growth.

We meet the live-in farmer, John, a pleasant man who gives us a brief history of his time working for Bill and their plans for the upcoming months.

We finish our self-guided tour and are in awe of the lush grounds, trees, waterway, fire pit and sitting area.

Just as we start to head out, Bill returns, updates us on the health status of his cat and proceeds to give us the $100 per person tour of the compound. Bill is knowledgeable about every tree and vegetable. He tells us about his plans for the Farm to Table restaurant. He has hired a chef to cook for the family and experiment with potential menu items. His future includes weekend tours of the farm to promote the restaurant. He shows us his personal *"retreat area"* where he occasionally escapes to recharge the batteries with a good book and a glass of scotch.

We head back to the house. Bill and I engage in a spirited ninety-minute discussion of Orange County, CA 1980's youth league and high school hoops. Bill's son played on the Woodbridge High team that won the California State Championship in the late 80's. I was heavily involved in the grades 3-8 youth program in Irvine. Even though we just met, the back and forth conversation sounded like two guys who had known each other for years.

Time to not overstay our welcome. I invite Bill to come to Las Vegas for the first four days of 2017 March Madness. Four days of college hoops for *"hoops junkies".* It would be great to see him again.

We head out to our next adventure and pull into Montana De Oro State Park. A hard-packed gravel pathway leads down to the beach below. We set out on foot and descend to the sandy beach area. A lone fisherman wrapped in a heavy jacket and wearing a wide brimmed hat and calf high boots stands in the shallow icy waters, fishing pole in hand, enjoying the views and the sounds of the crashing waves, hoping to catch a fish or two for dinner.

We park our socks and sneakers and stroll the beach for about a half mile. We come across two people riding horses and a large family of skinny legged birds. Time to turn around and head back. The stroll along the beach is easy. A challenge lies ahead ... a 160-degree uphill climb through very soft sand to the hard-packed gravel pathway. Slowly but surely we ascend one careful step at a time and rest at a well-placed park bench. The balance of the climb is a piece of cake.

Invigorated by the strenuous climb, we set out to meet with Jeanne Salter, a Help-U-Sell real estate broker. Leslie worked with Jeanne for a few years when we lived in Irvine a few decades ago. Her storefront office is in Grover Beach, a thirty-minute drive. Leslie and Jeanne enjoy a sentimental reunion with lots of tears and Kleenex.

Jeanne heads out to an appointment. We program *"Morro Bay"* into the car's navigation system, follow Bill's recommendation and enjoy a wonderful fresh fish dinner at The Galley.

The meal is well worth the price. The swordfish is *"melt in your mouth"* delicious. We engage in lively conversation with a couple sitting next to us at the bar. They were in their mid-eighties, a retired ranching couple who still owned 120 acres in the Paseo Robles area.

Being on vacation, dessert is a must. The local Friendly's soft ice cream hut provides the needed vanilla and chocolate sugar rush to top off another great day.

Back at the room, we settle in to watch the final forty-five minutes of the VP debate.

This part of the trip has been fantastic. We make a unanimous executive team decision to extend our stay for one more day! I plan to sit by the water and catch up on my writing and reading. Leslie is planning a road trip to Paseo Robles. She hopes to again meet up with Jeanne for dinner.

***

Wednesday, October 5th -
Los Osos, CA

We awake to another beautiful, cloudless blue sky fall day and are delighted we decided to stay one more night. Leslie's first words are "Boy my body is **FEELING** yesterday's uphill walk. Where is the Tens machine?" After showering and getting dressed, Leslie's body is covered with multiple Tens machines (Transitional Electrical Nerve Stimulation) patches bringing much needed blood flow to various aching body parts.

Another organic breakfast gets our day started. My goal today is to sit by the water, catch up on our travel blog and read. No more driving, picture taking, hiking, sightseeing, just a relaxing last vacation chill day. Despite not sleeping well, Ace Wahine Leslie opts for adventure and shopping and takes off for Paseo Robles.

I am in writer's heaven sitting in a rustic well-worn wooden lounge chair with feet up on a wooden ottoman. My fingers gently tap on the IPhone6 as the words flow freely from the vivid memories of the last two day's escapades. Time flies when you are having a great time with a great partner and travel mate. After two hours of writing and editing, the IPhone6 needs charging.

I switch gears and start reading *Armageddon How Trump Can Beat Hillary*, a New York Times bestseller by Dick Morris and Ellen McGann. The book is *"quite"* revealing to say the least about the ongoing political life of Bill and Hillary Clinton. I don't care if you are a Democrat, Republican or Independent. This book is a *"must read"* before casting your November presidential ballot.

The IPhone6 battery is charged. Time for a quick granola bar and saltines crackers lunch. I love the sea gulls and birds. I toss a few ground-up crackers on the small sandy beach. Within seconds, the leader of the flock cries out to his comrades with sounds only they recognize. The rest of the gull family and friends quickly show up and descend onto the beach littered with cracker crumbs. A quick snack for the fastest of the flock. After they fly away, a mature white sea gull decides he wants to be *"my new best friend"*. As he cautiously steps towards me, I try not to move a muscle for fear of scaring him off. He settles in a safe distance from me and proceeds to munch on the trail mix, granola bar and saltine cracker crumbs.

Time to finish Monday's story and start Tuesday's. I know our three Facebook followers are anxiously waiting for the happenings of the past two days.

A valiant effort on my part to finish the blogs falls short as the IPhone6 registers 1 percent battery life. So, charge the phone and get back to the book.

Before you know it, six hours have flown by. Time for an early dinner in Morro Bay at the Dutchman followed by, you guessed it, ice cream cones at Friendly's. We are creatures of habit and low on discipline especially when on vacation.

Leslie informs me she is exceptionally tired due to the lack of sleep from the night before (not my fault) or a cold coming on. Back at the room, Leslie is in bed by 7:30 PM. We watch the San Francisco Giants win an exciting wild card pitcher's duel between the Giants' ace Madison Bumgarner and the Mets' ace Noah Syndergaard.

Conor Gillaspie smacked a three-run homer in the top of the ninth off Mets All Star closer Jeurys Familia to give the Giants the win (3-0) in this *"one game winner take all"* playoff game.

It's an even year. Baseball fans are very aware that the Giants have won the last three even year World Series. Today, the Jade and

Sean Beardsley clan are happy campers to say the least. Being out of Nevada cost them twenty-two to one odds for the Giants to win it all. When we get home, I'll make a mad dash to the Southpoint to get down their wager to win the Series at reduced ten to one odds.

I finally finish Monday's adventure and post on Facebook. During the drive home Thursday, I will finish the blog for our faithful Facebook groupies.

***

Thursday, October 6th -
Los Osos, CA to Henderson, NV

All great things must come to an end, this trip included. Leslie is fully refreshed and her batteries charged from ten plus hours of sleep. We hastily get ready and toss our *"stuff"* into our suitcases. One final great breakfast. I *"be bad"* and order a double order of bacon . . . justifying my rapaciousness (gluttony by other standards) because **I AM ON VACATION**! The farm-fresh eggs are perfectly scrambled. The fresh coffee wakes up dormant brain cells and gets the heart pumping. Leslie chooses the organic frittata and an orange cranberry freshly baked scone. She is on vacation too!

Well, travel blog fans that's it. We gas up and head for the highway and home.

Last night our neighbor, Alyne, texts us a video of our cat Tee standing at her patio screen door crying for treats. Just can't get that video out of my head. We both know that our faithful house and kitty sitter, Diane, had most likely just five minutes before, given him a handful of his favorites. He just loves to play on the neighbor's soft spots. If Alyne ever opens the screen door, it will be all over! Tee will have a new home and become our neighbor. Alyne will be forced to buy him organic cat treats. That'll teach her.

Leslie drives the first-half of the 450-mile journey home. I get to write Wednesday's and today's final blogs.

Within a day or two, I will have the entire trip blog in one file and I will upload all the pictures from both phones. For the ridiculously LOW price of $49.95, you can receive the complete trip itinerary complete with hotels stayed at, thirteen-day blog and 100's of *"just gotta have"* pictures and videos. **PLUS, NO** shipping and handling fees!

We accept cold hard cash and certified checks, no credit cards or PayPal.

Act **NOW**! Place your order **TODAY** via text, email or Facebook. Include your shipping address and method of payment. Orders will be promptly shipped upon receipt of payment. No exceptions to anyone, including family members.

OR just call 800-JLT-BLOG 24/7. Operators are standing by ready to take your order.

Friends and followers, around 6:30 PM, after putting 2,568.4 miles on the SUV, we pull into the driveway. Until next time, **ALOHA!**

***

ADDENDUM
Traveling from Henderson to Maui

Wednesday, November 2nd, 2017 -
Henderson, NV

Good afternoon to our three faithful Facebook friends. Leslie and I leave for Maui tomorrow to begin a six-week stay. Nothing stupid will happen right? After all, I booked this trip many months ago and I purchased seat upgrades on the outbound segment from San Francisco to Maui. This upgrade includes one **FREE** checked bag for each of us. Simple right? Well, today, I log onto United.com to check-in and print the boarding passes. At the end of the check-in process, I am prompted for *"how many bags are you checking"*? When I put in two each, the website attempts to charge me for all four bags. Hold on Jack, I already paid for the first bag for each of us with the seat upgrade. Why are you trying to charge me for four checked bags?

Getting nowhere with the website, I call the United Airlines toll free 800 number and finally (after loosing my cool and screaming into the phone **HUMAN BEING**) convince the automatic voice recognition *"I can answer your questions computer voice recognition system"* to transfer me to a human being. When the agent comes on the line, it only takes a few seconds to comprehend that I am talking with a brand new, this is my first day, customer service employee. She could not understand that the seat upgrade charge (to the Emergency Row) that I purchased includes one checked bag for each of us on the outbound portion of our trip. After a few minutes of *"let me check"*, she informs me I am correct **BUT** (why is it there is **ALWAYS** a **BUT** with us?) now catch this one . . . the seat upgrade and one free checked bag each is **NOT** for the outbound SFO to Maui segment; hang on now . . . is for the **RETURN** flight!! "How can this be?" I asked. She replies "computer glitch, you booked this trip some time ago and since then, flight time changes have occurred." So I say, "Can you just fix it?" "No." "Can you just cancel the charge and rebook it?" "No." "Your one and **ONLY** option is to **NOT** check-in through the website. You **MUST** check in at the airport ticket counter and show the agent your receipt for the first bag free on your original receipt" (which, thank goodness, I saved).

Great, just great. So, instead of checking the bags curbside at the airport, we have to **STAND IN LINE**, check-in with a real person, pay the baggage fees for the second checked bag each and get the first bag checked for **FREE**.

GREAT way to start our trip ... another *"Lucy/Dezi"* moment!

***

Thursday November 3rd, 2017 -
McCarran International Airport
Las Vegas, NV

Good morning Facebook friends. Early this AM, Leslie and I arrive at the United Airlines check-in counter to resolve our one free bag each situation. As you recall, we purchased seat upgrades from SFO to Maui. The upgrade included one free checked bag each.

Yesterday, I unsuccessfully tried to check-in on line; their system wanted to charge us for four checked bags instead of two. However, the two telephone agents I spoke with yesterday informed me that the problem was caused by a variety of *"factors"* with their reservation system including a computer glitch, schedule changes to these flights and *"the merger"*. Maybe Wiki leaks or a Russian computer hacker doctored the reservation to show we are entitled to one free checked bag each on our return flight **NOT** the outbound flight. For the record, we did not plan to bring bags home in mid-December as we will return to Maui December 29th.

Anyway, the telephone agents yesterday **ASSURED** me that our conversation is fully documented in our travel record and the United counter customer service agent will be able to quickly *"fix it"* as long as I showed her my original receipt and itinerary. Cool, settled, piece of cake.

Not **SO** fast sports fans! We arrive at the counter and explain the mix-up to the agent. Our *"Fly the Friendly Skies of United"* customer service agent pulls up the reservation and proceeds to curtly tell me I am wrong, "There is no one bag free with the upgrade to emergency row seating you purchased!" So, I try my best (sometimes not succeeding but tried) to be friendly, explain the situation again, show her the information on the receipt ("this is not a receipt it looks like an itinerary" inferring that I was the **DUMBEST** customer of the day), and inform her what was relayed to me by the telephone agents (called two times yesterday, over sixty minutes invested). So what does the *"Customer Service Agent of the Month"* say? "They are just reservations agents. They don't know the policies." **Great, she just threw all of the United Airlines telephone reservation customer service agents under the bus!** Again, I reiterate the reasons the telephone agents told me yesterday as to why this occurred. She tells me, "the merger was five years ago!" Like how would I know? I didn't think I needed to read the history of United Airlines when I booked the tickets. Maybe I should next time.

Well, boys and girls, she hit a hot spot. Leslie holds me back from jumping over the counter to go nose to nose with her. The agent whips out her antiquated IPhone5 and pulls up the United policies for this upgrade. I say again, "But why do I have one free bag each on the return flight?" No reply.

Meanwhile Leslie is pleading, "Just pay the baggage fee, I don't want our bags to miss the flight." "**NO**, Leslie, I will handle it!" The agent asks if she wants me to have her check with a supervisor. Initially, I say, "No, I don't want to hold up the line" but she says, "**YOU** are my customer. I **WILL** take care of you." So off she goes. A good ten minutes later, (is she trying to wear me down . . . not this *"bulldog"*, a nickname given me by Jeff Perry and Rees Davis, clients from my consulting days. The bulldog *"never lets go"* until the situation is handled. Thanks guys.) Ms. Congeniality returns and reiterates the policy **BUT** to make **ME** happy, United Airlines, out of the goodness of their heart, will give us one free bag each even though the policy for our upgrade says no free bag. She cannot explain why our invoice and itinerary clearly states we have one free checked bag on the return segment. Maybe United gave us an early Christmas present. Whatever. My only concern now is that she will ship our bags to some remote outpost with one day a week United service.

As we gather up our boarding passes, our *"Friendly skies of United"* customer agent bids us adieu by saying with a sly hint of "I am right, **YOU** are wrong". "We **ALWAYS** take care of customers who are nice to us!" Well, rest assured, United will hear from me. I hope she has her resume updated. And I hope our bags arrive in Maui at the same time we arrive!

***

Thursday, November 3rd, 2017 -
McCarran International Airport Las Vegas, NV At the Boarding Gate for Both Flights

Is it just a coincidence or because of the long delay checking in at the United Las Vegas counter, why do the boarding positions printed on our boarding passes make us the last two people, other than the last minute standby passengers in line, to board the plane? I sense a conspiracy. How did the Las Vegas customer service agent pull this off? And where pray tell, did she ship our checked bags?

Thursday, November 3rd, 2017 -
From the Plane Somewhere Over the Pacific on the Way to Maui

Now ask yourself, what could *"happen"* at 39,000 feet that warrants a mention in my travel blog? Say it isn't so jolting Joe DiMaggio . . . what did Leslie do this time?

Our flight starts out uneventful. We get the free peanuts and beverages and settle in for a four hour and thirty-five minute flight from SFO to Maui. About ninety minutes in, mother nature calls. We both make our way to the restrooms located in the back of the plane. Along the narrow, crowded aisle, we rub butts with perfect strangers heading back to their seats. Ladies first. Leslie enters the bathroom on the left side while I wait my turn. Thirty-two seconds later, a flashing bright orange light next to the left bathroom door comes on. The flight attendants quickly jump into action. What is happening? One flight attendant is furiously pounding on the restroom door and very loudly calling out, **"ARE YOU ALL RIGHT IN THERE? Do you need help? Shall I have the captain turn back to San Francisco?"** Kind of reminds me of the first night in the hospital when Leslie had her right hip replaced. She had the audacity to pass out while I was trying to watch Sports Center. I had to quickly divert my attention from the TV and alert the nurse in charge. Within seconds, numerous nurses and staff including the person furiously documenting the events for, I assume, the insurance company, gathered to bring her back from going to the *"happy hunting grounds"*. Thought I had the Maui condo that night. Back to the plane. By now, the 230 plus passengers are in a panic. What is going on? I think to myself, what has Leslie done this time? Shortly thereafter, she emerges unfazed at the *"disturbance"* she has created. Looking sternly at me, she says in no uncertain terms, "Why were **YOU** knocking so hard on the restroom door? Didn't you see the **OCCUPIED** red light sign was on?"

"Ace (one of her many nicknames), that was not **ME** knocking, it was the flight attendant. Apparently, you pushed the **"I NEED HELP PANIC BUTTON"** located next the toilet."

"What button? I did not see or push any button?"

"Well Leslie you did. See that light there. It came on causing the flight attendants to jump into emergency procedures mode and startling the passengers."

"Oh no," she replied in her best Lucille Ball shrug and apologized to the stewardesses.

I just cannot go anywhere with her without *"something"* happening. Let's just say that on her way back to her seat, nobody offered to buy her a drink. She received a few fickle of fate finger *"salutes"* and many *"What the hell were you doing?"* stares from the passengers she passed. When she settled into her seat and buckled up, the Captain came by and said, "Lady, I don't care if you have use the bathroom again on this flight, **DO NOT LEAVE YOUR SEAT UNTIL WE GET TO MAUI! UNDERSTAND?**"

"But, But."

"NO **BUTS** lady, stay seated, period, paragraph end of story, kapech?"

One final observation from the flight cabin, can someone please explain to me what happened to rows sixteen to nineteen on this airplane? The seat rows jump from fifteen to twenty for no apparent reason. Did they somehow push the plane together to make is smaller? We noticed the same thing on the flight from Las Vegas to San Francisco.

Not to be upstaged by Leslie, our crackerjack Class Three flight attendant pulls a Leslie. On the last beverage service run, she stops her cart just behind my seat. After being served the beverage of my choice, sparkling water, I get up to grab something from the overhead storage area. I cannot safely drop the door for fear of having the overhead bin door plunk the flight attendant in the head. So I wait for her to move the cart down the aisle. No biggie, I can wait. But what does she do? She engages the couple in the row behind me in conversation. Five minutes, ten minutes, what are they talking about that is so important? Meanwhile, the other flight attendant working her beverage cart has progressed about ten rows down the aisle and is glaring at her *"partner"*. Sensing this conversation may never end, I say screw it, drop the storage door and call out loudly, "look out, incoming door". She gets the message, ends the conversation with her new best friends and goes back to serving beverages.

Reporting live from 39,000 feet somewhere over the Pacific ... **"Good night Chet, Good night David."**

***

Thursday, November 3rd, 2017 -
Maui, HI Airport Baggage Claim

Arriving at the baggage claim area, we anxiously await the arrival of our bags. Did the Las Vegas agent check them on this flight or send them to some remote village in the Far East? Patience is **NOT** one of my virtues. Slowly, checked bags fall onto the circular baggage claim carousal. Where are our bags? Finally, two suitcases and the golf clubs show up. However, Leslie's Hawaiian flowered, ocean colored luggage identifying wrap is missing from her large suitcase. Finally, my bag is the **LAST** piece of luggage that arrives on the carousal. Just a coincidence? I guess we will never know. But I did find a note attached to my bag that said, *"Make this bag the **LAST BAG** you send through to the baggage carousal."* I trust the handwriting expert I plan to hire can get to the bottom of this.

***